Three Rules
for
Writing a Novel

Books by William Noble

The Complete Guide to Writers' Conferences and Workshops, Forest Dale, Vermont 1997

Show, Don't Tell, Middlebury, Vermont, 1991

Bookbanning in America, Middlebury, Vermont, 1990

Make That Scene, Middlebury, Vermont, 1988

"Shut Up!" He Explained, Middlebury, Vermont, 1987

Steal This Plot (with June Noble), Middlebury, Vermont, 1985

The Psychiatric Fix (with June Noble), New York, 1981

The Private Me (with June Noble), New York, 1980

How to Live With Other People's Children (with June Noble, New York, 1978

The Custody Trap (with June Noble), New York, 1975

Three Rules
for
Writing a Novel

A Guide to Story Development

William Noble

Sanger, California

TheWriteThought.com

For David and Nicole Grosvenor

The Write Thought, Inc.
1254 Commerce Way
Sanger, California 93657
Info@TheWriteThought.com.

Library of Congress Cataloging-in-Publication Data

Kindle ISBN 978-1-61809-023-2
ePub ISBN 978-1-61809-024-9
Paperback ISBN 978-0-9818908-3-8

Noble, William.
      Three rules for writing a novel: a guide to story development /
      by William Noble.
      p. cm.
      Authorship. 2. Fiction—Technique. 3. Plots (Drama, novel, etc.)
      4. Setting (Literature) 5. Dialogue. I. Title.

PN218.N64 1997
808.3—dc21

                                             97-18127
                                             CIP

Contents

Rule Three:
Who Am I?

Introduction

A wise professor of mine once said, 'The symbol of a life isn't what we do or what we are; it's what we leave behind. I urge you to plant a tree, have a baby...or write a book!"

Even with more than fifty thousand books published annually, the latter is the choice with the smallest number of takers. Yet if writing a book followed the careful lines of a template, we'd master the process and...presto! Ho-hum. Another book. Millions in the pipeline or in circulation, and leaving one behind would be akin to willing your garden tools.

Fortunately, books, particularly novels, are, as the lawyers say, *sui generis*—meaning each is unique and of its own class or category. No two novels are exactly alike, and it's a good thing because our individuality is stamped on the cover of what we write. Take away that individuality and what have we got?

Groupthink and groupwrite. Who'd want to leave that behind?

We start, then, with the novel as a work of individual accomplishment and expression. And, yes, there are certain things that no two novels have in common: some would call it style or tone, others might call it character fulfillment or story angst. The literary answer might be more complicated, but the key is to ascertain the writer's impact on the page. Each writer offers something different, and that is where the uniqueness comes in. The serious novelist understands this because he or she knows what impact the reader should be able to take away from the experience. The uniqueness doesn't come from the act of reading (that would be too much to ask) but from the words themselves and how they are used.

It might seem strange to offer uniqueness as the prize for treading a well-worn path, but it's more a case of reaching a threshold (the end of the path) and stepping off into a personally chosen universe. Yes, uniqueness is part of any novelist's style, and we can celebrate that because it reaffirms the individuality in us all. But to present this gift to a reader, we must understand what goes before it so the uniqueness can shine.

And here is where we walk the common path. Some writers will puff up and say, 'There are no rules for novel writing except there are no rules for novel writing..." and others will shake their heads and murmur, "if there are rules, someone would have discovered them before this!" The answer, really, depends on what we seek to have the rules accomplish. If we want a detailed blueprint, coupled with a hundred do's and don't's framed by unbreechable parameters, such rules would squeeze the life out of most creative work.

But if we look to rules as guides only, as sparks for further inquiry, as reminders to maintain story integrity and vividness, we can build on what they tell us. If an artist paints a field of lilies by the numbers, the flowers may be clear and pretty, but they won't be as the artist sees them. If the artist sets up by a lily pond with only a pallet, brushes and an idea about colors, what will appear on the canvas is what the artist sees, and it may differ from what any other artist would see.

Novel writing works the same way—there are notions we must have, guides we should follow, but nothing should be so fixed we can't develop our own style with it First, we pay homage to our writer's eye, to the viewpoint in scene and story from which we tell our story. Whose eye or eyes will it be? Who's doing the story telling? This provides the broad foundation on which we can plant our more specific rules for writing the novel.

There are only three rules, general enough to guide without stifling, broad enough to support without controlling, question-provoking enough to spark without limiting:

—What's Happening?
—Where Am I?
—Who Am I?

We can apply generalized notions of writing technique to characterize these as plotting (What's Happening?), setting (Where Am I?), characterization (Who Am I?), but this would fall short of seeing these as *rules* rather than techniques. For example, no one doubts stories need plot, and there are ways to develop plot (such as asking "what if...?"), but when we ask What's Happening? we're seeking more than a simple plot line. We're casting our eye over the entire stage, sensing atmosphere and character reaction as well as the simple (or not so simple) facts of the story. What's Happening? means a lot is happening, more than just the storyline, and the writer needs to understand it

It's the same with Where Am I? and Who Am I? Both convey more than mere setting and characterization because they carry a sense of place and a sense of personhood into story development. When we ask questions like these, we have to be prepared to understand how the answers will affect the direction of the story and, at times, its underpinnings. Asking the questions—and answering them—provide pillars for story structure, and when balanced on the foundation of the writer's eye, we have a solid base to write a novel.

Three rules. That's all. *What's Happening? Where Am I? Who Am I?*

Read on.

The Eye of the Writer

"I like your sweater," a friend says.

"It was a present," we answer.

'The colors blend well."

We run our eyes over the sweater, unable to see the blend. "Right," we say.

"I mean, the blues and reds are smoothly mixed."

We shrug because we think the color is uniformly purple. "Right."

"Look here," our friend points at the neck stitch. "See how the blue becomes red but not all at once. Stitch by stitch, it changes. Gradually."

"I see purple, how come?"

"There's no purple here. Blues and reds, that's what it is."

"I still see purple…"

The eye of the beholder: if one viewer sees purple and another sees blue and red, it marks the differences between them. A work of art or a piece of writing will hold meaning in different ways to different people, but that doesn't lessen its significance or change its character.

Put another way…It is the artist/writer's *eye* we must follow to extract meaning from what we see or read. As readers we must walk in the shoes of one or more characters to the extent that we see things the way the writer wants us to see them.

As writers we must offer a point of view, or as the late editor, William Sloane, described it, a "means of perception" for viewing the scene. Through whose "means of perception" is the story being told? Whose point of view is highlighted? These are crucial questions that must be faced each time we create a story.

A point of view that doesn't work will cause a story to fall flat, to drag, and we know how long readers will put up with that! The writer's eye must be one of the first things we consider because it will control so many other things—characterization, mood and atmosphere, even plot development. Its importance is underscored when we realize how broad its effect can be. Novelist Janet Burroway puts it well: "Point of view is the most complex element of fiction. Although it lends itself to analysis, it is finally a question of relationship among writers, characters and readers…"

So, we ask ourselves each time we begin a scene: through whose eye is the story to be told? We have several choices, and in each case one will be more appropriate than the others.

There's the first person approach, the "I" perception where the entire story is seen through the lens of the story teller. The story unravels in the first person only, and there it stays:

I decided to see for myself whether John had moored the sunfish to our dock. So, before the others were up, I crept downstairs and let myself out the kitchen door, not sure what I'd do if I found the boat. What worried me was what I'd find under the forward combing…

One of the early decisions a writer must wrestle with is the point of view the story will take. We can see right away that using the first person offers the advantage of relative closeness between writer and reader. If the writer uses "I," as the lines above do, we are squarely inside the character's head, and the character doesn't make a move, doesn't develop a thought, without the reader stepping right alongside. The obvious advantage here is intimacy between character and reader, and this, then, gives the reader a reason to root for the character, to empathize with him or her.

Take the example above: even with this small selection, we know the character is unsettled, and there may be some threatening event to come. We observe as the character seeks to find answers, and we feel the character's uncertainty and worry as the search begins. Putting this in the first person allows us—the readers—to gain a closeness with the character because it's as if the character is telling us, one on one, what he is doing or contemplating, and why. It's as if we're having a private conversation with the character.

The writer's eye is crucial here because we want to build the intimacy between writer and reader. Using the first person—the "I" perception—will certainly help that along. The writer's eye will focus on creating the intimacy, and the point of view should do the rest. In the hands of an accomplished writer, the sense of intimacy simply envelops the reader. See how Raymond Carver works it in his story, *Cathedral,* where a blind man has come to visit the narrator and his wife. The visitor is the wife's former employer, but he and the narrator have never met. The narrator is uneasy with the blind man in his house, and as they spend the evening, the narrator speculates on his visitor:

I've never met, or personally known anyone who was blind. This blind man was in his late forties, a heavy-set, balding man with stooped shoulders, as if he carried a great weight there. He wore brown slacks, brown shoes, a light-brown shirt, a tie, a sports coat. Spiffy. He also had this full beard. But he didn't use a cane and he didn't wear dark glasses. I'd always thought dark glasses were a must for the blind. Fact was, I wished he had a pair...

As the narrator describes the blind man we find ourselves forming a clear picture, not so much because of the specific details of the blind man's appearance (his looks, his clothes, the way he carries himself), but because of the narrator's reaction to the way he looks, dresses and carries himself. This is clearly a first person point of view, we are seeing things through the narrator's perceptions...but what creates the intimacy here is the fact *the narrator has let us in on how he feels about the blind man's appearance!* "I" is used only three times, yet we have clear impressions about the narrator's feelings. "I've never met...I'd always thought...1 wished he had..." These are judgments, and the narrator is letting us in on his personal opinions, which, of course, color his attitude towards this blind man. Intimacy follows for us because now we know things no one else knows.

The writer's eye must decide how much intimacy to allow with the first person point of view. Carver gives us some, but had there been more, it's likely the narrator would come to dominate the story (when, in fact, it's the blind man who ends up dominating it). The writer's eye with first person point of view is a balance between developing intimacy among writer, characters and readers (as Janet Burroway suggests) and not allowing such intimacy to overwhelm the characterizations. Think of the axiom about too much of a good thing...intimacy with the characters works the same way—some, but not too much!

How do we control it? By not opening the flood gates of a character's mind, by holding something back. First person point of view does allow writer, characters and readers to get close to one another (closer, in fact, than other points of view), and the savvy writer will use the approach judiciously Watch how Ernest Hemingway handles it with his short story *Che Ti Dice La Patria ?* about a couple of young Americans driving in Fascist Italy during the 1920s. The young men are hailed by a uniformed Fascist on a bicycle and are told their license plate is dirty:

> I got out with a rag. The number had been cleaned at lunch.
> "You can read it," I said
> "You think so?"
> "Read it."
> "I cannot read it. It is dirty."
> I wiped it off with the rag.
> "How's that?"
> 'Twenty-five lire."
> "What?" I said. 'You could have read it. It's only dirty from the state of the roads."
> "You don't like Italian roads?"
> 'They are dirty."
> "Fifty lire." He spat in the road....

Though the story is in the first person, note that we don't get into the head of the narrator, at least not at this point. Whatever the narrator is feeling comes out in his words or his actions. He's frustrated, impatient, even confrontational, yet Hemingway doesn't allow us to get into the narrator's head—except through external means. We have to surmise what he is feeling, and in this sense our level of intimacy with him is not as great as it was with Raymond Carver's narrator. On the other hand, the mere fact that Hemingway uses the first-person point of view with this story should make it clear that some intimacy with the character is warranted. Hemingway wants us to feel intimacy, *but not too much intimacy!* Why?

Because his story was about more than rooting for the success of two Americans in a Fascist country. The travelers did have a couple of other incidents similar to the license plate flare-up, and in the final paragraph of this story Hemingway makes clear what his true purpose is:

The whole trip had taken only ten days [says the narrator]. Naturally, in such a short trip we had no opportunity to see how things were with the country or the people.

The writer's eye, then, was focused on something more than simple character intimacy, though it should be clear that by using the first person, Hemingway did want to establish some level of intimacy with the reader. It was his writer's eye that made the story more than a political exercise and gave it human value.

The same thing that makes the "I" perception useful for building intimacy also limits its application. When we're using the first person, our character's area of perception is cut off to what he or she can see or feel. Anything that happens beyond it, anything that another character thinks, for example, is outside the "I" perception and shouldn't be used.

I thought I saw him move his hand…this is clearly an appropriate use of the first person because we are in the narrator's head, and the point of view allows us to focus on what the narrator is thinking and what he sees. Put ourselves in the narrator's shoes, and we think and feel and see what the narrator thinks, feels and sees. BUT NO MORE THAN THAT!

This is a limitation on the first-person point of view. We want to build intimacy—fine; we want to keep the reader close— fine; we want to stand in the narrator's shoes—fine. But we can't see, hear or feel anything more than what the narrator does. Other things that happen, where the narrator is not personally involved, are beyond the first-person point of view.

*He gave me a disappointed look and thought about why I had left the door open…*this may have some "I" perception in it, but it's not a good use of the first-person point of view. The writer's eye, here, is unfocused. Why? Look at the means of perception. If we want to pursue the first person, how could the narrator know the other character was "disappointed" (I find it hard to conjure what could be a "disappointed look" —the other character may *feel* disappointed, but how can it be shown?). The misuse of the point of view is even more pronounced when the narrator tells us that the other character *thought* about why the door was left open. Here, the narrator is inside the other character's head, giving us that character's thoughts, and we know that proper use of the "I" perception would make that impossible. The only way the narrator could know these things is if the other character provided some physical response (such as slumped shoulders for resignation or clenched teeth for anger), or offered dialogue which highlighted how he was thinking or feeling ("I'm fed up with you," he said…"I've been thinking about what we should do," she said…). Absent some overt physical sign, the "I" perception has no business inside the head of another character.

That changes when we shift the point of view. If we go from first person to third person, the writer's eye expands because the opportunity to touch more people and events expands. We act more objectively (he ran, she saw, he danced…) because we go beyond the shoes of the single narrator. In its broadest form the point of view becomes omniscient, the see-all, tell-all perspective. The point of view rises above the characters and moves to the third person (not I see, but he sees, not I feel, but he feels). It can be a point of view without limitation in the sense that the story teller can be in the heads of all the characters, can see and reference all events and can interpret any and all things said or done. In effect, the omniscient point of view confers the God-like label on the writer, allowing the writer to describe what is happening, either objectively or subjectively, and enter the mind of any character. Janet Burroway, in her Writing Fiction, offers several items the omniscient writer can perform:

Interpret for us that character's appearance, speech, actions and thoughts, even if the character can't do so.

Move freely in time and space to give us a panoramic, telescopic, microscopic or historical view...

Provide general reflections, judgments and truths.

The omniscient point of view carries a major burden, of course, because the writer must be aware of all things occurring to all characters at the same time. It's a little like throwing several balls in the air and catching all of them before they hit the ground. With the omniscient eye, the writer must understand how a simple sentence such as "He decided to go to bed..." can affect all those in the scene:

—his wife who hadn't changed the sheets that day
—his daughter who was trying to tell him she was pregnant
—his house guest who wanted to pilfer an expensive set of cuff
  links from the bedroom
—his business partner who would call him in ten minutes to
  report a major theft...

Using the omniscient eye, however, doesn't mean we're required to jump into the heads of the affected characters at all times; what it does mean is we have that option, and it could give the story a more well-rounded feel if we could see how certain events affect others within the same scene. The burden the writer carries is to decide if and when he or she should take advantage of what the omniscient point of view offers. As Robie Macauley and George Lanning put it in their *Technique in Fiction*: the writer with the omniscient eye can "...borrow and use any one of several points of view as it suits his purpose...He can take a panoramic view, describing events that happen simultaneously or scenes that are widely separated in geography—things that a character narrator could not possibly cover completely..."

But note this: *can* does not mean *must!* The writer always retains the choice to limit even the omniscience he or she may have assumed. The question is: will the omniscience aid the story telling, add to the plot and/or characterizations, leave the reader close enough to the story so there's empathy and identification? That's the one drawback with the omniscient point of view: because the story moves over a varied ground and through a variety of characters and points of view, is there enough specificity to give the readers someone to root for?

One way to accomplish good things is to step back from the omniscient point of view and use a more limited eye. We're still in the third person (because if we were in first person, things would be limited automatically), but now we concentrate on the psyche of only one character (similar to the first-person viewpoint), and write about what that character sees and feels subjectively. In other words we can write: *He felt the first blush of uncertainty as he noted her stiff, unyielding stare. Would he be able to convince her his life was in the balance?*...But we don't get into the woman's head even though we're in the third person. What the man perceives is all we want. Through the limited objective point of view we see what the character sees (he noted her stiff, unyielding stare), but we don't know what she thinks or wishes to do. Yet because this is an objective viewpoint, we are in the third person, and because it is limited omniscient we, as author, can comment on his expectations (would he be able...). This would be much more difficult to do with first person. See how Leo Tolstoy uses limited omniscient in *Anna Karenina*, his novel of love and betrayal among Russia's nobility. Count Vronsky is smitten with Anna, who is married to Alexy Alexandrovich. Then, Vronsky sees Anna's husband for the first time, and Tolstoy describes what Vronsky feels:

Alexy Alexandrovich's manner of walking, with a swing of his hips and flat feet, particularly annoyed Vronsky. He could recognize in no one but himself an indubitable right to love her ...He saw the first meeting between the husband and wife, and noted with a lover's insight the signs of slight reserve with which she spoke to her husband...

Clearly, Tolstoy is using third-person objective, but note the limited omniscience here: "he could recognize in no one..." is an author's comment about Vronsky's attitude. Put it into first person ("I recognize in no one...") and it comes off overbearing, egocentric, controlling. In short, Vronsky would sound like a fool—which he isn't. There's more, though: "[he] noted with a lover's insight..." is an additional author's comment. If it were in first person, it would sound stilted; if it were in third person but not omniscient ("[he] called up his lover's insight...") it would sound contrived; either way the writer's eye is forsaken.

But concentrating on the limited omniscient point of view in the third person preserves the essence of this pivotal scene: we learn how Vronsky feels and what he sees; in the hands of many writers that might be enough. Tolstoy, though, offers us more: he comments on what Vronsky sees and feels, and in doing this Tolstoy adds substance to Vronsky's reactions and deepens the characterization. So, Vronsky has acquired "an indubitable right to love [Anna]..." and his senses are acute with "a lover's insight..." as he watches the meeting between Anna and Alexy. By the end of this description we have learned two things through Tolstoy's writer's eye: Vronsky is obsessed with Anna and he considers himself her lover.

Those are big steps in a few lines, but with careful crafting and characterization the writer's eye can make it happen.

It's obvious that point of view has great influence on the ultimate direction of a story. A plot seen from different perspectives will develop differently (look no further than William Faulkner's *As I Lay Dying* where there are more than a dozen points of view highlighted, chapter by chapter). It's equally true when we use dialogue or establish setting: depending upon whose "means of perception" we're following, what is said on the page or upon whom the physical aspects of the scene react will play a major part in story movement. For example, if there's dialogue such as the following:

"I didn't mean to hurt you," he said.

"Oh Charlie," she sighed, "you never think..."

With a limited objective point of view, this provides a balanced emotional rendering between two people. But if we turn it into first person, then we might have:

"I didn't mean to hurt you," I said, trying to keep a smirk off my face.

"Oh Charlie," she sighed, just like I knew she would, "you never think…"

Here, the man has become the scene driver, and instead of a balanced emotional rendering, the man has another agenda, and the scene changes course.

The key is this: plotting, dialogue, setting, mood and atmosphere are only means to an end. The writer's eye is the engine that starts them and keeps them going, and when everything works they way it should we'll be able to answer those three crucial questions:

—What's Happening?
—Who Am I?
—Where Am I?

Rule One:
What's Happening?

Structuring The Story

At a writer's conference in New England, an author introduces his audience to his new work of fiction. He relates that the plot is based on an ancient Greek legend—the myth of Daphne, Apollo and Zeus. In essence the author is saying, "I'm going to let you in on a secret. My plot is not new. It comes from somewhere else, and it's thousands of years old."

The author has found his Greek inspiration in Ovid's work—a love poem. Daphne, soft, beautiful and sensuous, bathes in a clear mountain stream. Apollo, by chance or by choice (it doesn't matter), watches her and becomes aroused to the point of abandon. Losing his perspective about courtship and love, he stands up, rampant and ready. Daphne is thrown into near shock and scoots into the woods, Apollo hot on the trail.

At the last moment before the inevitable rape, Zeus, blessed with imagination, turns her into a laurel tree. The still-aroused Apollo is left with a handful of bark. But laurel twigs whirl into a wreath, and a poet is born, as the crown settles on Apollo's head.

"Now," says the author, "suppose the setting could be changed to the New Hampshire woods, and suppose Daphne is a nubile college girl, and suppose Apollo turns out to be a virile, frustrated local man, and he comes on this latter-day Daphne, not only seductively naked, but *making love* next to the cool waters of a stream!"

She can't turn into a tree. The local man has more sense than to interrupt the love play. So…how about watching?…and stalking? What happens to his ordinary love life? Does he resent the pale, pudgy town girl who has been giving him what he wants for years, who is wordlessly slated to marry him and bear pale, pudgy children for him? Is this the future for him when, within his gate, is a liberated, rich girl who sparkles from an all-year-round tan acquired at tennis and swimming and other exotic diversions of the privileged?

"As you can see," the author goes on, "I found a plot." Indeed he did! By elementary changes in time, setting, cultural background he was able to map strategy and attitudes to bring everything into a contemporary frame.

The author seems to be challenging his listeners: What could you do with this ancient plot idea? Think about it...

The audience's creative wheels start spinning. What if...this plot were set in wartime? What if...the woman were a journalist and the protagonist a villager in a repressive South American country? What if...he intrigues her after frightening her and they become friends...then lovers? What happens to her old boy friend...his old girl friend?

And how about a modern literary reincarnation of the plot? Would F. Scott Fitzgerald's *The Great Gatsby* fit here? After all, Gatsby gazes on the object of his fascination from the safety of his dock. Daisy is "unattainable," "elusive," and uncaring about his feelings. It is amusing to think of his mooning after her. Yet if he became a physical threat, what a change we'd see!

"What if..." is the classic mechanism to take an old story or idea and enhance it with new trappings, to steal a plot and then make it one's own. What if...the time were changed? What if...the locale were changed? What if...the characters had different jobs or different looks or different sets of values?

But let's get back to that writer's conference in New England. At a coffee break after the author has described the Greek plot from which his new novel is taken, the audience reflects on the usefulness of the ancient myth in modern dress:

"So what happens to this modern Apollo? I can't see his just walking away from all this."

"If his modern Daphne doesn't stop romping through these woods in the nude, she'll get zapped by more than acid rain."

A woman interrupts. "I think your remark is stupid and patent-ly sexist. I'm not saying she won't be stalked, but she's not at fault. Look at me. I jog…I hike…and I don't think it's anyone's business. See, you're caught up in the whole bag of woman-as-lure. "

'Then why don't you steal the plot and change it your way?"

"Does the young man know this macho back woodsman— this hunk—is a threat? Does his girl friend tell him?"

The woman, again. "What if she doesn't?"

"That could be heavy."

"Good tension and conflict."

"Maybe toying with death."

A man speaks up. 'There are options, you know. We haven't even touched on Daphne." He turns to the woman. "Why don't you write it from still another angle?"

"You mean steal the plot, too?"

"Why not?"

If you write a lot, and others know it, you're apt to run into people who will ask: "Where do you get all those ideas?"

A good friend has a special answer for this. He writes fiction periodically for the men's magazines. He produces stories with heavy-breathing fantasy and graphic sexual detail. When someone asks him the usual question about story ideas, they invariably fol-low it up with: 'What does your wife think of what you write?"

He answers, "She thinks I tell a good story. She always asks me, 'Where did you learn that?'"

To preserve domestic harmony, he responds, "I made it up, of course."

Actually, what he "makes up" is two things—a story subject and a storyline. He gets the story idea and then he builds on it. One without the other is like an oreo cookie—the inside and the outside taste better when they work together.

So the question about story ideas is really two questions: where do our ideas come from and where do we get the format to carry them along?

Our friend who writes the erotic stories puts it this way: "One day I was on an airplane and happened to sit next to a woman who got to talking about her latest trip to Europe. She was a large woman, single and quite adventuresome. Also, I think she was oversexed. As she began to describe her amorous adventures in some of Europe's capitals, I realized I had the germ of a story. The story idea was simple—an erotic tale of sexual adventure and misadventure in Europe. But I was stuck on what motivation to use for my character's escapades. Then I realized that sexual fulfillment is a motivator. Call it self-discovery, if you like. But it meant that, in itself, the quest for sexual joy is enough to push a storyline along. So, 'A Nymphomaniac's Tour of Europe' was written and subsequently published in a well-known men's magazine." Then he chuckles. "It was actually anthologized, too."

The chuckle turns into a laugh, "Of course I never saw the woman again, and she never knew she was the model for the story."

Stories are all around us. They're as fresh and available as the air we breathe. Remember the opening lines of that television police drama about New York City some years ago? The announcer intones, 'There are eight million stories in the naked city…This is one of them!"

Actually it's a substantial understatement. There are millions upon millions upon millions of stories out there just waiting to be plucked like ripe fruit.

But stories must do something. They must go somewhere. It's not enough to say I'll write a story about a man going fishing. He must be going fishing because…or as he is fishing, an event occurs which affects his life… or his fishing is really a metaphor for something else. The story must be affected by some type of situation which moves it ahead.

One of the most popular novels in recent years is Peter Benchley's *Jaws*. Basically it is the story of a huge fish that kills people. But if we stop here, all we have is an idea that sits on itself. Without more it's like chewing air. Benchley's basic story of a man-consuming beast, in fact, has some pretty old roots. In ancient Greece there was the legend of the Minotaur, a beast with the body of a man and the head of a bull, that dwelled on the island of Crete and ate people. But again, without more, the existence of the Minotaur is simply a hideous fact, not a story.

The Greeks, however, were masters at story *telling*, and the legend of the Minotaur soon became interspersed with war and rescue and heroism and treachery. There was now a storyline, and a plot.

It went this way. Minos, the ruler of Knossos in Crete, declared war against Athens because he believed his son, Androgeos, was killed by the Athenians. At this time Athens was suffering from a series of afflictions—famine, pestilence, drought—and there was little spirit for a protracted war with Minos. The Athenians consulted their oracle and were told to give Minos whatever he might demand. Some years before, Minos's wife, Pasiphae, had become enamored of a bull, had unnatural sexual relations with it and produced the half man, half beast Minotaur. Minos, in his shame and anger, had the Minotaur, who feasted on human flesh, confined to the Labyrinth, an almost unfathomable maze.

Now against the Athenians, Minos exacted his vengeance. Every ninth year seven young men and seven young women would be provided as fodder for the Minotaur. They would be thrown into the Labyrinth, either to be feasted upon by the Minotaur or to starve to death if they couldn't find their way out.

But when the third round of tribute was due, one of Athens's great heroes, Theseus, offered himself as one of the sacrifices. In reality, of course, he intended to seek out the Minotaur and destroy it. He promised that if he were successful, he would, on the return voyage to Athens, fly white sails rather than the black sails that they had embarked with. And then Athens would be free of the tribute forever.

When he arrived in Crete, Minos's daughter, Ariadne, saw Theseus for the first time and fell in love with him. She decided to help him and gave him a ball of thread with which he could retrace his steps out of the Labyrinth.

The plan worked beautifully. Theseus found the Minotaur asleep, grabbed him by the forelock and killed him. Then, he found his way out of the Labyrinth, was joined by Ariadne and fled Crete.

Now, just as in the Greek legend, Peter Benchley has taken his monster-fish story and sparked it with certain dramatic situations which give it body, substance and—a storyline. There's terror and vengeance and heroism as the entire community becomes consumed with the presence of the fish off shore. But all these things are ancillary to the key ingredient at the foundation of the storyline—the chase to destroy the monster.

And what is the key ingredient behind the Greek legend of the Minotaur? Theseus's mission to destroy it.

What Benchley has done is to employ a classic device to move a story along. He has taken the story idea and given it motivation. He has used a plot motivator, and this has provided the storyline. Now the story has a why and a how.

The chase is but one of the thirteen plot motivators that can be found throughout literature. From the ancient Greek dramas of Aeschylus, Euripides and Sophocles to the modern prose of Saul Bellow, Ann Beattie and Robert Penn Warren, one or more from a limited list of plot motivators can be found acting to carry each story forward.

Thirteen plot motivators! Thirteen.

Most of us remember hearing at some point that there really are only 20...or 30...or 40 different ways to tell a story. Or that there are only 16...or 36 different plots ever devised.

The truth is the list can be expanded or contracted on the basis of how general we wish to be. One thing is certain, though: there really is a limited number of basic storylines to follow. Goethe, in fact, said, "It is almost impossible in the present day to find a situation which is thoroughly new. Only the matter of looking at it can be new, and the art of treating it and representing it."

In his renowned work of more than 60 years ago, Georges Polti came up with 36 dramatic situations which he claimed covered all available story opportunities. Again, depending upon how general or specific we want to become, there really is little room for dispute.

And we should reemphasize that! An attempt to exhaust every possibility is not only a herculean task but an impossible one as well. There really isn't anything new, though we want to be clear about what is basic plot and what is ancillary. For example, when we speak of ambition, one of the thirteen plot motivators, do we also talk of greed? After all, ambition run amuck becomes greed. But is greed really the source for a basic dramatic situation? Is it any more basic than jealousy, arrogance, self-righteousness? Is it as basic to storyline as are plot motivators such as ambition, rebellion and catastrophe?

There are certain items which become basic to story construction, and we've chosen to call them "plot motivators." They aren't plots, nor are they dramatic situations. They simply move the plot along and provide drama. There are thirteen in all which cover most available story opportunities for the writer.

But why plot *motivator?*

Because a plot—the story within a story—without some direction is like a large boulder in a bubbling stream. It's a lovely scene. You see it, you might even be able to touch it, but it doesn't move! Plot motivators make a story move, and they are the prime devices by which a writer can steal a plot and make it his own..

Take Benchley's *Jaws*. Many have compared it, at least superficially, to Herman Melville's *Moby Dick* in the sense that there is an unremitting chase or search for a great white fish. Here again we have a similar plot—a human-devouring beast that must be destroyed. But look at what Benchley has done. He has asked "what if…" the scene becomes the south shore of Long Island…the fish is a Great White Shark…the hunters are motivated by more financial reward than anything else…

Yet before Benchley's plot will really work, he has to ask why? Why must the fish be destroyed? The answer lies in the plot motivator, i.e. vengeance. Ahab in *Moby Dick* and his counterpart, the fishing boat captain in Jaws have both suffered grievous harm from the great white fish, and so they set out to destroy it to salve their own concepts of revenge. Vengeance moves the plot along; it motivates it!

Following are the common plot motivators that appear and reappear through literature. At any given time, of course, more than one plot motivator can exist side by side, affecting the story. The point is that these are the wheels that make the story go; they are the underpinnings for the various dramatic situations. You can take any story idea, attach one or more of these motivators to it, and you'll have a plot and a storyline.

In no particular order of importance the plot motivators are:

Vengeance
Catastrophe
Love and Hate
The Chase
Grief and Loss
Rebellion   Ambition
Betrayal
Persecution
Self-Sacrifice
Survival (deliverance)
Rivalry
Discovery (quest)
Ambition

As good as plot motivators are in developing a story, there are times when they need further substance and direction. Think, for instance, about Ernest Hemingway's well-told story, *The Old Man and the Sea*. The plot is simple and straightforward: Santiago, an old Cuban fisherman, sets out in his small boat to pursue his livelihood, alone and with just the barest of gear. Far from shore he lands the largest marlin he has ever seen, a fish that if he gets to port intact will rectify, perhaps forever, the misery he has endured throughout his life. Eighty-four days he has gone without catching a fish, and now his salvation is at hand!

Enter the plot motivator—survival. Hemingway paints a vivid portrait of Santiago's fight, not only to land the huge fish but also to get it, intact, back to shore where he would be honored and recognized for such a feat. And it is truly an epic battle for survival, for the fisherman is almost overwhelmed time and time again, first by the huge marlin itself and then by the predators who are drawn to the boat by the trailing blood of the marlin as it remains lashed alongside. So survival is clearly the plot motivator for this story, and a battle for survival is fine story material.

Yet what if the battle for survival was not just a naked struggle but possessed other elements which gave it additional dimension? What if the elements honor and dishonor were added? He *must* land the fish, he *must* bring it in! And with survival as the key plot motivator throughout the story, will it be survival with honor or with dishonor?

What Hemingway has done is to use a plot motivator with something we have chosen to call a "story spicer." It is a device which will add body to an already good story. It will make a plot bolder and more substantial.

Story spicers, in and of themselves, are not strong enough elements to be lumped with plot motivators. They simply can't push a story along by themselves as plot motivators do, yet without them a storyline might appear thin.

Are there a limited number of story spicers, just as there are plot motivators?

Here again the answer depends on how general or specific we wish to be. We felt there were thirteen basic plot motivators, and we feel there are thirteen basic story spicers. The great bulk of literature through the ages shows this again and again. But note, this book is not an attempt to be self-limiting or inflexible on the subject of plots; rather, we have extracted well-defined mechanisms that will help in stealing a plot and using it to good purpose .

So if you can find more than thirteen story spicers, use them by all means. Meanwhile, here are the ones we've uncovered:

Deception
Unnatural Affection
Material Well-Being (Including Increase or Loss of)
Criminal Action (Murder)
Authority
Suspicion
Making Amends
Suicide
Conspiracy
Searching
Rescue

Honor and Dishonor
Mistaken Identity

Imagine the following dialogue between a speaker at a writer's conference and his audience of eager listeners:

'There's no problem in stealing a plot. We all do it," the author says.

"Plot motivators are the key. Right?"

The author nods. "You take a story idea, apply a plot motivator, and you have a viable plot. I've shown you how this has been done by every writer since the ancient Greeks."

"I'm still kind of fuzzy," one student says.

"All right," the author says patiently. "Pick a story—something you've read that you liked."

"How about *Catch-22*?"

The author smiles. 'Joseph Heller's book."

"Yes."

"Now, we know that the book was essentially a story of one sane man's struggle with the insanity in the military. It had overtones of anti-war, but it was really about the sheer irrationality in the military. Agreed?"

There are nods and murmurs of assent. "Okay, let's play what if…" The author looks at the student. "What if…we pick another institutional setting. Not the military but the…"

"Business world!" the student says.

There is a burst of laughter from the others. But there is general agreement. The author continues. "Now, let's pick a plot motivator, something that will give direction to a story about the sheer irrationality in the business world."

Another student speaks. "In *Catch-22* Yosarian was really just trying to survive. Survival was the main plot motivator."

The author nods. "There may be some who would disagree with you, but I'll concede that was at least one of the plot motivators. Okay, pick another for our plot about the business world."

"How about…self-sacrifice?"

More laughter. 'That's a pretty rare commodity in the business world," the author says. "But okay. We have a story about irrationality in business where self-sacrifice is the prime motivator. Now, we don't have to follow Heller's style and make this a satire; it can be a serious, well-defined story. A businessman continually bumping heads with the institutional irrationality of the marketplace who sacrifices himself for some broader purpose." The author pauses and looks around. "How about a story spicer?"

The first student speaks up. "Conspiracy," he suggests. "There's a conspiracy which either is directed at the businessman or is one in which he is participating. In either case it dooms him in the end."

The author is grinning now. He pans the room benevolently. "We have a plot with substance and detail. A story about the business community and its strange ways, about a member of that community who, because of sanity amidst irrationality, ends up sacrificing himself for some higher purpose as the victim of a conspiracy. We have a plot, do we not?"

There are nods all around.

'Then," the author smiles, "please use it. We have stolen it, and it is yours."

Motivating the Story

1. Vengeance

"Vengeance is mine, I will repay!" said The Lord.

Vengeance, that man-eating shark of an emotion, tears at the innards while it propels the protagonist into action. The urge for vengeance is obsessive. To write about it properly, one must portray it as consuming, all-encompassing. Vengeance is an obsession. That is the primary thing to remember.

We have been told that long-standing Greek custom requires a man to avenge the murder of his brother. Until he does, the dead brother will not rest quietly. He may cause havoc from the grave. Even a mild, self-effacing victim could turn into a demon if the crime against him is not avenged. The surviving brother or brothers are duty bound to seek vengeance.

The plot motivation is clear: the brother seeks the killer, finds him and does away with him. Peace reigns.

But look how an accomplished writer molds and fits this plot motivator for the contemporary scene. Harry Mark Petrakis, whose work has been nominated for the National Book Award, explores the issue in his novel, *Days of Vengeance*. He considers these questions: what if…the setting for the opening scenes is rural Greece in the first decade of the twentieth century; and what if…the victim is slated to go to America to join his uncle; and what if…he is a kind and trusting young man, and before he emigrates he is killed by a pathologically envious contemporary; and what if…; the brother emigrates in the victim's place; and what if…the killer emigrates to America as well?

Vengeance is clearly the plot motivator in this story, but something more is needed to give fullness to the tale. So Petrakis adds a story spicer—the search. The story moves from Greece to Ellis Island to Chicago to the bestial labor camps at the mines and railroads in the western United States. It revolves about the obsession for vengeance while the avenger searches for his victim across the face of the continent. The storyline is a neat mixture of plot motivation— vengeance—and story spicer—searching.

In Euripides's *Medea* vengeance is the concept of the scorned woman. Medea had been left by Jason for another woman, and in her fury Medea poisons her rival and then kills the children she had borne with Jason. Story spicers in this ancient tale include honor and dishonor and the commission of crimes—specifically, murder. But the motivation for the story, the track that the story moves upon, is vengeance. Medea wants revenge; why she wants it and how she gets it are ancillary to the essence of the story.

Shakespeare deals with vengeance in a number of his works, but in *The Tempest* it is quite clearly the prime plot motivator. What if…one brother, Antonio, drives another brother, Prospero, into exile and usurps the family throne; and what if…Prospero lands on a barely inhabited island in the South Atlantic and is somehow blessed with magical powers; and what if…these magic powers cause Antonio to become shipwrecked on the island and to come within the control of Prospero? How the vengeance is wrought and what other discomforts are experienced by Antonio and his family liven up the basic story, but it is Prospero's urge for vengeance that carries things along.

"Revenge is a kind of wild justice which the more man's nature runs to, the more ought law to weed it out." Francis Bacon made this observation several centuries ago, and it's an apt expression about the pervasive disharmony that accompanies the urge for vengeance. It results in powerful emotions and forceful actions because it implies an ultimate payback.

And no clearer example can be uncovered than in the work that many consider the model for revenge-seeking in the annals of literature: Aeschylus's *Oresteia* or *The House of Atreus*. Called a revenge trilogy by critics, *Oresteia* consists of three dramas that begin with the start of the Trojan War and with the murder of the war hero, Agamemnon, by his wife, Clytemnestra. The trilogy ends with the murder of Clytemnestra by her son, Orestes, and his subsequent persecution by his mother's ghost and the Furies until he receives final absolution through the Gods.

Though this work is explored in greater detail elsewhere (Betrayal), it offers a good example for our purposes here as to how revenge-seeking carries with it the seeds of its own perpetuation, crime begetting crime with no seeming end. Agamemnon, on his way to the Trojan War, sacrifices his daughter, Iphigenia, which brings his wife, Clytemnestra, to hate him. She kills him with the help of her lover, Aegisthus. (His father, Thyestes, had been forced to eat the flesh of his own children by Agamemnon's father, Atrius.) Orestes kills Clytemnestra and Aegisthus to avenge his father, Agamemnon. The Furies then persecute Orestes.

The Greeks were well aware that a tale founded on revenge brought out a strong storyline, one with which people could identify and take sides. It allows the writer to develop a variety of themes such as the arrogance of power, the retrieval of honor, the urge for wealth and position, the righteousness of simple justice. All of these (and more) are explored in *The House of Atreus*, and none could have achieved such fine portrayal except within the clamor and the wrench of vengeance sought and vengeance done.

It is plot motivation on a grand scale because Aeschylus deals with universal themes of love and hate, life and death and man's essential subjugation to a higher will. Vengeance is not without its cost. No mortal is immune from the ultimate payback.

Some twenty-five hundred years later, the same panorama of values and judgments, obsessions and satisfactions are displayed on an equally grand scale in Herman Melville's classic, *Moby Dick*. Here we have vengeance sought not against a human, but against a white whale, and the struggle is a testament to man's urge to erase a lifelong scar that pulses with his own fallibility. If...the whale could be destroyed, that would underscore the righteousness of the vengeance. If...man could exact his revenge and survive, that would be a testament to his essential superiority over non-human beings.

The plot, which carries many of the same themes that Aeschylus uses in *The House of Atrius*, concerns the whaling voyage of the ship, Pequod, out of Nantucket. Ishmael, a schoolmaster with a yen for sea travel, signs on and becomes friendly with a tattooed harpooner, Queequeg. The ship is enroute to the Indian Ocean in the hunt for whales, and the first few days of the voyage are fairly calm as the ship is handled by the first mate, Starbuck. Captain Ahab, the skipper, is nowhere to be seen, but after a time, he appears on deck, a rigid man with a dour expression and a white scar running from his cheekbone right down to and under his collar. He has only one leg, the other just a stump supported by the bone from the jaw of a whale. It is soon evident that his obsession to find and kill the white whale is total, and after a few days, he calls the men to him at the foot of the mainmast. In solemn ceremony Ahab takes a gold piece and nails it to the mast, promising that the first sailor to sight the white whale will get it. Then, he orders liquor broken out so that each member of the crew may have a cup. Drink! he orders. Drink to the death and the destruction of *Moby Dick*!

In the end, the only one to survive is Ishmael, and he does so by clinging to the strangely designed coffin once made for his friend, Queequeg. The vengeance Ahab sought with such passion comes to nothing. It is the same message Aeschylus sends out in *The House of Atrius*—only the Gods can exact vengeance. A mere mortal attempts it at his ultimate peril.

"Vengeance is mine," said The Lord.

So it is.

2. Catastrophe

Catastrophe...a series of calamities or disasters that end in supreme despair or ruin. Catastrophe—a situation filled with various misfortunes that, taken together, amount to destruction.

Catastrophe as a plot motivator is a surging force on a story, a most powerful influence. Catastrophe, by its very nature, carries along the elements of good story making— tension, of course, high drama, essential conflict, life-and-death struggles. It really isn't hard to understand the impact of catastrophe on storyline.

Through the ages writers have used catastrophe to move their plots along. Homer, in *The Iliad and The Odyssey*, uses it over and over. In fact, in the opening book of The Iliad, he writes of a pestilence that has invaded the camp of the Greeks who have been besieging Troy for almost ten years. It seems that Chryses, Apollo's priest, wants to gain his daughter back from Agamemnon, Commander of the Greek armies. Agamemnon has been using her as a concubine, and he doesn't want to give her up. So Chryses prays to Apollo for intervention, and Apollo responds by sending a pestilence. In The Odyssey Homer writes of shipwrecks, of life-and-death struggles with the one-eyed Cyclops, of having a ship's crew changed into swine, of a descent into Hades and the battles with Scylla and Charybdis—events which border on catastrophe because Odysseus, the protagonist, survives by just the barest margin. Catastrophe as a plot motivator is effective even if it doesn't occur, so long as the threat of its happening is there and the consequences seem very real and frightening.

Catastrophe, actually, comes in several shapes, and as a plot motivator its shape ultimately determines the storyline. For example, the most common type of catastrophe is of the natural variety—earthquake, flood, famine, drought and the like. We build a story on the foundations of a natural catastrophe, as Albert Camus did with *The Plague* in 1947. This story is set in Oran, Algiers in the 1940s, and the leading character is Bernard Rieux, a young doctor. For several days Rieux finds rat bodies on the landing of the stairs to his apartment each morning. The rats have died from internal bleeding, and the concierge grumbles about having to clean them up. Day by day the number of rat bodies increases, and soon truckloads are being carted away Then the concierge comes down with a fever and Rieux treats him for it and for painful swellings. Rieux calls some of his colleagues around Oran and finds that they, too, have had such cases.

The head prefect is notified, but he doesn't want to take any strong action because of his fear that the local population might be unduly alarmed. He cautions patience, even though one doctor makes it plain to him that he thinks the city is afflicted by bubonic plague. But people begin dying, and shortly the death toll rises to thirty a day. The prefect is then implored to do something drastic…but still the death toll climbs. In the local papers, the weekly count of deaths has become a daily count. Armed guards are set up at all the entrances and exits to and from the city, allowing no one to enter or leave. Citizens are forbidden to send or receive mail, and the telephone lines become so heavily overburdened that the only reliable way of communicating with the outside world is by telegraph. Body disposal becomes a problem, and the authorities begin to cremate the remains in older graves to make room for the new bodies. Two pits are dug in a field, one pit for women, one pit for men. But even these pits become filled, so still another, larger pit is dug and this time there is no attempt to segregate the sexes. Men, women and children are simply thrown into the larger pit and covered with a layer of quicklime. Rieux works in a ward at the infirmary, but there is little he can do to stem the onslaught of the disease. The available serum is ineffective, and most of the patients die. All Rieux can do is try to make their hours and days a bit more comfortable.

Camus weaves various characters through the story, interpreting their reactions to the plague as a commentary on good and evil, God and man, retribution and penance, the fulfillment of one's life. These heady themes all play through the book while Camus works his plot along, grinding the horrendous conditions ever more severe.

And finally, with the coming of cold weather in the middle of winter, the plague dies away. But, of course, the lives of those it affected will never be the same.

Can we steal Camus's plot? It doesn't have to be a plague, or even a natural catastrophe. It can be any momentous event which throws people into situations where they can be manipulated by the author into professing views or taking action on the grander questions of our time. A volcanic eruption, perhaps? Or an out-of-control forest fire? What about the slowly disintegrating layer of ozone in our atmosphere which protects us from the scorching rays of the sun? What if…we take Camus's Doctor Rieux and make him a coal miner caught in a huge underground explosion with many others? Or a meteorologist in the center of a massive tornado scourge? Or a ship's captain threatened by a massive hurricane? The actions of the characters are conditioned by the catastrophe, and the movement of the story is controlled by reactions to the threat of catastrophe, the catastrophe itself and the after-effects of the catastrophe.

Now, suppose we take a natural catastrophe and enlarge it with a man-made catastrophe, a double dip so to speak. Here again the same general principles apply. Survival is part of the circumstances, but we continue with major emphasis on the catastrophe. In John Steinbeck's *The Grapes of Wrath*, we have a natural catastrophe, the dust-bowl drought in Oklahoma in the nineteen thirties, and the man-made catastrophe, the Great Depression, fusing to become a double-layered event that questions the very nature of capitalism and social justice. Are injustice and oppression and misery natural products beyond our control, or can man do something about his lot? Are we, each of us, individual islands of self-concern or are we inexorably tied to one another, interdependent and all part of a greater whole?

The Grapes of Wrath is the story of the Joad family's journey from their barren Oklahoma farm to the promise of migratory farm work in California. Without catastrophe as the plot motivator, the story would become little more than a travelogue, but because Steinbeck has given the plot substance by means of the series of disasters and calamities that befall the Joad family, the story is exciting, provoking, moving and forceful.

Many have traced the plot of *The Grapes of Wrath* to the Bible— specifically to the Book of Exodus. In both instances the story concerns people led into the wilderness with the hope of something better, in a search of a "promised land." Both stories open with the presence of catastrophic conditions. In the Bible, the Egyptian Pharaoh is refusing to allow Moses to lead the Israelites out of Egypt and as a result the Lord visits a series of calamities on the countryside. In one night all the Egyptian cattle die. A hailstorm kills off mature herbs and trees in the fields. A plague of locusts ruins any remaining vegetable and fruit plants. And then come three days of inky black darkness. Finally, after the Lord and Moses set up the Feast of the Passover and every Egyptian first-born dies, the Pharaoh lets the people go. For John Steinbeck this is the blueprint for *The Grapes of Wrath*. His plot has its own tortuous turns and twists, but the essential story is the same: catastrophe motivating a journey for some kind of redemption.

In our modern age, of course, it is nuclear catastrophe that we face, and ever since the atomic age became reality in 1945, writers have spewed forth literature based on its possibilities. What if?... What if?...Actually, it was in 1914 that it was mentioned first—by H.G. Wells, in *The World Set Free*:

The catastrophe of the atomic bombs which shook men out of cities and businesses and economic relations, shook them also out of their old-established habits of thought, and out of the lightly held beliefs and prejudices that came down to them from the past.

Since 1945 it's been what if...

...we have already had World War III, the major cities of the United States are destroyed and a small town in Florida, cut off from the rest of the world, tries to cope by reversion to a primitive lifestyle? *Alas Babylon*, by Pat Frank, 1959.

...we have a set of bombers flying towards Moscow because of a defective missile-alarm system, and there is no way to recall them? *Fail-Safe*, by Eugene Burdick and Harvey Wheeler, 1962.

...an obsessed Red Chinese Colonel plots to drop a nuclear bomb on New York City and provoke total war? *Thirty Seconds Over New York,* by Robert Buchard, 1970.

...a scientist dies at Los Alamos in 1946 of radiation sickness and during the eight days of his dying his colleagues discuss and weigh the consequences of producing and using the bomb? *The Accident,* by Dexter Master, 1975.

Perhaps the classic use of catastrophe in our nuclear age is found in Nevil Shute's *On The Beach,* published in 1963. Here, as with almost all the literature in which catastrophe is a plot motivator, there is also the motivator survival. Yet it is the catastrophe itself that spurs the story on. A "short, bewildering war" in the Northern Hemisphere has resulted in the annihilation of all human life there, and now the heavy, lethal cloud of radiation is making its way inexorably towards Australia, with Melbourne the last major city as yet unaffected. There are about nine months left before radiation will blot out every living thing.

Then, of course, the real—and final—catastrophe dawns...the end of all known life.

3. Love and Hate

The idea of love—and hate—is clearly represented in the ancient literature. After all, it is Aphrodite who really sets in motion the events leading to the Trojan War. Paris is asked to judge a contest of beauty among three of the goddesses: Athena, Hera and Aphrodite. He chooses Aphrodite, and in return she offers him the most beautiful mortal woman in the world. Paris wants Helen, the wife of Menelaus, King of Athens, and steals her away. Then he is challenged to a duel by Menelaus, a duel he would never win because he is not a fighter. In truth, he is a lover. Enter Aphrodite… she sweeps him up and places him in his bedchamber, eager, anticipatory, ready!

Aphrodite then disguises herself as an old servant and goes to Helen and whets her appetite for Paris. Soon, it's Helen who goes to Paris, and they make warm, passionate love.

While Aphrodite smiles at what she has created and relishes the beauty prize Paris has bestowed on her.

Helen accompanies Paris to Troy, Menelaus fumes over his wife's treachery and soon the armies of Athens and other Greek city-states begin their march on Troy. And the ten years of the Trojan War begin.

Now, let's update this drama about three thousand years. What if…the ultimate male fantasy is to make love with the most beautiful, desirable woman in the world; and what if…four men come together and agree that the object of their longing is a gorgeous, sexy movie queen named Sharon Fields, the embodiment of all their unfulfilled desires; and what if…they hatch a plan to kidnap this movie queen in order to play out their untamed sexual fantasies; and what if…after the kidnapping they install Sharon Fields in a mountain cabin and then fall to bickering among themselves;

and what if…Sharon Fields becomes the object of a wide search and she and her kidnappers are besieged in their mountain cabin; and what if…one of the kidnappers falls madly in love with her…

What we have here is the plot of *The Fan Club*, a 1974 novel by Irving Wallace. Did Wallace purloin the essentials of the famous story about Helen of Troy? Perhaps, but so what? Actually what Wallace has done is to take the Helen of Troy story further and in a different direction. In *The Fan Club* we concentrate on the interrelationships between Sharon Fields and her kidnappers. In *The Iliad*, where we find the details of Helen's kidnapping, emphasis is on the fortunes of the contending armies and their champions. Homer did not dwell too much on just how Helen and Paris actually do get along—on their daily conversations and such. But not so in *The Fan Club*. We come to know each of the kidnappers intimately, and we see clearly their motivations and desires. In the process we also come to know Sharon Fields intimately, more intimately perhaps than anyone could ever know Homer's Helen of Troy.

Yet the essentials of the two stories remain the same: a beautiful, desirable woman is kidnapped, the consequences start a chain of events that have destructive results for all concerned. For Paris, Helen and Menelaus there are the ten years of the Trojan War; for Sharon Fields and her kidnappers, there is only degradation, distaste and ultimately, for the kidnappers death.

Even though love reigns in the Greek legends, there is hate, too. The Greeks and their gods hated as fiercely as they loved. "No Olympian god is so hated…he thinks only of strife and wars and battles…" Homer writes of the god, Ares in *The Iliad*. Ares is the spirit of carnage, the slayer of men, interested only in blood and death and slaughter. He may be one of the divine gods, but in Greek legend none has less respect from the other gods and none is so feared and despised. Throughout *The Iliad* his partiality for the Trojans is apparent, and Homer describes him in less than glowing terms.

But the clearest object of his hate was another god, or in this case, a goddess, Athena. "I begin to sing of Pallas Athena," goes one of the ancient *Homeric Hymns*, "the glorious goddess, owl-eyed, inventive, unbending of heart, pure virgin, savior of cities, courageous...From his awful head wise Zeus himself, bore her arrayed in warlike arms of flashing gold, and awe seized all the gods as they gazed..."

Athena is the spirit of the warrior, yet she is not war hungry, as is Ares. She might urge the Greeks on in battle if their morale were to drop, she might inspire them to heroic deeds. She is at all times rational and protective—unlike Ares who is destructive and demonic. Homer writes of Athena with great passion and respect, and Odysseus, his most famous character, is the object of Athena's constant love and protection.

But there is hate between Ares and Athena, based as much on their conflicting natures as anything else. The bloodthirsty Ares versus the noble Athena. They have a battle in the twenty-first book of *The Iliad*, and it will be the only real contest they fight. But the hatred between them is palpable. Diomedes, the Greek hero of numerous battles, finds himself face to face with Ares, and the blood-lust of the god is a vicious thing to behold. Athena, who has come to the aid of Diomedes in other situations, sees his peril and appears to him in the flesh, leaping on his chariot and taking the place of his driver. Ares throws his spear at Diomedes, but Athena deflects it almost casually. And then, injecting her power into the spear-throw of Diomedes, she causes Ares to be deeply wounded and to go howling off in pain.

If the gods can hate one another, man can also. Hate is hardly relegated to the divine circle. And as a plot motivator it can have a powerful force on a storyline, just as love can. Hate and love, as opposites, can usually deal with the same set of circumstances and motivate the plot in separate directions. For example, let's go back to *The Fan Club*. What if...Sharon Fields is kidnapped, not because she is a love goddess, but because she is a hated symbol! Perhaps in the way the Symbionese Liberation Army treated Patty Hearst in 1974. Now, after the kidnapping, the hatred begins to pour out. Anger, even physical abuse, may occur. (In *The Fan Club* it took die form of sexual abuse.) We come to know the kidnappers intimately, and the person kidnapped. The kidnappers bicker among themselves, violence erupts, and finally there is death and destruction. All arising out of hatred, not love. Same set of circumstances, same number of characters, same outcome. Same plot motivator, too—but in mirror image!

As a plot motivator love is most effective when it is in motion—that is, when it expands or contracts or takes on a different aspect. Love should never be static, it must have a life of its own! Then the story will move, as well. The same is true of hate.

Look at how Ernest Hemingway deals with love in *A Farewell to Arms,* his 1929 novel set in Italy during the First World War. Though the book has anti-war overtones, it is first and foremost a love story. Lieutenant Frederick Henry, a young American with an Italian ambulance unit, meets Catherine Barkley, a British hospital nurse. At first there is just casual interest in one another, but then Henry becomes wounded and is moved to a hospital in Milan. Catherine is there, too, and they fall in love. Catherine manages to be with him constantly, and he slowly recuperates. They dine in cozy little restaurants, ride the countryside in a carriage and become closer and closer. From time to time Catherine comes to his hospital room where they make love.

Then, Henry is due to go back to the front, his wound now healed. They spend his last days and nights together in a hotel where Catherine tells him she is now pregnant. Henry is deeply upset about leaving her in the midst of war, but she assures him she will be all right. He goes back to his unit and soon finds himself in the middle of some of the heaviest fighting. The Italian army begins the ill-fated retreat from Caporetto which ends in a chaotic frenzy of disorder, and Henry must try to cope and save himself. As the retreat continues Henry comes to the conclusion that he has no place in the war, and he sets out on his own back to Milan and Catherine. When he gets there, he discovers that the British nurses have gone to Stresa, and he then borrows some civilian clothes from a friend and makes it to Stresa where he finally locates Catherine. The bartender at the hotel where he and Catherine are staying warns him the authorities will arrest him the next day for desertion. He offers Henry and Catherine his dingy for an escape to Switzerland. All night Henry rows, and by morning his hands are so raw that Catherine insists on taking over. Henry protests, but to no avail, and they finally reach Switzerland. They spend the next few months at an inn outside Montreux, and they discuss marriage. But Catherine will not be married while she is pregnant. They make plans to be together after the war ends.

Then it is time for Catherine to have the baby, and after hours of labor, the baby is born dead. Catherine begins to hemorrhage, and as Henry sits with her, she dies. For Henry it is the end. There is no place he can go, no one to talk to, nothing he can do. As he leaves the hospital and walks back to his hotel it is raining.

A tragic love story about a love that grows, blossoms and finally ends. It doesn't die, it just ends. The love has a life of its own in this story, and that is the key to using love as a plot motivator. Hemingway referred to *A Farewell to Arms* as his *Romeo and Juliet*, and there are certainly similarities. While Shakespeare plays his story out against a backdrop of family feuding and some political turmoil, Hemingway sets his story in wartime. When we think of classic love stories, of course, Romeo and Juliet comes immediately to mind, and if there are star-crossed lovers in Shakespeare's drama, is it any less so for Hemingway, just because *A Farewell to Arms* is set in the twentieth century? Henry and Catherine are equally beset by a hostile environment, they carve out their love in the midst of all that turmoil, they pledge themselves to one another, and their love never dies. It simply ends.

4. The Chase

"There he goes!" The shout rings out, and action speeds up. The chase is on, and if it's done well enough, we'll identify with those doing the chasing or those being chased. It's a simple formula for a good story. There's conflict (why else would there be a chase?), there's movement and there's a natural storyline. The chase itself could be the entire story in that it would comprise a beginning, a middle and an end, and we could weave a complete plot through it. That's essentially what Jules Verne does with *Around the World In Eighty Days,* his Saga of Phineas Fogg who races his arch rival in a variety of contraptions for a prize put up by a New York newspaper. The chase is for the title of winner, and is to be completed within the prescribed time. The entire story deals with the race—the chase—but in the course of it Verne weaves in love and adventure and scientific know-how. Without the chase there simply would not have been a story.

The chase as a plot motivator seems to work best where stories lend themselves to adventure, mystery, suspense. The reasons are obvious: the necessary ingredients of a chase include action and conflict, and the writer has a fertile opportunity to stretch out the chase or narrow it by creating tight escapes or despair or even temporary capture. Each time, the tension between the characters is heightened because the chase gets down to a basic human level, an eyeball-to-eyeball confrontation. Each close brush gives us more to identify with in the characters, and it provides additional fuel to stoke up the fires of suspense, mystery or adventure.

When is a chase not a chase?

When the object of the chase is already there, in place, waiting to be captured. This is more like a search, a quest, because no one is running away, no one is trying to elude capture. Using the chase as a plot motivator means that someone (or something) is after someone else, and the latter is or should be aware of it. That awareness, in fact, creates the tensions that add up to suspense: will he/she be caught? How does he/she get away?

If we set up a hunting story, the chase is the most important plot motivator. Story spicers such as searching and rescue come naturally into play because a hunt implies a search and rescue. But there is this difference: with a search the quarry is often someone or something that hasn't done anything wrong. They may or may not want to be found, but it isn't because they are trying to elude capture. With a chase, of course, the opposite is true. The quarry is trying to avoid capture, is trying to get away not be found. Searching stories also involve someone looking to be found, someone who has been lost or abandoned. Not with chase stories.

Thus, if we use a hunting motif for a chase story, we ought to be able to understand the confines of the motivator. And, of course, one of the most famous hunting stories has to be Herman Melville's *Moby Dick*, the obsessive hunt for the white whale. More chase stories than we imagine pattern themselves on *Moby Dick*—and for good reason. The conflict is between man and animal, good and evil; the characters are outsized, dangerous; and the motivation is pure obsession, a lust for vengeance rarely equalled throughout literature. These are the ingredients for a rich and lively tale.

Take Walter Clark's 1950 novel, *The Track of the Cat*, a thinly disguised reincarnation of *Moby Dick*. The Bridges family live in a remote Nevada valley on a large cattle ranch at the turn of the century. Word comes that a huge black panther (translate: white whale) has been killing their cattle in the mountains, and the two oldest Bridges brothers set off to kill it as the first snowstorm of the year settles in. First one and then the second brother is killed by the panther, and so the third and last brother and a mystical, legend-spouting Indian take up the chase. Before it's over, the hunters become the hunted as the cold and the panther's cunning and the lack of food take their toll. The blackness of the panther is evil incarnate, of course, but the irony in this story is more direct: the third brother is frail and abhors killing while his older brothers relish it. Yet in the end it is the third brother who finally kills the panther. (Unlike Captain Ahab who is finally done in by his white whale. But then, isn't Walter Clark just applying a what if… scenario?)

Chase stories don't always have to be so serious or ponderous. They can be cast in the adventure, suspense or mystery mode and still make us laugh. Story spicers such as suspicion, even suicide or criminal action can be added, and the action can be light with humor spilling from the pages. This is what Thomas Berger does with *Who Is Teddy Villanova?*—a 1977 novel that is really a spoof of the detective mystery. The protagonist is Russel Wren, a former English literature professor turned private eye who tries throughout the entire book to prove that he is not Teddy Villanova, an arch fiend and international criminal. The story of the chase is just this: Wren's hunt for Teddy Villanova or for information that will prove, first, that he is not Teddy Villanova and second, just who and where Teddy Villanova really is. In the course of the book, Wren consistently avoids his secretary's demands for back pay, is knocked around over and over, is questioned repeatedly by the police, is held at gun point and is generally one of the most ineffective private eyes to cross the detective, mystery, suspense scene.

The spoof continues in the way Wren speaks: with outlandish, flowery, Victorian phrasing, overblown and often quite pointless. He is the antithesis of the hard-boiled, no-nonsense operative who speaks little but acts with great verve and success. He is the chronic loser, and even when he is hired to find Teddy Villanova, the amount he is offered is insultingly small. Near the end of the book, Berger has Wren saying, "I still don't understand the part I've played, but I assure you, I'm nursing a massive grudge against someone." In this we see the essence of his ineffectuality. He doesn't even know who his enemy is! Yet the chase goes on and the chuckles pile up.

Though the heart of most chase stories involve the hunt, sometimes the chase isn't to capture the quarry so much as to expose and thereby render the quarry ineffective. The purpose of a chase is to generate action, to move the story along, and the end doesn't have to be so perfect. The chase itself is what motivates the plot, not the ultimate result.

This is the way things happened in *The Bedford Incident*, a cold-war drama written by Mark Rascovich and published in 1963. The author pondered—what if...*The Bedford*, an American destroyer on duty in the North Atlantic, comes in contact with a Russian submarine trying to penetrate U.S. radar defense, and what if...the captain of The Bedford knows he can't fire on the submarine but must try and make the spying mission as difficult as possible, and what if...The Bedford is the most modern electronically equipped killing machine in the Navy and the submarine an equally equipped marvel in the Russian submarine services...

The Bedford's captain, Erik Finlander, is a veteran of the Second World War and an insatiable foe of submarines ever since the destroyer he sailed on in the war had been sunk. Once contact with the Russian submarine has been established, Finlander drives his ship and his crew to frightening lengths in order to win the only battle open to them—ship-handling dexterity. He hopes to force the sub to surface and thereby admit the superiority of Finlander's vessel and skill.

But as the conflict increases in intensity, the tension aboard *The Bedford* grows as well. Tacitly, both ship and submarine wage a bitter maneuvering battle with more and more control of the struggle given over to electronic devices that make them both lethal killing machines. In the end both ship and submarine perish, the victims of humans having too much power at their command without a corresponding check on the human frailties that can cause misjudgment in the use of that power.

Look carefully now...isn't that the ghost of *Moby Dick* peering through the pages of *The Bedford Incident*? The obsession of the captain for the undersea creature that almost destroyed him in his youth, the rising tension on board as the chase and the search continue for a quarry unseen but felt, the naked clash of good with evil (if, in fact, one considers the Russians the embodiment of evil. And at the height of the cold war, when *The Bedford Incident* was written, there was more general support for that view than there is today.)

The chase is on...'There he goes!" And with the spectre of *Moby Dick* hovering just barely in view, the storyline is spice (by elements of search and rescue and deception and suspicion and honor and dishonor.

The hunt goes on, and the *Moby Dick* saga is stolen again.

5. Grief and Loss

Except in matters of love, there is probably no more universal theme in literature than death and its effect on those who have some thread of contact with the event. How do we react to death? How *should* we react? What to do next? What do we remember? Are our lives richer for knowing the deceased?

Questions like these are the fodder that causes dynamic stories to sprout. When we mourn, we aren't just feeling sad because someone we felt close to has died; we are marking the end of life for a part of us, as well. It is the part we shared with the deceased, that private part which contained special experiences and intimacies, special fantasies and unspoken dreams. No more will we hope or plan or wonder. We have only the reality of living to endure.

Death and the way it affects us is a powerful plot motivator because we can't run from it. We *must* stand and deal with it, have no choice. From Aeschylus's *The Death of Achilles* right to Erich Segal's *Love Story* and beyond, the annals of literature are bulging with stories about death, or impending death, and our reactions to it. It is a superb technique for mirroring human values and human foibles because of the universality of the theme. The prospect of death—or the inevitability of it—or the fact of it—remains a constant throughout the story, and each character can be fleshed out and judged against the never varying constant. It is as if the story is bundled within a rolled-up carpet, and as we unroll the carpet the story unravels too, but never does it stray off the carpet. Grief and loss, which are the natural effects of death, preserve the constancy of it and cause the same reactions. If there is death, do we grieve? If we suffer a loss, do we hurt?

One way writers have dealt with this theme is to provide a kaleidoscope of characters and to weave their reactions and interreactions together against the backdrop of a central character's death or dying. Reactions differ, of course, just as individuals differ. Some are noble, some are coarse, some malicious, some just plain evil. None remain untouched, however, and in the interplay of their grief, we build a story.

Two great novelists fashioned stories this way, approximately a generation apart. Though they used the same mechanism, here we have one example when a plot is not stolen. As we'll see, there's just too much dissimilarity.

The first of these stories is William Faulkner's 1930 work, *As I Lay Dying*. It is the story of the dying and death of Addie Bundren and the way her husband, Anse Bundren, and her sons, Cash, Darl, Jewel and Vardaman, and her daughter, Dewey Dell, deal with it. As Addie lies propped in her bed, she can see out the window, and she watches her son, Cash, build the wooden coffin that will hold her. As he finishes a section he displays it for her approval, his only reason being an obsession with fine workmanship. Cash would be heartbroken if the coffin were irregularly finished. Addie has indicated she wishes to be buried in Jefferson, a town a full day's ride from the farm, and Anse is determined that her wish be fulfilled. But two other sons, Darl and Jewel, want to take a wagonload of lumber into town and earn three dollars for the family to use on the trip to Jefferson. At first Anse doesn't want them to make the trip, fearing they might not return in time to take Addie's body to Jefferson. But he finally gives in.

Then Addie dies, while the boys are still away and before Cash can finish the coffin. Vardaman, the youngest, returns to the house with a fish he has just caught, in time to be present during his mother's death throes. He entangles his mother's death with the death of the fish and he is severely upset.

Meanwhile, a torrential rainstorm has delayed Darl and Jewel with the lumber, and on top of that they must repair a broken wheel on the wagon. Cash, though, keeps working through the rain and finally finishes the coffin. As Addie's body is laid within it, Vardaman, who once almost suffocated in his crib, bores holes in the top of the coffin so his mother can get out.

There is a short graveside service and then the family begins the trek to Jefferson with Addie's body. Their destination is the family cemetery. But before they go very far, they come to the river, now swollen by the heavy rains. With a great deal of effort they succeed in getting the wagon with Addie's body almost across the river, when a huge log floats downstream and upsets the wagon. Cash's leg is broken in the melee, and he nearly drowns; the mules pulling the wagon are drowned, the coffin slips overboard but is finally collared and pulled to the bank.

Anse looks at the scattered remnants of his entourage, and he is tempted to ask a nearby farmer for the loan of a set of mules. But then he reconsiders…whatever is to carry Addie to her grave must be his and his alone. He will ask for no help from anyone. Instead, he offers to trade a spotted horse—a special favorite of Jewel's which he had worked morning and night to pay for—without asking Jewel if he could bargain it away. In this way Anse is able to get the mules to continue the journey.

Jewel, however, is quite upset at what his father has done; he hops on the spotted horse and rides off, leaving Anse's bargain for the mules hanging. But later Jewel has a change of heart, and without telling anyone in the family, he simply places the spotted horse in the barn of the person who has been bargaining with Anse for the mules.

By now Addie has been dead so long the buzzards are following the wagon. But still the family plunges on. It is nine days before they finally get Addie buried, and in the end it is Anse who is most rejuvenated by Addie's death. Before starting the trip home to the farm, he buys himself a new set of false teeth—something he has needed for a long time—and he has acquired a new wife. For each of the others, the death trip costs something precious: for Jewel it is his favorite horse; for Cash it is the use of his leg; for Darl it is his sanity (he sets fire to a barn where Addie's coffin lies the night before she is buried, and Anse turns him over to the authorities who send him to a nearby asylum). For Dewey Dell it is her self-respect, for a drugstore clerk seduces her by convincing her he has some medicine which can abort an illegitimate child she is carrying.

In the end, Faulkner has us believe that the roads through life and through death are not two separate paths but only one, and that it's absurd to try and distinguish between them. As Addie says on her deathbed: "I could just remember how my father used to say that the reason for living was to get ready to stay dead a long time."

Some quarter-century later James Agee deals with the same theme in his *A Death in the Family*. Again, we see the reactions of a host of characters to a single death. In this case it is the death of Jay Follett, husband, father, son, brother and respected citizen of Knoxville, Tennessee. It starts early one morning when Jay arises before daybreak to go to the bedside of his father who has been taken gravely ill. Jay and his wife, Mary, have quiet breakfast together and decide not to wake their children Rufus, who is six, and his younger sister, because Jay expects to be back by nightfall. But he doesn't come back, and Mary hears a stranger's voice say that Jay has been killed in an automobile accident. Agee then delves into how this death affects the various members of the family.

For Mary it is a cold slap of reality. Death is common, she comes to understand; many people suffer as she does. And she I turns to her faith for consolation.

For Rufus, it is another of life's confusing moments such as his nightmares, or the reasons why older boys ask his name and then laugh and run away or why his mother has made him promise never to mention the color of a black maid's skin.

For Ralph Follet, Jay's brother and a drunk, who happens to be an undertaker, it provides a means for some small measure of self-worth. He will prepare his brother's body for burial; no one else will be allowed to do it.

With these and other characters Agee portrays efforts to understand Jay Follett's death in the grief and the love they share. The plot is simple—a man has died and we witness how those close to him react. The action, really, is in the portrayal of the reactions and how the feelings of the characters interweave, such as Rufus's urge to show off his new cap, bought for him by a great-aunt who wishes to ease the loss he will be feeling. He runs to his parents' bedroom but finds only his mother with face drawn and two pillows behind her back, his father's place empty. It's something a six-year-old boy just doesn't understand.

Story spicers in works like *As I Lay Dying* and *A Death in the Family* don't amount to much. We might fit in making amends, or honor and dishonor, but essentially, stories like these rely more on an exploration of emotion than on a connected series of events. Still, what plot there is will be spurred by the sense of grief and loss felt by each of the characters.

Let's be irreverent and call these "House of Death" books because that's what they really are. It's a fairly common story framework where the person who is dying or already dead and those the event affects are locked in close proximity with one another. The author weaves a story out of memory, fantasy and self-proof with the plot moving forward at a gradual pace.

This is what James T. Farrell does with *The Death of Nora Ryan*, a 1978 book about a woman who suffers a stroke and about her various children who gather by her lower-middle-class Chicago bedside and hold a vigil until she succumbs. Just as Faulkner and Agee do, Farrell has his characters develop in the light of the enveloping tragedy. There's Eddie the successful novelist, and Steve the successful doctor and Clara the sister who stayed at home…and an assortment of other siblings who spare time for their mother's death but who are barely touched by it all. In the end they return to their ordinary lives, their memories refreshed by thoughts of the way things used to be but their outlooks neither changed nor helped. They are the same people before the event as they are after it, and that, in itself, is the story. They are not ennobled by their mother's dying nor are they made more contemptible. Except in the immediate sense, the House of Death has little effect on them.

6. Rebellion

A rebellion is a...revolution is a...*coup d'état* is an...insurrection. "If you've seen one, you've seen them all," a former vice-president of the United States once remarked. He was referring to an urban ghetto where minorities struggled, passing their days in abject poverty. But his remark—insensitive and inaccurate though it was—could be applied to situations where active challenge to established authority takes place. "If you've seen one challenge to authority, you've seen them all," may not be without exception, but stories which contain a strong dose of rebellion or *coup d'état* or revolution or insurrection seem to follow similar lines.

There's authority being challenged, and most often it is a government or political entity rigidly enforcing its own standards or rules. But it doesn't have to be political. How about *One Flew Over the Cuckoo's Nest,* Ken Kesey's fine work about the challenge to authority in a mental institution? In a sense the mental institution is a separate state, at least to those who are confined behind its walls. Randall McMurphy, the protagonist, is the primary challenger to the institution's authority, and the challenge he makes is not so much to overthrow authority as to attempt to relax the rules. He ridicules, he teases, he creates mischief in order to demonstrate to Miss Ratched, the head nurse and his major adversary, that the rules are silly, pointless and in some instances downright dangerous. His rebellion is more of the spirit than for material gain, though he is obviously striving for some form of power.

And that's the next similarity about stories that use challenge to authority as a plot motivator. There's that search, that urge for power. We rebel to throw off someone else's yoke, but in doing it don't we also look to gain power? Take *The Caine Mutiny,* written in 1951 by Herman Wouk. It's the story of an aging minesweeper during the Second World War, her skipper's rapidly developing paranoia, the effect on the crew and the ultimate challenge. It's the saga of Willie Keith, a Princeton graduate who becomes a junior officer on the S.S. Caine, as the ship readies herself for sea duty in the South Pacific. Her new captain is Philip Queeg, a veteran of the battle of the Atlantic, tired now and worn. As Queeg begins to distrust every one of his officers and men and actually wonders whether there are plots to unseat him, Willie Keith and the other officers conspire to take command from him. They consider him dangerously unreliable, and they fear for their lives. And then, as The Caine wallows perilously in the fury of a typhoon, Queeg appears lost and confused, and his command is taken over on the spot. The challenge has succeeded, and in the ensuing court-martial the actions of the officers in taking away Queeg's command are ratified. Queeg's power over them has been stripped, and they are now free to develop their own destinies. They have acquired power for themselves.

In stories where rebellion and a challenge to authority become the plot motivator, there will usually be some aspect of survival as well. Perhaps it might even be a co-plot motivator, whether we're concerned about the one whose authority is being challenged or the one who is doing the challenging, the way either or both survive the challenge is most important. Surviving the rebellion... how it is done...what will replace the old order...are significant circumstances to write about. What does surviving do to the characters, to their relationships? What about those who don't survive?

Obviously, rebellion coupled with survival is fertile pickings for story spicers. Honor and dishonor are almost always there, as well as conspiracy and authority. In fact, it would be rare to find a story motivated by rebellion that didn't contain at least these four story spicers.

In Shakespeare the question was always hanging there— is the new order any better than the old? Macbeth, King Lear, Julius Caesar, among other Shakespearean dramas, show us that man's political motives are often narrow, self-concerned and not particularly benign. However, it doesn't always have to be that way. In the early 19th century Johann von Schiller wrote his famous William

Tell, a story about a strong, silent hero who emerges from obscurity to rally a rebellion and then retreats back to obscurity. Schiller based the plot on a popular legend that grew out of the animosity between Austria and the Swiss in the fifteenth century. Schiller played what if…the Emperor of Austria sends his personal representative, Gessler, to rule over the forest cantons of Switzerland, and Gessler finds to his anger that the Swiss hold their lands in fief to the Emperor himself and not to his appointed representative. The prosperous, independent Swiss show Gessler to be a paper tiger with only limited authority over the citizens. Now, what if… Gessler determines to exert his own authority and mounts a cap on a pole in a public place, requiring that each man bow to it.

Then, Gessler goes even further and sends his own men to the farm of Henry of Halden, demanding he turn over his best team of oxen. Henry's son, Arnold, refuses, and attacks Gessler's men, driving them away. But Arnold realizes he had better go into hiding, and while he is away, Gessler's soldiers come back and torture Henry and put out his eyes.

So, what if…popular miscontent rises and Walter Furst, William Tell's father-in-law, becomes the leader of the free Switzerland movement. They meet in great secrecy and decide to revive their ancient parliament, though they delay the cry for a popular uprising until the Christmas season.

At this Time William Tell and his sons walk past the pole with the cap on top, and really more by accident than design, pay no attention. Tell is immediately arrested, and his father-in-law pleads with the guards for his release. But William Tell submits to his captors, and as he is being led away Gessler rides by.

He spies Tell's son, Walter Tell, and has an apple placed on the youth's head. Use your bow, he commands Tell, and see if you can shoot the apple from your son's head.

Tell protests, but Gessler is adamant. "Do it!" he commands. So, Tell takes out two arrows and neatly fits one in his crossbow. He aims at the apple on Walter's head and splits it.

"Why did you take two arrows?" Gessler asks.

Tell refuses to answer until Gessler promises not to harm him, no matter what the answer.

Now, what if…Tell says that if his arrow had missed the apple and hurt his son, he would have shot the remaining arrow into Gessler. Gessler, angered by this impudence, forgets his pledge and has William Tell arrested on the spot. He decides to imprison Tell in his castle for life.

On the boat that will take them to Gessler's castle, William Tell is in chains. But a storm comes up and the boat is pitching furiously. What if…Gessler, in fear for his life, implores William Tell to save them, and he unbinds the chains. Tell takes over the helm and guides the boat close to shore where he leaps to safety, then disappears into the forest.

Later, he finds a path on which Gessler must travel to escape the fury of the storm. And he waits for the tyrant. While he is in hiding, a woman and her children come along, hoping to intercept Gessler and plead for clemency for their husband and father who is in prison for a minor offense. Finally, Gessler approaches with his hangers-on and many, many citizens. The woman stops him and makes her appeal for clemency. But Gessler denies the plea.

And that is all William Tell waits to hear. He sights, aims and shoots an arrow from his crossbow, hitting Gessler in the chest. He emerges from his hiding place and announces that it is he who has shot Gessler. Then, quick as he appears, he disappears back into the forest, leaving Gessler to bleed to death in front of so many he has oppressed. And in the ensuing period a free Switzerland is born.

Thus is hatched the modern legend of William Tell, the quiet, unassuming forester who is aroused to action only by the injustice of the tyrant. A bigger-than-life hero, really, someone we could imagine in graphic color depicted on the cover of *Zap!* comics or a modern reincarnation of the western movie tyro, Shane. The hero who does his heroics for the betterment of mankind and not for any personal glory or reward.

Clearly, Schiller stole his plot here. There's no question the William Tell story came from a centuries-old legend, and even if Schiller stayed close to the truth of the legend, the storyline did not come from thin air. In fact, Schiller admitted that he went into the old Swiss Chronicles and discovered the apple-shooting sequence, though not too much else. There were many loose threads—partial story ideas, characters and events, but they weren't tied together in any sort of frame. He had to do that himself. Still, if he hadn't found the incident of William Tell shooting the apple from his son's head, there might not be a modern William Tell today.

And we wouldn't see still another example of an author stealing a plot—and admitting it!

The nature of stories that use rebellion (or revolution, insurrection, *coup d'état*) as plot motivator is that there has to be action, often violent action. Rebellion, by its very nature, implies challenge, conflict, some form of resistance. Action—and reaction—build the story, even though we may be dealing with something other than political events. The rebellion of a young child against its parents, for instance…or the rebellion of employees against an unreasonable employer…or the rebellion of a husband (or wife) against the other spouse…anything, in other words, that creates a challenge and demands some type of redress. "Every revolution was first a thought in one man's mind," wrote Ralph Waldo Emerson many years ago. If we remember that, then rebellion as a plot motivator can be seen in its simplest form. It is just a way of telling a story.

7. Betrayal

Suppose we have a character who is to do something, take some action, be somewhere; others rely upon him, and he knows it. If he deliberately ignores what he's supposed to do, and this brings harm or suffering to anyone, we have the essence of a story. If we start painting in the corners and filling in the spaces, we can label the story as one of betrayal. He has betrayed those who have relied upon him.

Betrayal...treachery...deception...cheating...all of these and more are what has happened, and when we dig a little bit, we're almost certain to have a good story, because stories of betrayal bring out the rawest emotions and precipitate the strongest reactions. It's natural. If we place our trust in someone or rely on them and they *deliberately* take advantage of that to gain something for themselves and we suffer directly for it, the seeds of vengeance are going to sprout in a hurry.

It happens in real life all too often. Betrayal and vengeance go hand-in-hand, one bringing the other out, in a circle of disillusionment and hate that sparks violence and death. Somehow when we're betrayed, it's different from being attacked without provocation. It's worse because we've seen our faith and trust not only slammed back in our faces but hurt us as well. We're victims in a special way because we've allowed ourselves to be deluded.

So, stories of betrayal carry many possibilities, but it all comes down to one basic situation: a person who has put trust in another, has that trust shattered. The result can be a dynamic tale.

It's easy. Many have done it. One of the latest is Joyce Carol Oates in her 1981 novel, *Angel of Light*. Maurice Halleck is a high federal official, director of the Commission for the Ministry of Justice. There is a scandal and Halleck is accused of taking a bribe so a multi-national corporation can continue its illegal activities in South America. Halleck is forced from office, and in disgrace he allegedly commits suicide.

His wife, Isabel, has been having an affair with Nick Martens, an old friend of Halleck's, and in fact Martens eventually succeeds to the post Halleck occupied. In flashbacks the author shows that the relationship of Halleck and Martens goes back more than 30 years, and that when they were both young, Martens actually saved Halleck's life. This brought such gratitude from Halleck's family that Martens's education and career were insured.

At this point, enter Halleck's two children, Kirsten, young, drug-dependent, boarding school educated, anorexic and emotionally unstable, and Owen, a dull, thick-witted Princetonian with an urge to succeed in corporate America. Kirsten is convinced Halleck was murdered by Isabel and Martens, and slowly she convinces Owen. Their mother has betrayed them and their father. They must seek vengeance...

And here we have the plot of *The House of Atreus*, refined and updated. Mother and lover kill husband...lover takes husband's place...children find out...children plot to kill mother and lover.

In refining her plot, Oates brings in a group of terrorists who believe that perhaps Kirsten and Owen have a point about who murdered their father and that it was done for political purposes. Owen, in fact, is killed in a terrorist bombing of his house after he has killed his mother. But this is done simply to keep things current, and it doesn't deflect the basic storyline.

What about story spicers here? There's conspiracy (mother and lover conspiring to kill father and husband), deception (mother and lover keeping their affair quiet), criminal action (murder, murder, murder), suicide (Halleck's alleged death), honor and dishonor (the memory and reputation of father). Note how important a story spicer like deception becomes. The plot is motivated by betrayal, but it becomes all the more significant when the wife and the lover conceal their affair in the hope of succeeding to the power held by the husband. The deception hides the betrayal and provides still another motive for vengeance... *They tried to keep it from us!* the children say...*they knew they couldn't have achieved what they wanted if they didn't hide the affair!*. The act of deception is a betrayal in that it allows the mother and her lover to ignore their responsibilities to the father and to the children.

Shakespeare dealt with betrayal in the eternal love triangle, though certainly not humorously. But in this case it is a story of imagined betrayal which leads to sorrowful consequences. In truth there has been no betrayal, but events transpire on the basis that a betrayal has supposedly occurred. Othello is the play, and the story shows that betrayal can motivate a plot even though it doesn't actually take place. The important thing to remember is what the characters think goes on—their suspicions, their false assumptions.

In the story Othello, a Moor and a general in the Venetian army, falls in love with and secretly marries Desdemona, daughter of Brabantio, a Venetian senator. Othello picks Cassio instead of Iago as his lieutenant and Iago vows vengeance for the slight.

Then the Turks attack Cyprus, and Othello is dispatched to take charge of the defense. Iago, nursing his anger, proceeds to get Cassio drunk while on duty, and this causes Cassio's demotion. Desdemona, meanwhile, has joined Othello with the army, and Iago subtly implants the idea in Othello's head that Desdemona and Cassio have been having an affair. Although he resists mightily, Othello's suspicions slowly become aroused. Cassio, of course, is chagrined at what happened to him, and he seeks advice from Iago about how to regain his rank. Have Desdemona plead your case, Iago advises him. She knows you, she will sway the general.

What it does—as Iago hoped—is to arouse Othello's suspicions even further. Then, to, tighten the noose, Iago plants a handkerchief on Cassio that Othello has given to Desdemona. This convinces Othello that Desdemona has betrayed him with Cassio. Late at night he enters the bedchamber he and Desdemona share. She is asleep. Othello stares at her, sure now that he must kill her....

Yet I'll not shed her blood;
Nor scar that whiter skin of hers than show,
And smooth as monumental alabaster.
Yet she must die, else she'll betray more men...

And he smothers her with a pillow. Subsequently, Iago's plotting is uncovered, and he is arrested. Othello tries to kill him but fails. In despair he then kills himself.

And the betrayal, which is nothing more than a seed planted in Othello's mind by a revenge-bent Iago (again, betrayal and vengeance working together), has claimed its victims. As Shakespeare sees clearly, betrayal can be just as effective as a plot motivator even if it actually never occurs. What the mind thinks is the clearest reality, and this is more than enough for an effective storyline.

Stories of betrayal can blossom in settings far removed from the eternal love triangle. In fact, when we think of betrayal's alter ego—treachery—politics and espionage are relevant, for here we can have betrayal on a grand scale. What if . . .a U.S. Ambassador is blackmailed by the enemy? What if…a group of terrorists get their hands on a nuclear bomb through the misguided actions of a high-level scientists? What if…the secrets of a vital U.S. defense position are stolen? What if . . .someone entrusted to guard the person of the president of the United States is secretly planning to kill him?

All of these storylines have been used before, and yet they represent only a slice of the plots available with betrayal as a motivator. Politics calls up an urge for power, and success can bring a heady victory. The rewards can be substantial, and that is why a character—or characters—can rationalize that the ends (political power) can justify the means (betrayal).

This is what Piers Paul Read does with *The Villa Golitsyn*, his 1981 book about the search for the betrayer of an English officer and his men in the undeclared war between Indonesia and Malaya in the 1960s. The Foreign Office has suspicions it is Willy Ludley, a member of the embassy staff during that period and now retired and living in the South of France on a comfortable family fortune. Simon Milson is sent by the Foreign Office to The Villa Golitsyn, Ludley's home, to ferret out the facts, and the bulk of the action takes place here. (There is a similarity to Agatha Christie's *Ten Little Indians* in that the search for the criminal takes place within the confines of an isolated mansion, the characters and their motivations are spelled out, their interaction is scrutinized and clues and blind alleys abound.) There is Priss, Ludley's wife who is a tease,

Helen, a young girl who arrives unexpectedly at the Villa, Milson, himself, searching for an answer.

Questions about Ludley hover over the pages. Why does he drink so much? Why did he flee Jakarta so rapidly after the torture-killing of the officer and his men? Why has he lived in semi-isolation for more than twenty years?

These questions and more keep the story going. But the underlying theme is the motivation for seeking answers to the betrayal, and this is the essence of the book. If we were going to steal this plot, wouldn't we like to follow a theme which provides that the Foreign Office is "always afraid that the ideological bacillus which had raged through Cambridge in the 1930s might have infected later generations."

Did the betrayal occur, or didn't it?

That is the question!

8. Persecution

"Of all the tyrannies on human kind, the worst is that which persecutes the mind," wrote British poet John Dryden more than three hundred years ago. Persecution is that unfairest of all agonies because it is opposition raised to vicious, uncompromising harassment, it is contentiousness on a scale that allows little in the way of mercy, understanding or approval. One is persecuted because one is different, and the very nature of persecution carries along deep-seated conflict and tension—the very elements that go into the making of a good story.

Persecution is made of more than just opposition. It is based on a distinction in social level or religion or origin— items which go far beyond a simple intellectual dispute because persecution usually ends in severe personal harm or death.

Persecution can be made most vivid when it is accomplished in the name of or directed at a single individual (even with the pervasive effects of the Holocaust as background, books such as *Sophie's Choice* by William Styron, The *Diary of Ann Frank*, and QB VII by Leon Uris remain the story of one person). "Opposition may become sweet to a man when he has christened it persecution," wrote George Eliot in the nineteenth century, and that's certainly true. If we're harassed and opposed, and we know our lives are on the line, we call it persecution and somehow the battle seems more just, more right. For the persecutor the battle may seem equally just, but the bottom line is that both persecutor and the one being persecuted see their conflict as a struggle over basic, innate characteristics which, if left alone, would finally overwhelm and defeat the other.

Persecution is a powerful plot motivator, and it has formed the basis for many, many stories. Shakespeare recognizes the device and uses it in *Richard III*, his tragedy of the hunchbacked member of the House of York who persecuted all those standing in his way to the throne of England. Richard, to be sure, is the villain in this story, and through his conniving and treachery, lies and deceits he gains the throne. But the plot fairly bursts with his persecution of friends and relatives alike.

The story opens with Richard announcing his intent to play upon the suspicions of King Edward that under an old prophecy the King's issue would be disinherited by one of his heirs whose name begins with the letter "G"—a clear reference to Richard's brother, George, the Duke of Clarence. George is arrested, thrown in the Town of London where Richard, promising to free him, murders him instead.

This is but one in a string of murders that Richard conceives and carries out all in pursuit of the throne after King Edward dies. Along the way he stabs a deposed King (Henry VI) and his son, the Prince of Wales. He eliminates a variety of noblemen and followers, his own wife, the two young princes residing in the Tower who are in the direct line for the Crown and finally his own ally, Buckingham. In each instance, Richard senses a threat that can only be neutralized by doing away with the individual. Sometimes he is quite subtle about his scheming, as in the manner in which he is finally crowned...Buckingham, his ally, is told to emphasize at a meeting at the Guildhall that the late King Edward (whom Richard did not kill) had illegitimate children and was, himself, a bastard. He should imply that the late King's line was flawed and that Richard, whose family had impeccable royal credentials, should assume the throne.

The big lie works well enough so that the Lord Mayor and the citizens of London decide to offer Richard the crown. Buckingham suggests that he appear on a balcony with two bishops and seem to be deeply absorbed in a prayer book, affecting a strong sense of piety. Play hard to get, Buckingham suggests...

Mayor
Do, good my lord, your citations entreat you.

Buckingham
Refuse not, mighty lord, this proffer'd love

Catesby
O, make them joyful, grant their lawful suit!

Richard
Alas, why would you heap these cares on me?
I am unfit for state and majesty
I do beseech you, take it not amiss
I cannot nor will I yield to you...

But of course he does give in and he is crowned. Then, noting that the little princes are in the Tower, he fears for the security of his reign. He summons James Tyrrel (referred to as a "discontented gentleman") after Buckingham has parried a request to kill the little princes. Tyrrel agrees to do it, and goes to the Tower and smothers them as they lie sleeping in one another's arms. The agony of the moment is captured in Tyrrel's words:

The tyrannous and bloody deed is done,
The most arch act of piteous massacre
That ever yet this land was guilty of...

Richard is finally forced to fight for his throne with Henry Tudor who has been in exile in France and raising an army. They meet on Bosworth field, and the night before the final battle the ghosts of all those whom Richard has killed haunt his dreams, appearing one by one to condemn him.

Here, then, is a plot filled with the persecution of any who stood in Richard's way for the throne. In many ways it is just an updating of some of the old Greek tragedies where the number of bodies strewn about almost exceeds the cast of characters. But the theme is a viable one: opposition seen as so threatening that persecution must follow.

Did Shakespeare create this story? No. Scholars tell of a similar tale, the play *Richard Tertius*, in Dr. Legge's Latin chronicles. And then there is *Richard Crookback*, authored by Ben Jonson some years earlier.

What, then, is there to steal? If we update *Richard the Third*, we can see a modern equivalent in Mario Puzo's *The Godfather* where an undisputed leader persecutes his enemies (real or imagined) unmercifully. There is killing and treachery on a scale to rival *Richard the Third*, and while there is nothing to match the execution of the little princes, how about the artfully contrived simultaneous ambush slayings of the Barzini crime family? The plot motivator in both instances is persecution of enemies based on deep, fundamental differences.

What about a story spicer in *Richard the Third*? As befits a complicated plot there are several here. Perhaps the most significant is the resort to criminal action—specifically murder or murders—to achieve the necessary ends. If Richard had, somehow, attempted to outmaneuver those he felt opposed him, without giving in to murder, think how less effective and substantial the plot would have been. In fact, it would be little more than an innocuous history lesson. Also, of course, it probably wouldn't have been very realistic, given the tenor of the times approximately five hundred years ago. People did kill people to be crowned king. People even killed women and defenseless children. So, any plot dealing with the story of *Richard the Third* requires murder and treachery to make it real.

Shakespeare uses other story spicers as well. There is conspiracy in that Richard employs both Buckingham and Catesby to further his scheme and help him persecute his enemies. It is no less a conspiracy though Buckingham and Catesby are part of his retinue and owe him allegiance. The conspiracy is in agreeing to perform some illegal act together, and murder is certainly an illegal act.

Then, there is deception. Quite obviously, Richard deceived the Lord Mayor and the citizens of London by feigning indifference for the Crown. And there is the way he manipulated the suspicion of King Edward so that Richard's brother, George, would be tossed into the Tower, and there is his reassurance to George that he intends to free him— only to murder him instead. Deception, deception—it bursts from *Richard the Third*, but only to spice the underlying persecution. It cannot hold the story by itself.

Persecution as a plot motivator is equally effective when it can be portrayed through the eyes of the one being persecuted as through the eyes of the one doing the persecuting. In Nathaniel Hawthorne's *The Scarlet Letter*, written in 1850, we agonize with Hester Prynne in the early days of the Massachusetts Bay Colony as she is convicted of adultery and forced to stand in the public pillory holding and acknowledging her illegitimate child. The good citizens of puritan Boston have forced her to wear a red letter "A" embroidered on her breast to signify to one and all that she is an adulteress. The young minister, Arthur Dimmesdale, urges her to reveal the name of her lover, but she steadfastly refuses, and while she is in the pillory, her husband, Master Prynne, an English physician, arrives from Antwerp, Belgium and comes upon the scene. He has not laid eyes on her for two years because he had sent her on ahead to Boston. When he married her, she was very young, and from the beginning it had been a loveless marriage. Though the minister, Dimmesdale, continues urging Hester to divulge the name of her lover, he can't bring himself to admit, publicly or privately, that it is he.

In the meantime, Master Prynne determines to find out who impregnated his wife. He assumes a false name and succeeds in becoming Dimmesdale's doctor. His suspicions of Dimmesdale lead him to inflict various forms of mental anguish on the minister, including the implication that a scarlet letter is now burned into his flesh. Finally Dimmesdale can withhold the information no longer, and he joins Hester in the pillory where he publicly confesses to being her lover and the father of her child. The same day, he dies in Hester's arms.

The persecution of Hester by her puritan New England world provides a tale rich in social commentary and moral judgment. The plot is not complicated—a woman bearing an illegitimate child in early America—but the manner in which she is treated by her friends, neighbors, family and lover is what motivates the plot. Her persecution is symbolic for anyone's persecution when they defy the dictates of a religious and moral norm, and in showing this the author highlights the sheer ferocity of popular reaction.

Hawthorne's story is about the universality of sin, and in this sense there probably isn't a piece of work anywhere that doesn't touch on the issue. In a more specific way, too, the persecution of someone for flaunting moral values is a theme that has been picked up again and again. How about *Lady Chatterly's Lover*, written in 1928 by D.H. Lawrence? A titled English lady falls in love with her husband's game keeper, and they conduct a torrid affair under the nose of the husband. The language is rich in sexual detail and imagery, but an equally important aspect of the book is that what's going on violates the moral, cultural norm. It simply isn't done in upper-crust England in the nineteen twenties to get it on with the local gamekeeper. So, after agonizing about alternatives, the couple know there is only one choice —they must leave England forever, if they wish to remain together. It is the threat of persecution for their actions that motivates the plot here, and in the course of the book, Lawrence takes dead aim on a society that would treat others so viciously for partaking of simple sexual pleasure. In a broad sense, Lawrence did steal Hawthorne's plot, but he concentrated not on the aftereffects of the sexual activity but on the activity itself, detailing the persecution as threatened rather than already experienced.

Are there story spicers in Hawthorne's and Lawrence's work? Clearly, an item which provides solid substance throughout is the idea of authority. What is going on in both stories is that traditional authority is being ignored and the characters are pursuing their own personal gratifications. In puritan America it is the authority of the church and the community, and in the twentieth century in England it is the authority of the family and the traditional class system. The use of authority or the reaction to its use is a strong story spicer because it implies a good guys-bad guys theme— you're either for us or you're against us! Story conflicts like these make for good plots.

A fertile source of persecution drama has been the black-white racial conflict. Persecution and authority again come together here, and it's a framework that goes back hundreds of years. See, for example, *Uncle Tom's Cabin* by Harriet Beecher Stowe which was published in 1851 and its modern equivalent, Richard Wright's *Native Son*, a story of mob violence against the black man. It is persecution, not for strongly held beliefs or principles, but because of skin color, though of course a black skin carried certain innate expectations to the white man, and if they weren't fulfilled, the black man paid dearly.

On an individual level the story of one person's persecution can be a lesson for us all. In Harper Lee's To Kill a Mockingbird, written in 1960, the persecution is actually double-edged, affecting a black man and a white man. In a drowsy Alabama town sometime during the nineteen thirties, Atticus Finch, a widowed lawyer and the father of the narrator, Scout Finch, a young girl seven or eight years old, is assigned by the court to defend a black man, Tom Robinson, who is accused of raping a nineteen-year-old white girl. Though there are other themes in the book, persecution is what motivates the story because without it this would simply be a series of recollections about rural Alabama that could be found in the history books. But the author has used persecution to paint a vivid picture of southern life before the onset of the war. She has employed a classic device to build tension and conflict—a trial.

Atticus Finch, once named as Tom Robinson's counsel, sets to investigate the facts and discovers that he believes Tom to be innocent. The fact that a black man is going to stand trial for allegedly raping a white girl in the South in the nineteen thirties and that he will be judged by other white men is a form of persecution with which we are now all too familiar. Even Atticus Finch acknowledges that his client has probably been prejudged and will be found guilty. But he persists with a vigorous defense, and for that he is severely judged by his friends and neighbors. The family of the girl also attempt their own form of retribution, even threatening Atticus and Scout with physical harm. This is a family of poor, ignorant whites, who live off the refuse in the town dump and wait each month for their relief checks. They would love nothing better than to bring down a respected member of the community, to brand him as a "nigger lover."

But in the case of Atticus, at least, the persecution is of fairly short duration, and at the end of the book he is reelected to the state legislature. The question of Tom Robinson's fate is not so nicely disposed of, except that we see the fruits of persecution in bold relief. The black man is still not free, he is still the object of bias and bigotry even when his accuser is a white girl from a disreputable family. At least, Atticus tells Scout, since the jury took so long to decide Tom Robinson's fate (he is convicted), it indicates some progress toward erasing the stigma of being black in a white man's courtroom. Small consolation, though, to Tom Robinson.

Let's steal Harper Lee's plot—a lawyer defending an unpopular defendant and becoming the object of persecution and threats. What if…a social worker storms through the inertia-laden welfare system on behalf of a severely distressed client who happens to be both unpopular and unattractive?…or a doctor goes against conventional medical wisdom in order to uncover a new drug or to heal an especially unpopular patient?

If we stay with Harper Lee's plot, the story will involve someone with professional credentials, though, of course, the protagonist can be anyone practicing any trade. The point is to challenge the norm sufficiently to create a reaction so severe it becomes persecution. Then, we add a story spicer or two, and we have a complete storyline.

On a broader scale the persecution inherent in the black-white conflict is portrayed by Nadine Gordimer in her 1981 novel, *Burgher's Daughter*. Here we have an entire national setting—South Africa and its apartheid policies—for the events and the reactions. But, just as Harper Lee's book shows, it comes down to the story of one person, or one family, against a background of racial persecution.

In this case, however, the family is white, and they are persecuted for their support and work with the black-liberation movement. Early in the book, Lionel Burgher, the father, a physician and Communist, dies in prison to which he has been sentenced because of his efforts for the black majority. His daughter, Rosa, is now the object of government surveillance and in order to survive she must live a life of secrecy and deception. Because of her constant concern for who is watching or listening, she moves through life like some carefully programmed robot, always aware of what effect her actions will have on others, not free to be spontaneous or carefree. But she harbors doubts about her dedication to the black movement and would like to travel abroad. Only the government won't permit it, requiring her to remain in South Africa.

She persists, however, and after much effort she finally gains a one-year travel permit on condition she stay away from anyone the South African government feels has anti-government attitudes. As she travels she finally finds the free expression and spontaneity she lacked before, and she has a fulfilling love affair with a Frenchman who provides her with a greater sense of herself.

But in the end she returns to South Africa to take up her father's work. And in the final pages she, herself, is now in jail becoming again the remote, carefully controlled person she was before. The apartheid dilemma is once again played out as a vivid mix of inhumanity and survival.

The persecution suffered by the Burgher family is the prime plot motivator, for without it, the political discord is little more than a mild debate and the suffering of the characters clearly unmotivated. Once again, authority is an ever-present story spicer since the persecution emanates directly from this source. Suspicion is also present, as are honor and dishonor since, after all, it is the dignity of the individual that this book is about. We honor that dignity or we dishonor it, by our treatment, and for Nadine Gordimer, honor wins out.

In persecution we have a plot motivator that can cut across economic, social and political lines. Its power is that of high emotion and the fulfillment of some overriding purpose. Evil or just, the elements of persecution call forth vivid action and a continuous testing of one's principles and goals.

Persecution propels a story with the force of the moral equation it always poses: is persecution ever justified and if so, when?

9. Self-Sacrifice

The young woman's eyes are bright with grief and determination. Her brother is dead, and he must be buried. Her sister stands with her in the early morning glow, and the sister isn't sure she wants to bury their brother.

I *will* bury him, the young woman says.

But the King has forbidden that he be buried, the sister reminds her.

He has no right to stop me, the young woman exclaims. She turns to her sister…

Be what seems right to you;
Him will I bury. Death, so met, were honor;
And for that capital crime of piety,
loving and loved, I will lie at his side.
Far longer is there need I satisfy
Those nether powers, than powers on earth; for there
Forever must I lie…

The young woman is the Greek princess Antigone, daughter of Oedipus and sister of the dead Polynices who has been killed in an expedition to win the throne of Thebes. Creon, the King of Thebes, has decreed that Polynices's body should remain unburied, but Antigone will not allow that to happen even though she knows that violation of Creon's decree will mean death.

Here, then, is the storyline for one of the great Greek tragedies by Sophocles. Antigone explores the basic question of whether one's duty is first to the gods or to the state. When the laws are in conflict, which should prevail?

For the ancient Greeks, leaving a body unburied was the most heinous of all events because it meant the soul would be sentenced to grievous torment. Proper burial was not only the obligation of the family but an act of piety demanded by the gods, and failure to appease the gods brought untold misery and suffering. Thus Antigone's dilemma...does she obey King Creon's law or does she follow her conscience and the will of the gods?

It's a classic case of self-sacrifice. Antigone, knowing the consequences of her actions, pursues her goal because it represents a purpose higher than the vengeance exacted by Creon on Polynices's body. Self-sacrifice is just this: giving oneself up because something or someone is more important. A cause, an ideal, even an act of self-regeneration is what motivates self-sacrifice. Think of it as a balancing...which of two or three alternatives is more important? Do they balance one another? If one weighs more, do we bring them back in balance again by self-sacrifice?

Antigone, even though she is engaged to Creon's son, Haemon, is sentenced to die, and she is placed in a cave which is then walled up. But the prophet, Tiresias, warns Creon that the gods are not happy with the way he has handled things. Bury Polynices, he suggests, release Antigone, or Haemon will die.

Creon realizes that Tiresias's prophesies have never proven false. He rushes to have Polynices buried and to release Antigone. At the mouth of the cave he hears Haemon, inside, crying out with grief. When he enters he finds Antigone dead, hung by a rope from her own garment, and Haemon rushes at his father, spits at him and then falls on his own sword. He, too, is dead in seconds.

When Creon's wife hears about her son, she kills herself. Creon, in deep anguish, then admits he has been wrong. He gives up his throne and has himself exiled from the city.

The self-sacrifice, here, of course, is Antigone's, and in the dilemma over whether to obey the laws of man or the laws of the gods we have an often-used plot. Lloyd Douglas uses it, for example, in *The Robe*, and Henryk Sienkiewicz uses it in *Quo Vadis*, both of which highlight the conflict between the birth of Christianity and the opposition of the Romans. Self-sacrifice for a higher ideal—in this case a place in the Christian orbit—makes hommage to Roman law a lesser responsibility. One sacrifices oneself for this greater ideal even though it may mean death.

We can take any moral imperative and apply the self-sacrifice formula. It doesn't need to be religion-based, just something that demands a right—or righteous—course of action. We sacrifice ourselves because we have a conscience.

And speaking of conscience, one of the most remarkable examples in literature is found in Leo Tolstoy's *Resurrection,* the story of a Russian prince, landed gentry in Czarist Russia, who sacrifices almost all he has for a prostitute. The story begins when Prince Nekhludoff seduces Katusha who is just sixteen years old and the ward of Nekhludoff's aunt. She becomes pregnant and has the baby, but it dies soon after birth. Nekhludoff, meanwhile, pursues a military career, ignorant of what is happening.

In fact it is ten years later that Nekhludoff, now wealthy and a playboy, sees Katusha again, and then only by chance. He sits on jury duty in a murder trial in which one of the defendants is Katusha, who by now is a prostitute. It seems clear that she has been falsely accused in the murder case, but is convicted and sentenced to four years in Siberia. Nekhludoff Finally recognizes her. He goes to a lawyer to appeal her case, and he realizes that his life has been empty and self-serving. The pursuit of pleasure is nothing but degeneration, and he decides that what he really wants is to marry Katusha and give up his lands and estates.

Nekhludoff goes to the prison and reveals himself to Katusha, but she reacts coldly. She stuns him by showing pride in being a prostitute, and he is bewildered. But he returns to see her another time, and once again she treats him with disdain. Then he asks her to marry him, and she gets very angry and flees back to her cell.

A friend tells Nekhludoff to arrange for Katusha to work in the prison hospital as a nurse, that she will be well treated there and have a healthier existence. Nekhludoff is able to do this.

By this time, however, his urge to marry Katusha has waned, though he is still determined to go through with the marriage. He goes into the countryside intending to dispose of his estates in preparation for the trip he will take to Siberia with Katusha. While he is getting rid of his lands, he sees his aunt, and she tells him about the birth of Katusha's son and the fact it had died in the midst of the poverty and misery he sees about him. Nekhludoff is now more determined than ever to give away his lands, and he sees to it that the peasants share a communal ownership in everything he gives them.

Nekhludoff then goes to St. Petersburg, hoping to convince the Senate to overturn Katusha's sentence. But to no avail, and in fact one senator considers Nekhludoff's morality in the case offensive enough so he demands the sentence be upheld. And it is.

Nekhludoff goes to see Katusha once again, asking her to sign a petition to the emperor for clemency. While he is with her, Nekhludoff feels himself falling in love with her again, and this time Katusha returns his love, but she decides she is not the kind of woman he should marry. She will be bad for him, she feels.

The long march to Siberia begins, and Nekhludoff follows the prisoners, seeing Katusha whenever he can. He learns the way revolutionists think, because they are part of the prisoner group, political and non-political prisoners together. One of the political prisoners falls in love with Katusha and approaches Nekhludoff. He tells him that he wishes to marry Katusha but that she wants Nekhludoff to decide for her. He answers by saying that he would be happy to know Katusha was well cared for. Later, in a far-off Siberian town, Nekhludoff finds out that Katusha's sentence has been commuted to simple exile in a less remote portion of Siberia. He tells Katusha who says she prefers to remain with the political prisoner who loves her, though she refuses to say whether she returns his affection.

And me? Nekhludoff asks. What will become of me?

You will have to live your own life, Katusha says.

Here is the penultimate in self-sacrifice. Nekhludoff gives up literally everything except his life to help Katusha, to make amends for what he did to her when she was just sixteen years old. His conscience reacts when he sees her in the courtroom, and he begins to question his life and the values he has always lived by. He sacrifices worldly pleasures, comfort, career and family in order to achieve some form of spiritual atonement.

And isn't this really one of the lessons in the Bible? How many of Christ's disciples gave up all that Nekhludoff does and more in order to gain some form of spiritual atonement? They followed

Christ, living as he did, hoping for salvation and peace. Nekhludoff does pretty much the same thing, though for him it is a single journey for a single purpose. But clearly, Tolstoy's model might have begun, at least, with the Bible.

Note the story spicers that appear in *Resurrection*. There's making amends, certainly. (In fact, this one will appear frequently in stories of self-sacrifice.) There's loss of material well-being, rescue, and honor and dishonor. A bagful of spicers for a vivid story of self-sacrifice.

A woman's a woman and a man's a man, and well…through the ages one or the other has sacrificed a lot for love. This is especially true when the love isn't returned. Nekhludoff's sacrifice for Katusha is essentially for love, and his ultimate hope is to help her, even though in the end they go their separate ways.

Literature is full of such sacrifices for love, and one of the more notorious is that depicted in Somerset Maugham's *Of Human Bondage*, where the woman—Mildred—is not such a likable character as is Katusha. Mildred, in fact, spends years duping a young medical student, Phillip Carey, into giving her money, supporting her, rescuing her and slavishly waiting on her—all because he loves her. Carey, with his club foot (one aspect of the bondage in the title), is enthralled with the worldly wise, older woman, and for years he thinks she returns his feelings. Though, of course, it isn't so; she goes out with other men, goes off with them too and uses Phillip only when she has nowhere to turn. In fact, Carey's love for Mildred is the other aspect of the bondage in the book's title.

How does she view the way Phillip feels? After she has another man's child and Phillip is back in her life because she needs money and a place to live, she considers that now she should settle down with him…"She had no doubt of her power over him…He had so often quarrelled with her and sworn he would never see her again, and then in a little while he had come on his knees begging to be forgiven. It gave her a thrill to think how he had cringed before her. He would have been glad to lie down on the ground for her to walk on him. She had seen him cry. She knew exactly how to treat him, pay no attention to him, just pretend you didn't notice his tempers, leave him severely alone, and in a little while he was sure to grovel."

What Phillip sacrifices for Mildred isn't his fortune or his power. What he gives up is his honor, his sense of self-respect. He becomes her slave, her rag doll she can kick around whenever she feels like it. For Phillip the cause is sufficient—his love for her. He would do anything for that. And, of course, he does.

Did Maugham steal Tolstoy's plot? Only in the very general sense that a man will give up things he might hold dear for the love of a woman. Maugham doesn't get into the biblical yardstick of spiritual atonement the way Tolstoy does. For Maugham, Phillip Carey's actions are sufficiently explained by his love for Mildred and his hope of having her love him back. Fulfillment—spiritual, physical or any other kind—would follow naturally.

There are infinite variations on the man-woman theme with self-sacrifice. Perhaps the woman becomes the man's slave, or they jointly sacrifice for the love of a third person— a child or a parent—or they sacrifice themselves for each other or they sacrifice themselves not out of love but out of vengeance on one another.

Men and women don't have to be in love in order to sacrifice for one another. There are other motivations just as strong. Take Jan de Hartog's 1960 novel *The Inspector* which concerns the actions of Peter Jongman, a member of the criminal investigation department in the Amsterdam police department. The story is set in 1946 and Jongman is on the trail of a white-slave trader who takes young girls to South America and places them in brothels against their wishes. Jongman is a bit unsettled. In his youth he had wanted to be a sailor but instead had opted for the security of a police career. Then, during the war, he stayed in his comfortable job while the Nazis held the country. He was able to free a few anti-Nazi criminals, but compared to the work of the underground his contribution wasn't much.

Now, as he follows the white-slave trader to London and confronts him, his eyes lock with a thin-faced girl, Anna Held, whom the slave trader is about to ship out. Jongman demands the girl be set free, and the white slave trader shrugs and answers, "What do any of them matter? They are Jewish bitches that slipped through the net! This one is from a medical research camp. She is no good to anybody. She has even been sterilized!"

In the ensuing days Jongman finds that Anna wants to go to Israel, and he thinks of how little he really did during the war. If he were to help her get to Israel, wouldn't that make up for some of his doubts?

The journey, then, to Israel becomes his regeneration. He must undertake it in defiance of most of the governments in the world who back the British in closing off all emigration to Israel. He also runs the risk of losing his wife and family because, of course, he will make the trip alone with Anna. So he is faced with the ultimate form of self-sacrifice: he stands to lose his job, his wife and family and his life.

Is it done for the love of Anna? Yes and no. He comes to love her, but he has no urge for sexual relations. It is a platonic love, a joy simply in giving to another human being without expecting anything in return. He comes to see that what he is doing is necessary to save his soul, and that if he survives, he will not be the same smugly assured, narrowly based person he was. For him there is no doubt—the sacrifices are worth it.

Self-sacrifice is really nothing more than giving up something we have or something we hold in esteem in order to gain something else we consider more important. Another person stands to benefit in all this, and so we sacrifice ourselves or part of ourselves for that other person. Antigone does it for the soul of her dead brother, Polynices; Prince Nekhludoff does it for Katusha, Phillip Carey does it for Mildred; Peter Jongman does it for Anna Held. The relationships which offer the opportunity for self sacrifice are as varied as the human mind can extend because what we're limited by isn't who can or can't sacrifice for whom. Anyone can play this game, anyone can be a self-sacrificer. The only limitation is whether one really sacrifices or not. The key is just what is being given up, why, and what is expected in return. Self-sacrifice demands a substantial commitment. Without it there really wouldn't be much of a story.

Suppose, for example, a man finds his wife is very ill, and he is faced with a dilemma: should he give up his girlfriend in order to devote all available time to his wife in her last months, trying to make those last few months as comfortable as possible? If he does, and in the course of caring for his wife he finds that he has really been in love with her all this time, do we have any self-sacrifice in his breaking off with his girlfriend? Perhaps, in the beginning, but even so, how much of a sacrifice is he really making? What is the cause or ideal he is seeking in such sacrifice? To make his wife's final time comfortable? As a humanitarian gesture it is certainly admirable, but is it strong enough to support something we think of as self-sacrifice? Especially when he is seeing the girlfriend right up to the moment he makes the decision?

Now, what if…his wife wants to go on a final journey, somewhere far away, and it is dangerous and costly and questionable that either or both will return safely. To give up his girlfriend in these circumstances is much more story-provoking. Here he gives up much more, including the possibility of remaining alive. That is self-sacrifice.

Giving up one's life is the ultimate sacrifice. Stories of a hero striding fearlessly into almost certain death so that something or someone else can live have come down to us from the Greeks (the legend of Theseus and the Minotaur, for example). They embody the idea that even in death there will be some kind of purification and regeneration. The person who sacrifices will live in the minds of those he saved, and his memory will be treated with deference and respect.

A natural place for this type of situation is in stories of intrigue, suspense, revolution, even war. Any circumstances where the concept of death and dying is a normal outgrowth of the action. Stories with political undercurrents are especially appealing…

Take *Days of Wrath*, written by Andre Malraux in 1936. It's the story of Kassner, a Communist who has been arrested by the Nazis in Germany. Kassner is one of the Nazis' most-wanted people, but they don't know that the man they have is Kassner, and so they don't kill him summarily. Instead they spend nine days torturing him, trying to get him to divulge who Kassner is and where to find him. He is kept for hours in a pitch-black cell, disoriented and terror-filled in a way he never felt when he was facing danger out in the streets. But he doesn't break, though his mind is swirling with jumbled thoughts, and he is close to losing his sanity.

Then he hears a tapping on the wall…"Comrade, comrade, take courage…" That's all, nothing more. Suddenly from the adjoining cell he hears sounds of the guards beating someone—muffled noises and shouts. Shortly, he's hauled from his cell and sped off into the countryside. He's given two days to leave the country.

His head is filled with questions. But then he hears one of the guards talking. Another man, it seems, has admitted he is Kassner. He has given himself up for a certain death.

And the real Kassner doesn't know who the man is. But this nameless stranger gives his life so Kassner can live and continue his work.

Malraux, quite obviously, is writing a form of revolutionary fiction here. Remember the date—1936, the zenith of strains between the Nazis and the Communists throughout Europe. Malraux was a Communist himself, ardently subscribing to the revolutionary philosophy, so of course he paints his hero in glittering hues. But that doesn't detract from the fact that this story is motivated by self-sacrifice. A good writer can recognize strong motivations and dramatize them so the story can go forward, even if he or she may not be in agreement with those motivations. The point is that Malraux believed the ideals of revolution were good enough motivators to construct a story of self-sacrifice.

A man dies for his political beliefs. Isn't that a strong enough motivator? Especially when he allows someone else to live and perpetuate those beliefs?

10. Survival

Some plot motivators are simply better than others at generating a storyline, and stories about survival are clearly among the best. Why? Because a survival story contains the major elements for any tale—natural tension over whether survival will in fact take place, a backdrop that constantly menaces the characters, and built-in conflicts. There can be conflict over the *way* to survive, *who* will survive, and even *when* to survive.

For example, in the classic survival story we have someone in an alien environment, remote from other people (or in company with others in the same position) and dependent upon his or her skills. How the characters cope and whether or not they succeed are the keys to the story. We can use what if...over and over: what if...the setting is the jungle and the characters are all city-oriented? What if...the characters are arch rivals and only one holds the key to survival? What if...one of the characters falls in love with another character and affects both their wills to survive? What if...survival depends on the skills of one person and he/she refuses to help? What if...coping with survival brings out hidden talents and hidden flaws in each of the characters? What if...one or more of the characters doesn't want to survive? What if...the menace to survival turns out to be something different from what everyone thought? What if...among the survivors is someone who has criminal designs on another? What if...the survivors turn on one another out of desperation and frustration?

What's clear is that survival is an excellent springboard. And we can make some pretty accurate generalities with respect to using survival as a plot motivator. For example, survival will usually follow some catastrophe, some event that has cast the survivors to the place where we find them. So, it would be possible to treat the plot motivator, catastrophe, in the same way as we treat survival, except that the emphasis would be placed on surviving. Paul Gallico does this with his 1969 book, *The Poseidon Adventure*. It is the story of a luxury cruise-ship caught by an underwater earthquake (the catastrophe). The ship capsizes but somehow stays afloat, and a small party of passengers must make their way from the overturned main deck up through the bowels of the ship to the tip of the floating hull. How they do it is the story of survival, and the leader is an athlete turned minister who uses his mountaineering skills to lead the people to safety. Even as the characters survive, however, the elements of the catastrophe are all around and so they must be treated. There's the menace of drowning or some other death while crawling through the ship's innards, the fact that there was no way to prepare for the disaster, and the stark depiction of ruin and shambles all around.

Yet where catastrophe presupposes death and destruction, survival emphasizes life and rescue Survival comes after catastrophe and should carry with it a greater degree of hope.

In addition, catastrophe stories tend to be monumental, taking in large numbers of people and places. But survival stories can be limited to one person in one place. The basic question continues to surface: will he/she survive or not? The ordeal, in other words, can be reduced to a single individual's struggle.

In survival stories, too, the story spicer, rescue, is almost always in the picture. Will the survivor/survivors be rescued or not!? Perhaps one can survive and not be rescued, in the sense that one can rescue oneself, but usually the hope for outside rescue permeates these stories.

No more vivid portrait of the hope for rescue and the urge to survive can be found in all of literature than that of Daniel Defoe's legendary character, Robinson Crusoe. Of all survival stories, this one comes to mind first. Robinson, a young Englishman with a taste for adventure, is aboard a ship which breaks up on reefs off the coast of South America in the latter part of the seventeenth century. Only he survives, of all the crew and passengers, and he washes ashore on an uninhabited island. He is able to retrieve food, ammunition, water, wine, clothing, tools, sailcloth and lum-

ber from the stricken ship, and thus begins his thirty-five year so-
journ on the island. Yet Robinson never loses hope that he will be
rescued, even though he sets about building himself a permanent
shelter and furniture. He learns to trap and plant, and creates for
himself a self-perpetuating little world.

His first sight of other humans occurs after 24 years, and they
are cannibals who devour human flesh before his eyes. But because
he still has guns, he is able to rescue a prisoner of theirs who becomes Friday, his long-time and trusted servant. Now, after a quarter century of seeing no one, he has companionship, but of course
Friday can speak no English. So Robinson begins to teach him.
Another ten years pass, and then an English ship appears off the
island. Robinson and Friday rush down to greet a ship's party as
they come ashore. The party, however, is just the Captain and two
crew members, victims of a mutiny.

Robinson and die Captain, along with Friday and the two sea-
men, retake the vessel, and finally Robinson Crusoe returns to his
native England, after 35 years. The major thrust of the story, of
course, is not the rescue but the manner in which Robinson survives. He washes ashore with absolutely nothing—only what he is
able to save from the ship. He is not skilled in outdoor survival, nor
in planting, carpentry or hunting. Yet he is able to pull it off because of sheer determination, a little luck and an intelligence that
refuses to panic but carefully and methodically creates a way of
life. This is a perfect story of survival, combining the elements al-
luded to above: he is in an alien environment, remote from others
and dependent solely upon his own skills. There is as much fascination in how he survives as in whether he survives. And that is really a key to survival stories: readers like to watch the step-by-step
process of survival, they can easily identify with the protagonist as
he/she struggles and copes, and they can not with approval as he/
she takes each hesitant step.

The remote-island setting is perhaps the most familiar device
for stories of survival because it provides a very appropriate format
for man-against-nature plots. The conflicts and the tensions are
apparent from the beginning; the writer doesn't have to go about
constructing them, as is the case with stories of rivalry or betrayal

or even persecution. Man-against-nature is the classic survival story, and it can be even more exciting if man-against-man is added to the mix. Then there is a double conflict and the undoubted appearance of other plot motivators.

Man versus man…try *Lord of the Flies*, William Golding's fine book written in 1955. Here we have the remote island setting. A group of young English boys, the oldest of whom is twelve, are the victims of a plane crash on a tropic island after the outbreak of world-wide nuclear war. They are alone, without parents or other adults, and they must learn to cope. The story is essentially that—coping, surviving in an alien environment and without adult assistance But the man-versus-nature theme is quickly subverted to the man-versus-man theme as the boys in just a few weeks begin to fashion themselves a society built along familiar English lines. They call an assembly and elect a leader. They set up rules, give everyone tasks to do. But shortly things begin to deteriorate. In the tropic heat they shed their clothes, and they find pleasure in painting their bodies. They elect two chiefs, Ralph and Jack. Ralph is the methodical one, concerned with preserving the structure of whatever civilization they have, while Jack is the maverick, a rebel who quickly comes to odds with Ralph. "Rules are the only thing we've got!" says Ralph, while Jack responds, "_____to the rules!"

The boys split into two groups, forming rivalries and hatreds. The fat boy in the group, Piggy, becomes the ultimate scapegoat who succeeds in saving the boys at the cost of his life. This story is really an allegory on the human condition and the fact that the civilized behavior we have spent thousands of years developing can actually be dissipated in a matter of weeks. At first the boys think of their situation as high adventure, but it doesn't take long for them to realize they are alone in an alien world, unprepared except for what little they have learned in their short lives. This is when, even as they try to follow the highly civilized example of English society in setting up a governing structure, they begin to succumb to the primitiveness all around them. The adventure turns to nightmare as torture and cruelty replace the early optimism that English manners can serve anywhere, anytime.

Did Golding steal this plot? What if…a group of children are captured and placed aboard a pirate ship sometime in the nine-teenth century and exposed to murder, seduction and the grim outlaw life. And what if...the gradual maturing of the children causes them to accept or reject this way of life with equal fervor, even as the pirate ship goes about its deadly business, murdering and pillaging at will? And what if...rivalries and hatreds occur be-tween and among the children as they seek or reject special favors from the pirates?

A quarter century before *Lord of the Flies*, Richard Hughes wrote *A High Wind in Jamaica*, a tale of children living aboard a pi-rate vessel based on a true incident. Hughes's story, like Golding's, is a view of the child's world in the midst of chaos and remoteness, *as viewed by the child or children*. In both books the setting is outside the normal bounds of civilization—an uninhabited tropic island or an outlaw pirate ship. Laws and rules and manners are what the individual participants say they are, and yet there is a certain rough civility. Emily, ten years old and precocious, is accosted one night by the drunken pirate-ship captain in *A High Wind in Jamaica*, but she bites his thumb and he moves off. For days she and the captain avoid one another until Emily is injured when a dropped marlin spike severely damages her thigh. The captain comes along, sober now, but instead of attacking her he takes her to his cabin where he dresses the wound and allows her to sleep in his bunk.

The rough civility in *Lord of the Flies* is apparent from the time the boys decide to organize along accepted English govern-ing principles, with elected leaders and rules of conduct. That even within these bounds of civility there can be cruelty and viciousness is also apparent. And in this sense there is little distinction from what goes on in *A High Wind in Jamaica*. The point of both books is this: survival in an alien world is a learning process that forces us to examine the very essence of who we are and to cope with what we find. Seen through children's eyes, survival is different and much less fearful because of the essential innocence of childhood. That innocence becomes clouded as children mature, and the fear-lessness with which survival was once approached is now replaced with uncertainty and, at times, total fear.

The remote-island setting for books like Lord of the Flies and

Robinson Crusoe or fictional extensions like the floating derelict in The Poseidon Adventure or outlaw-pirate society in A High Wind in Jamaica are only a few of the possibilities where survival as a plot motivator could take shape. What if we use…an abandoned railroad car…or a remote cave…or a prison cell or prison camp…or a sealed bank vault? Each provides the necessary alien atmosphere for the story to take shape. But these aren't the only settings we can use.

Suppose survivability depends, not on place, but on person? Suppose it isn't where we are that's so important but who we are that helps to motivate the story? Suppose we take an otherwise ordinary person and place that person in extraordinary circumstances and see what they would do? There's little of the remote-island kind of setting in this approach, though of course such a setting could be used. But the story of survival doesn't have to work within the confines of a narrow physical atmosphere. It, instead, can have elements of the chase and mistaken identity, and the menace can be more human than environmental (in other words the survivor is fighting off other people rather than a stark, forbidding element).

Such a story is what John Buchan wrote in 1915. The Thirty-Nine Steps has become the basis for many tales of mystery and suspense in the ensuing years. Graham Greene writes of Buchan that he was "the first to realize the enormous dramatic value of adventure in familiar surroundings happening to unadventurous men." His story is essentially one of survival in the face of a well directed, well financed adversary against the background of the events leading to the First World War.

Richard Hannay, a mining engineer in London, is suddenly confronted by another tenant in his building, Franklin Scudder, who tells a fantastic tale about plans for the assassination of a Greek diplomat who is about to visit London. Scudder is badly frightened because his knowledge of the plot has brought him to the attention of The Black Stone, a secret organization that wants nothing better than to start a war between England and Germany. The assassination will help in the plan immeasurably. Hannay lets Scudder stay in his flat, but he returns one day to find Scudder with a knife through his heart. Then he notices two men patrolling in front of the building.

He's convinced now that The Black Stone knows who he is and that his own life is in danger. He retrieves a little black book from Scudder's body that he had seen Scudder makes notes in. Then he escapes from his flat in disguise, planning to stay in hiding for a couple of weeks and then divulge what he knows to the authorities.

He goes to Scotland, but he finds that the London papers have reported Scudder's murder and his own description and that he is suspected of committing the murder. He finds a refuge, but one day a plane flies overhead, and he assumes The Black Stone has found him, so he flees again (notice that Hannay has nothing on his mind but surviving, and thus this is a story of survival—an ordinary man in extraordinary circumstances). Another time he is briefly captured by The Black Stone but succeeds in getting away.

He reads Scudder's black book and sees it is in code which he arduously tries to decipher. He succeeds, finally, and finds that Scudder has told him only part of the truth. Yes, there will be the planned assassination of the Greek diplomat, but also there is to be an armed invasion of England, with airfields already laid out and mines to be placed along the shoreline. A French envoy with plans for the placement of the British fleet is to be intercepted so that the exact arrangement of the mines can be made. The operation is to commence at a place where there are thirty-nine steps and a high tide at 10:47 P.M. No other information can be uncovered by Hannay.

Then he has a stroke of luck and meets someone with high connections in the British government. All the while, of course, The Black Stone is still after him, and so he must be very careful. But he finally gets to someone in the government and convinces him about the plot.

There is to be a secret government meeting concerning the information Hannay has provided, but Hannay is not invited. However, his sixth sense tells him he should go. Without telling anyone, he appears at the house and sits in the hallway waiting to be called. While he is waiting, one of the officials at the meeting comes out, and Hannay recognizes him as a member of The Black Stone—someone he had seen when he had been briefly held by them. Hannay turns out to be right, and the man, who by now has escaped, is seen as an impostor for the First Lord of the Admiralty. While in the meeting, the impostor has scanned the entire defense structure of England from drawings and figures on the tables.

Hannay, finally, has been rescued, and his ordeal as a survivor is now over. The book goes on showing how Hannay uncovers the secrets of the thirty-nine steps and the time and place in the reference to high tide. The end result is that even though England and Germany declare war on one another in a matter of weeks, the war will not be fought on British soil, which the author points out might have happened if the plot by The Black Stone has succeeded.

Buchan's thriller is the model for so many works which followed, particularly because of the presence of another plot motivator, the chase. The story revolves around Hannay surviving while being chased by The Black Stone and by the authorities. How he survives is important, of course, but more important is why he should survive. It is the theme of good guys versus bad guys, and here, at least the good guys will win. In one sense the alien atmosphere we find in *Lord of the Flies or The Poseidon Adventure* or any of the other works set on remote islands is also present here. Isn't Hannay's situation just as alien to a civilized, law-abiding man as forbidding terrain would be to a group of young English boys! Hannay must try and stay alive and deliver some vital information to the proper people, efforts he has not had to make, nor been trained for. So, in this sense, at least, his world is just as alien, just as forbidding.

An up-to-date equivalent of *The Thirty Nine Steps* is James Dickey's *Deliverance* where four men decide to white-water canoe a wilderness river before it will be lost forever to a dam and the demands of civilization. These are not macho types, but soft, paunchy suburbanites with a mild yen for adventure. But their fun turns to terror as they run across some vengeful backwoodsmen, and before it's over one of the adventurers is killed and the others have barely survived. The key to this story, as with Buchan's tale, is the actions of ordinary men suddenly confronted by difficult, unusual circumstances. How do they handle it?

One falls apart, another calls on a reserve of courage and endurance to lead them through while a third remains badly injured. The fourth has been killed. Here again, the chase plays an important part because the men are stalked by the woodsmen who have every intention of killing them. They start out as the hunted, but in the end they become the hunters, and that is how they survive. The chase and survival work hand in hand with these stories.

Actually, what is survival but a state of mind? No matter where we find ourselves we either cope or we don't. Stories of survival are essentially this. And when we write them, we are limited only by the settings our imagination can cook up.

11. Rivalry

Lydia, the heroine, is young, vivacious and addicted to reading sentimental romantic fiction…

Jack, the hero, is handsome, rich and determined to win Lydia….

Anthony, Jack's father, wants him to marry someone Anthony will choose….

Lydia's aunt favors Bob, Lydia's other suitor, who is also rich and aspires to become a man about town….

Jack has been seeing Lydia under an assumed name because he realizes that if she knew him under his real name, she would have nothing to do with him. For her the true pursuit of romance is what she has found in the melodramatic, sentimental love stories she reads incessantly. The person she will fall in love with must be dashing, certainly, but also penniless. And Jack, if she knew the truth, is far from penniless!

So is Bob, Lydia's other suitor, but then he has Lydia's aunt pushing his availability. To the aunt, Jack appears just as Lydia sees him—poor, struggling, yet handsome and debonair. Bob, the other suitor, however, has all the characteristics one would want in a husband—reliability, saneness, wealth, loyalty, ambition—and family approval.

Anthony, Jack's father, however, becomes determined that his son should marry the *right* person, and he astounds Jack by proposing it be Lydia. But Lydia doesn't know Jack under his real name, and Anthony doesn't know Jack is already taken with Lydia, but in his disguised capacity. The father, who doesn't know Jack and Lydia already know one another, decides his son should meet Lydia, which complicates things even more because Lydia only knows Jack in a disguise.

What to do? In his disguise Jack attempts to convince Lydia that because her aunt doesn't like him, he must pretend to be someone else...and he reassumes his natural identity. But Lydia, her dreams of love with a poor, though good man no longer a reality, will have nothing to do with him.

In the meantime, Bob, the *other* suitor, has discovered he has a rival. So he challenges Jack to a duel...only he has never seen Jack and so he assumes his rival is someone else, only it is actually Jack-in-disguise because that is the only way Bob has heard about him. He also hears that Jack is friendly with the character Jack has assumed—himself in disguise. So he gives the challenge to Jack to transmit to the person whose identity Jack has assumed.

Before the duel can be fought, Lydia rushes to the field of honor, now taken with the fact that Jack, even though he may be rich, would fight a duel for her. A new, romantic scene blossoms before her...she realizes that Jack and the person she wanted to be her hero are the same individual! Ah, that a man, any man, would fight a duel on her behalf!

Bob, the other suitor breathes a sigh of relief because now he is forced to fight a duel no longer...and he can reassume his man-about-town role.

"It almost seems," wrote Samuel Butler in the nineteenth century, "as though the nearer people stand to one another in respect of either money or genius, the more jealous they become of one another..."

A good point, because in the dramatic situation above *the rivals* for Lydia, the heroine, are both rich and both determined, and jealousy is inherent in the scope of the rivalry. Jealousy and rivalry don't always go together easily because jealousy will sometimes spring from covetousness that someone has something or someone the other wants. Rivalry, of course, implies that neither has the prize as yet. However, jealousy and rivalry come together when they are both founded on the idea that one is aware of a competitor for something or someone and that there can be only one winner.

In fact, in the dramatic situation above, we are talking about the essence of rivalry—it is Richard Brinsley Sheridan's classic satire on affectation and eighteenth-century English upper-class manners, The Rivals. The plot is basic—two men in love with the same woman—but, of course, it's only the beginning. By injecting the plot motivator, rivalry, into the story, Sheridan has brought along a variety of elements: jealousy, competition, conflict, success. But most important he has also used the story spicer, mistaken identity. The entire story is moved along because everyone has a mistaken notion about everyone else. By carrying it to outlandish extremes, Sheridan has used a basic humor-technique—exaggeration. The Rivals is comedy even though it may be a bit stiff for our taste today. Sheridan satirizes the superficiality and the empty-headedness of the upper-class English by showing them as objects of derision. He exaggerates their foibles, and in so doing he makes us laugh.

Did Sheridan steal this plot! Take a look at the Shakespearean comedy, *Two Gentlemen From Verona*. Two good friends, Valentine and Proteus, go their separate ways, Valentine to Milan to pursue his fortune at the palace of the Duke. Proteus stays in Verona happily content with his love for Julia. In Milan, Valentine meets Sylvia, the Duke's daughter, and falls in love. The Duke, however, wants Sylvia to marry Thurio, a wealthy though foolish landowner. Then Proteus shows up in Milan, sent there by his father who wants him to become more worldly. Valentine introduces him to Sylvia and confides that he intends to put a rope ladder up to Sylvia's room and steal her from under her father's nose. Proteus, however, can't bear the thought of Valentine going off with Sylvia because he, Proteus, has also fallen for her in spite of his earlier vows of love for Julia. So Proteus goes to the Duke and tells him of Valentine's plan. The Duke then banishes Valentine from Milan.

Julia, however, now shows up in Milan disguised as a page and thinking Proteus still loves her. She comes to Sylvia's house and stands in the shadows while Proteus sings love songs to Sylvia. But Sylvia will have none of it, saying she still loves Valentine and that Proteus should be ashamed of the way he is treating Julia.

Proteus doesn't give up so easily and decides to send messages to Sylvia via the nearest page—who happens to be Julia in disguise. In the end Proteus sees that Sylvia truly loves Valentine and that Julia, her disguise now lifted, is the one for him. Valentine returns from exile, gains the Duke's favor and is betrothed to Sylvia.

There are differences with The Rivals, of course. But Shakespeare uses the identical story spicer, mistaken identity, and he has one of the suitors in disfavor with the young woman's authority figure. In The Rivals the two young men almost fight a duel. In *Two Gentlemen From Verona* Proteus and Valentine end up wrestling and fighting for Sylvia. Shakespeare's use of deception as a story spicer comes off in a bit more subtle fashion than in Sheridan's work—Proteus betraying Valentine to the Duke—but in both stories deception is a definite factor in the way the plot moves. In Thurio, Shakespeare has a character very similar to the other suitor in *The Rivals:* wealthy, a bit priggish with social-class aspirations.

So…did Sheridan steal Shakespeare's plot? Maybe steal is too strong a word. After all, we really don't know if Sheridan had ever read Shakespeare, though it's fairly common knowledge that Shakespeare's plays and poems were well recognized and read by the last third of the eighteenth century. Suppose we say that two fine dramatists happened to fashion similar stories, even though they lived two centuries apart. As we've said, what's the crime in a bit of plot larceny?

More than a century after Sheridan, Edmond Rostand uses rivalry as a plot motivator in his *Cyrano de Bergerac.* The story is well known: Cyrano, a poet, loves Roxanne, but he composes love poems for his friend, Christian, letting Roxanne think Christian is the poet. Note the similarity with Shakespeare and Sheridan: Cyrano and Christian as rivals…and as the objects of mistaken identity.

Humor is here, too. Cyrano shows off his oversized proboscis: "A great nose indicates a great man—genial, courteous, intellectual, virile, courageous…"

But, more important, the plot is a love story with rivalry the motivating factor. The fact that Christian is oblivious to having a rival only heightens the tension and allows us to identify more with Cyrano. Yet love is the object of the rivalry, and as with *The Rivals* it is the basis of the story.

The general concept of rivalry can be traced back to the early Greek legends. On a broad scale it is found in the continuing rivalry between the city-states, Athens and Sparta. On a more personal level, we need look no further than the conflict between Ajax and Odysseus for the armor of Achilles. During the ten years of the Trojan War Achilles was considered the most fearsome of the Greek warriors. In single combat he destroyed the Trojan hero, Hector, and then paraded his body, lashed to a chariot, around the walls of Troy. But later, Paris, son of the Trojan King, Priam, was able to kill Achilles by shooting a poisoned arrow into his heel, the one place he could not protect. Now it was time for a new Greek champion to emerge and both Ajax, considered second only to Achilles in strength and courage, and Odysseus, claimed that honor. They finally put their cases to Agamemnon, the Greek king. Agamemnon chose Odysseus for the armor, and Ajax went absolutely raving mad, ultimately killing himself.

But for sheer plot magnitude on the theme of rivalry, there is little that can surpass Sir Walter Scott's 1819 epic, Ivanhoe. A veritable cornucopia of rivalries are present here, involving love and politics and manliness and property and even religion. It is the time when knighthood is the reigning norm, when Prince John is Regent in England, ruling in place of his brother, Richard the Lion-Hearted who has gone to fight for Christendom in the Crusades. Richard is thought to have been imprisoned somewhere in Austria and Prince John is taking steps to solidify his own rule. The plot in *Ivanhoe* fairly bristles with rivalries, though the most significant are those between Wilfred of Ivanhoe and his enemies. First, there is the Knight Templar, Brian de Bois-Guilbert, an arrogant, pugnacious character whom Ivanhoe meets on horseback in the tournament lists. Ivanhoe enters the tournament disguised, and it's only after he has unhorsed Brian de Bois-Guilbert and has distinguished himself in armed combat that he reveals himself.

Then there's Reginald Front-de-Boeuf who acquires the ancestral castle of Ivanhoe from Prince John after it is seized when Wilfred follows Richard to the Crusades. Reginald continues to maintain his claims, and at one point has an injured, captured Wilfred locked away in his castle...only he doesn't realize it's Wilfred.

Then there's Maurice de Bracy, captain of Prince John's Free Lances, who has fallen for Rowena, ward of the Saxon, Cedric of Rotherwood. Here we see a familiar rivalry because it is Rowena that Wilfred loves too, and in fact it is because of that love that Cedric, Wilfred's father, has banished him and caused him to follow Richard to the Crusades.

When Wilfred (severely injured) and Rowena and Cedric are captured by Reginald and Maurice de Bracy and Brian de Bois-Guilbert and taken to Reginald's castle, de Bracy comes to Rowena's apartment and makes his feelings known. And in the process outlines some of what Wilfred faces...

"Thou art proud, Rowena, and all the fitter therefore to be my wife. Know that my rival, Wilfred of Ivanhoe, is in this castle. It only remains for me to betray the fact to Front-de-Boeuf who would make short work of one whose manor he claims as his own. Richard gave Ivanhoe to Wilfred; John has given it to Front-de-Boeuf. There would be no rivalry for its possession if I were to say one word to the lord of this castle..."

Then there is the Christian-Jewish conflict, for this is a time of strong religious passion. Prominent throughout the book are Issac of York and his daughter, Rebecca. Periodic assaults on Issac and Rebecca by various Normans, including Prince John and Reginald Front-de-Boeuf, mirror narrow religious attitudes and establish the intolerance of the high-riding Normans. But in the end there is a resolution of sorts because Brian de Bois-Guilbert has fallen for Rebecca and offers to renounce his knighthood and a place in Europe for a home and a life with Rebecca in Palestine. This plan is doomed, because Rebecca is to be burned at the stake as a sorceress, and when she demands to be judged by trial by combat, Brian de Bois-Guilbert is named by the Templar Order against her. Wilfred comes to Rebecca's aid, and he and Brian finally meet in combat...only Brian falls over dead before a strong blow can be delivered.

Story spicers abound in *Ivanhoe*. There's deception (as when Wilfred appears in the tournament in disguise), rescue (as when Wilfred comes to Rebecca's aid in the final battle with Brian de Bois-Guilbert), honor and dishonor (as in the code of chivalry that all characters try to follow), criminal action (as in the capture and imprisonment of Wilfred, Issac, Rowena, Rebecca, Cedric by Reginald, Brian and Maurice de Bracy), conspiracy (as in Prince John's continual efforts to solidify his throne against Richard and do away with the influence of any of Richard's supporters), authority (as in the struggle, mainly political, over who will continue to rule England—Prince John or Richard).

Do we want to steal a plot? There's enough in Ivanhoe for all of us to use and still leave a field of possibilities for those coming along afterwards. Rivalry as a plot motivator can find its way into almost any type of situation. In politics, love, religion, physical prowess, the military—any case where two or more people or groups are vying to win something or someone.

Or how about the world of business? Let's deal with a contemporary situation. "A minute or two before or after two-thirty on the afternoon of the twenty-second of June, Avery Bullard suffered what was later diagnosed as a cerebral hemorrhage. After fifty-six years, somewhere deep within the convoluted recesses of his brain, a tiny artery finally yielded to the insistent pounding of his hard-driven bloodstream. In that instant of infinitesimal failure the form and pattern of a world within a world was changed. An industrial empire was suddenly without an emperor…"

So begins Executive Suite, a 1952 novel by Cameron Hawley that was also made into a movie. It is the story of what happens to the Tredway Corporation, a large, dynamic multinational business in the twenty-four hours following the sudden death of the man who had taken it from a small, family-owned business almost in bankruptcy and molded it into a major corporation. The storyline is rivalry in its raw, pure form with the overriding question pumping through the pages—who will be the next Chief Executive Officer of the Tredway Corporation?

Hawley introduces several contenders, each of them a vice-president of one area of the business, and then he portrays them scheming and plotting against one another to take over the top spot. One tries to manipulate stock holdings, others attempt to influence large shareholders to support them. At times the contenders grow obsequious or demanding as they try to thrust themselves forward. For Hawley, the author, the world of business is not a sharply drawn battlefield of good guys and bad guys, but a place where there are simply better people and worse people, where a businessman's ambition is not so much to be skewered as to be defined and directed. In the various power plays that the characters let loose, one school of thought feels that the financial people ought to be in charge of the business, that there should be emphasis on "safety" and conservation of capital; others feel that there really should be no frontier to business expansion, that a business that doesn't grow is in the throes of dying. In the end, Avery Bullard's successor is someone cut from Bullard's mold, dynamic, forward looking yet balanced. The rivalries have determined who that successor will be.

Stories with a business background are a natural for a plot motivator such as rivalry. The essence of business is competition, and the essence of rivalry is...competition! One feeds the other in a most positive manner, and while the ultimate objective may be money or power or prestige or simply to win for the sake of winning, it is the sense of competition that breeds the rivalry and makes it formidable.

Can we steal the plot of Executive Suite? Some say Arthur Hailey modeled his *The Moneychangers* in 1975 after it. The well-loved president of a major bank in the midwestern United States is dying, and as soon as that fact emerges, there is a power struggle for the top spot. Two vice-presidents are involved (not five as in *Executive Suite*) but their differing ideas about where the bank's business should be directed create the rivalry and the competition. One feels that the bank should be a community resource, that it should help the poor and the disadvantaged to upgrade their lives; the other is interested only in the bottom line, the larger the better. In the rivalry between these two concepts we see the same kind of conflict that was apparent in *Executive Suite*, only now it's a quarter-century later. In *The Moneychangers*, an international financial manipulator is pushing the bank for a huge, dangerous loan, and the question is just how far will the bank go in its thirst for profit. Hailey's book, of course, contains various elements not present in *Executive Suite*: there is bank theft, for example, a counterfeit-credit conspiracy and close-at-hand racial problems. Hailey's characters tend to be more good guy-bad guy extremes than do Hawley's, but essentially in both books we have the same storyline: a large business leader fades away, and a power struggle for succession occurs. The rivalry is intense and clearly defined between those preferring short-term return and those favoring a longer-term commitment to more human values. Along the way in both books there are story spicers, of course (in *Executive Suite* the question of material well-being is important because it keys the issue of safety versus expansion; in *The Moneychangers* criminal action plays a part as does honor and dishonor in the banks' ultimate relations with the local community). But it is rivalry that motivates each plot, and it is rivalry that draws each storyline.

Way down, then, at the center of it all, there is that spark of competition that started it off. Because, in the final analysis, we are only rivals when we decide to compete. Rivalry is competition.

12. Discovery (Quest)

What if…there's a terrible war, and in its aftermath a young man, a veteran of that war and now displaced, decides to leave his scourged land and find a place for himself elsewhere. He is driven by some inner sense of destiny so that he cannot stay at any one location for very long. Each time he begins to think of settling down, the turmoil within him boils over and he must wander again, never certain where he is headed but absolute in his belief that somewhere, some place will claim him finally.

It is in his quest to fulfill his destiny that this young man wanders, and his life is dotted with adventure and danger and episodes of near-death. A wealthy and influential woman falls in love with him and then kills herself when that love is not returned…a shipwreck nearly kills him and leaves him stranded on the shores of Africa…a local hero resents him so much that a bitter feud develops and leads them into physical combat…a mystical flight of fancy reveals just what his destiny will be and how he will attain it…an assailant wounds him not once, but twice, as the ultimate battle is fought.

This is the story of *The Aeneid*, the famous epic poem of Publius Vergilius Maro (Vergil) written in the first century B.C. It is the tale of the founding of Rome by the Greeks. For Aeneas there is no going home again, and Vergil paints him as a wandering hero carrying his destiny while he searches for the place he will finally settle. It is the story of discovery, the founding of Rome and the beginnings of a civilization, the place which would become the heartstone of the ancient world.

In some ways Vergil follows the lead of Homer in fashioning the plot for *The Aeneid*. There are Aeneas's wanderings— quite similar to those of Odysseus in *The Odyssey* with the usual assortment of outsized characters and gulp-filled dangers, and there are the battles which are fought to establish a civilization on the shores of the Tiber River—quite similar to the battles and the conflicts in *The Iliad*. Aeneas differs from Odysseus and some of the others, however, in that his sole motivation for carrying out his destiny is not riches or fame or power but simply the knowledge that the responsibility has fallen to him to found a new nation. That, in itself, is sufficient compensation.

When we look at discovery as a plot motivator we must see it, not as a formula for a chase or a search (though undoubtedly that could be part of the mix) but as a means of gaining something or someone through metaphysical considerations. In other words, it isn't enough to seek physical or tangible rewards; there must be some extra-physical meaning or compensation. For example, the quest of Aeneas is not only for a final home place but for a place where he can found a whole new civilization. His destiny is much broader than merely finding a safe haven for himself and his men. His is the destiny of the prophet.

There is a sort of other-worldly quality to this plot motivator because stories of discovery often are grounded on elements of self-perception. Whatever we quest for, we have to come to terms with ourselves or the journey hardly seems worth the effort. If Aeneas had decided that the journey and his destiny were simply too long and too difficult to achieve, or that he was content at one of the intermediate stops along his way, or that he really wanted power or riches or the continuing love of one of the beautiful women he encountered, the story would have ended. It would have become an adventure yarn in ancient dress, a story not of epic proportions but simply of minor historical value. By retaining the metaphysical trappings, the Aeneid raises the element of discovery to another level and gives it substance and influence.

People wander in stories of discovery. They travel, they search, they seek. There is always a purpose in the wandering, though it might not seem so on superficial investigation. But as with *The Aeneid*, a vague though inner-directed sense of destiny keeps Aeneas going, and his wanderings— to Carthage, Sicily and up the Italian coast—are actually quite purposeful. When he and his men come to the site of the seven hills which would become Rome, they know from a prior prophecy that this is where they will settle.

If wanderings are the name of the game with this plot motivator, then certainly the travels of *Don Quixote de la Mancha.* meet the test. In many ways this seventeenth century novel by Miguel Cervantes is the standard by which all other quest novels are judged. "For my absolute faith in the details of their histories," Quixote says, "and my knowledge of their deeds and their characters enable me by sound philosophy to deduce their features, their complexions and their statures." He is speaking of knight-errantry, that cultural and philosophical spur to action that consumed adventurers and dreamers in the Age of Chivalry. Quixote had read so many chivalric romances that his real world and his fantasy world had melded into a montage of damsels in distress, knightly tournaments, quests, weird and beguiling enchantments. He is so taken with the practice of knight-errantry that he decides to follow its customs and seek out the challenges that the world could present him. He would rescue damsels, he would slay monsters, he would prove his worth in tournaments, he would fight evil and dishonor wherever he could find them. He would revive the long-discontinued practice of knight-errantry. In short, his quest is to deal with a world as it had been centuries before, and to prove his valor as a man under these circumstances.

Of course he is mad, but that doesn't really detract from the book. Cervantes had the avowed purpose of ridiculing the practices of chivalry, and so he established his character in the midst of the most unromantic poses he can find. Quixote is old and poor, his horse, Rosinante, is a mangy old nag, his squire, Sancho Panza, is nothing but an illiterate peasant, his suit of armor belonged to his great grandfather, his mistress, Dulcinea, the one to whom he would dedicate his deeds of valor, is a kitchen-maid who happens to have skill in salting pork.

From all this Quixote sallies forth…and in his first adventure he meets up with some traveling merchants not far from his village. They laugh at him, and then they knock him around when he challenges them to meet him in combat.

Back home he has his cuts and bruises attended to, and his

friends, the village priest and the local barber, decide to stop the madness before it goes too far. They burn all his books about chivalry and romance and the code of knight-errantry.

But Quixote is undaunted. His books have been carried off by a wizard, he believes, and he readies himself for another effort to carry the values of knight-errantry to what he believes is awaiting world.

Late at night he and Sancho Panza sneak out of the village, Quixote on his spavined horse and Sancho on a runty donkey. On the plains of Montiel they see some windmills, and Quixote thinks they are strange, threatening giants. They must be attended to, he decides, and so he sets his lance and kicks Rosinante's flanks until there is a headlong charge, and one of the vanes picks him right out of the saddle and sends him flying.

Why, the giants turned into windmills, he exclaims to Sancho as he is dusted off. Sorcerers must have done this!

Thus Quixote's series of adventures continues. He encounters a lady in a carriage escorted by men on horseback and, thinking her held prisoner, demands her release. There is a sword fight of sorts which Quixote miraculously wins, sparing the life of his victim if he will return to Dulcinea and become her servant; he intervenes in a love quarrel and is soundly beaten for his pains; he mistakes dust clouds for two medieval armies in combat, only to find instead that the clouds are flocks of sheep, and when he intervenes, the shepherds throw rocks because he has scattered the sheep; one night he comes upon a funeral procession but mistakes it for a parade of monsters and attacks, sending the mourners in all directions. For this Sancho names him the Knight of the Sorry Aspect.

The adventures pile up, but the point is that it is the quest of Quixote to re-establish the code of conduct for the knight-errant that moves the story along. Monsters and threats and ladies in danger and feats of valor are the grist for his mill, and he seeks them out with bravery and conscience. It is not enough to read *Don Quixote de la Mancha* as a satire on the ridiculous extremes to which chivalry pushed its adherents; it must also be read as a morality lesson. Is it right to deride someone who wants to perform decent, humanitarian tasks, even though the way they do so may be a bit silly? Can a person not choose the way he or she will live a high-minded life? Are the habits of the past so dead that they can never be resurrected and applied with equal value?

In the end Quixote answers these questions in the simplest way. Before he dies he renounces knight-errantry as foolish nonsense, never realizing that even though the acts he performed might have been ridiculous in a modern age, the manner in which he conducted himself was in the very spirit of the great knights-errant. He was the true embodiment of the chivalric gentleman. He had succeeded in his quest.

Story spicers in a story like this—or in *The Aeneid*, for that matter—abound. From deception through conspiracy to honor and dishonor (especially this latter) each of the spicers appears, lending substance to a fine tale. Would *The Aeneid* be so powerful if elements of rescue hadn't been present? Would *Don Quixote de la Mancha* be so finely drawn if searching and mistaken identity weren't present? Clearly, in a story which is motivated by discovery, each of the thirteen story spicers could be used.

For example, if we steal the plot of *The Aeneid* and substitute a buried treasure for the destiny of Aeneas to found Rome, then we could introduce story spicers such as criminal action, material well-being, even suicide and suspicion. Not that these aren't present, but to a much lesser extent than they might if we change the plot around to emphasize the physical rather than the metaphysical aspects of the quest. The point is that the nature of the quest will determine the extent and even the usefulness of the individual story spicers. Some work with one type of quest, others work with another. Dabble, experiment, float them and see which sails best.

A quest is really a search for truth, for some definable product that will enlighten us. In The Aeneid and *Don Quixote de la Mancha* the quest is essentially positive, a reaffirmation that goodness and virtue can be attained. But there is another side, where a quest seemingly pursued with right-thinking motives can result in something else. Stories of discovery don't always have happy endings, the quest need not be so uplifting.

This is the way it works out in Joseph Conrad's *Heart of Darkness*, the plot of which became the storyline for the 1979 movie,

Apocalypse Now! In Conrad's tale, Marlowe, a young sailor, is to take command of a river steamer that will navigate the inner reaches of the Congo River in Africa to help bring out ivory that has been cut and is awaiting shipment. The sailor hears tales of the legendary Kurtz who lives among the natives, educating them while at the same time sending back record shipments of ivory Over and over Marlowe hears of Kurtz's reputation and his skill at gaining the natives' respect and confidence. This runs counter to the feelings of the company district manager on the scene who resents what Kurtz is trying to do. He'll ruin the natives, the district manager feels—he's botching up the ivory business.

The quest here is Kurtz's. Can he discover how to help the natives, enlighten them while at the same time providing the company with record quantities of ivory? At first it all seems to be working, but when Marlowe and the district manager finally arrive on scene in the deep-up-country portion of the Congo River, they come face to face with the real truth. Instead of enlightening the natives, Kurtz has been debased by them. He attends native rituals, has killed a number of times in order to get ivory and even hangs shrunken heads outside his door. Kurtz admits to Marlowe the truth of what he has become, asking only that he be allowed to die among the savages he has come to embody. Instead of educating the natives to become like him, he has become more like them.

And in this ironic fact we have the culmination of Kurtz's quest—the truth he seeks is, in effect, a pattern of evil. His discovery is darkness, not light.

Irony can play an important part in stories of discovery. It's a natural plot technique. We establish the nature of the quest right off, and then we slowly build the action towards some kind of resolution. Either we achieve the quest or we don't, but if we don't—or perhaps even if we do—what we ultimately get may not be what we were looking for in the first place.

Take C.P. Snow's 1935 novel, *The Search*. It's the story of a young scientist, Arthur Miles, who, from the age of ten, wants nothing more than to be a scientist, to discover something that will make him notable within the scientific community. For him science is the complete discipline, and his passion for scientific research, the long, arduous hours collecting and evaluating bits and pieces of information are like a sacred journey with the light of eternal truth as the ultimate objective.

Does he find it! Well…yes and no. He becomes a crystallographer and gradually garners the respect and admiration of his colleagues as his learned thoughts and discoveries begin to make the rounds. At one point he falls in love, but even this must give way to his obsession with science. His quest is for immortality within the scientific community and recognition outside it. As he draws closer and closer, his chosen field is suddenly rocked by new thoughts and discoveries, events which make Miles realize he is now on the outside looking in. No longer is he at the cutting edge of his profession—he is now trying to run to catch up.

And in so doing he reflects on whether it has been all worthwhile. He decides that the obsession he held for science was misplaced. Science is but a pleasurable enterprise, providing momentary ecstasy, but for him such ecstasy seemed to arrive only in his youth. In adulthood the ecstasy gives way to pleasure and drive. His quest for immortality in science now becomes, instead, the vehicle for a career change. Ironically, his discoveries in the science field make it possible for him to get close to what he wants, but the closer he gets the more elusive the prize until he decides the quest isn't what he wants anyway.

So he gives up science altogether and starts a career studying and writing about economics. And he is finally content. His discovery has produced an x-ray of himself.

The quest for personal peace is a common theme in stories about discovery. In some there are rites of passage that must be endured, in others only death will finally provide the relief. Personal peace may come through divorce or bankruptcy or sexual release. A final tribute or a final battle may offer lasting comfort. We seek to discover something about ourselves, and the circumstances of that discovery make for a fine plot.

For example, in Margaret Atwood's 1973 novel, Surfacing, we have the story of an unhappy, divorced commercial artist, her lover and two friends travelling to the artist's family cabin in a remote section of Quebec in search of the artist's father who has apparently disappeared. While the search goes on, strains among the four travelers begin to appear, and the artist withdraws into a private world full of childhood memories and events. She finds what she considers to be secret clues to the whereabouts of her father, as well as other symbols and signs she believes were left for her by her parents when she was a small child. Pretty soon communication among the four dries up, and the artist slowly sinks into the equivalent of a breakdown, totally immersed in the events of her past. But in effect what is happening is an act of regeneration. The artist has come to the wild, remote Quebec countryside to remove the pain and the anguish of living in a world which holds nothing but discomfort, abuse and disappointment. As she regresses into her past, her quest for some kind of personal peace becomes possible. It may be a private thicket of problems, but at least it is her own thicket and not the product of someone else. In a metaphysical sense she has purified herself, and in so doing she has found peace.

Even where the quest seems to be based on gaining the most tangible of all rewards, there can be another dimension which provides the true essence of what is sought. For example, we wish to discover buried treasure, and so we begin our search. Quite obviously we're looking for material rewards, so can we really call it a quest! It's just a way to get rich, right?

Not necessarily. If our search for treasure brings into question not whether we'll succeed, but why we are trying in the first place, or that what we seek is really just a symbol for something else, then we've gone beyond the physical and into questions of the very nature of the quest.

Such is the intent of Bruno Traven in his 1935 work, *The Treasure of the Sierra Madre*, set in the mountainous wilds of Mexico. It's the story of three down-and-outers who go into the Sierra Madre mountains searching for a lost gold mine. They find the mine and the gold it holds, but then the trouble starts. Traven treats the gold quest in the political sense, as a statement of the sorry mess the profit-making, capitalistic system causes. The men seek to get rich: they can taste the new life that will open up for them…but in their yearning for material rewards—the very reward the capitalistic system offers—they run afoul of the evils of the system.

The three men team up for the gold search, strangers to one another but united in their obsessive quest for the gold. It fills their waking moments, and they talk of little else as they make their trek into the Sierra Madre. The gold mine they seek was once worked by the Spaniards but has long since been abandoned and is reputed to be under an Indian curse. No matter, they proceed anyway, and they do find the gold.

They mine all they can carry, and with pockets bulging they start back to civilization. At this point one of them begins to question why he should have to share with the others. Why shouldn't he keep it all for himself? Another grows ill in a remote Indian village they pass through and reluctantly trusts his gold to the other two. Later, greed becomes a compulsion, and one of the remaining two forces his companion into a clearing in the forest and shoots him in cold blood.

Now he has the gold, and the rich life beckons…

But as he is trudging along, he is suddenly confronted by Mexican bandits. They surround him, and with little concern for the gold dust he is carrying eye his other possessions.

Then—swipe! One of the Mexicans unsheathes a machete and severs the prospector's head from his body…and the gold dust is scattered across the countryside.

An unique plot? It has several story spicers such as honor and dishonor, searching, suspicion, criminal action, material well-being, but these only add substance. The plot is motivated by the quest for gold which turns out to be the basis of evil.

But then, this plot really isn't new. If we go all the way back to the fourteenth century, we see the same story elements in one of Geoffrey Chaucer's *Canterbury Tales*. Specifically, it's *The Pardonner's Tale*, about three men who follow a hedonistic way of life—drinking, gambling, dancing, overeating and wenching. One morning, as they are drinking in their favorite tavern, they hear a bell toll and find out a friend from another town has died. Death must reside in the other town, they decide, we must find Death and slay the monster! And so they set off, but before going too far they meet an old man whom they treat in a shabby fashion. He tells them they'll find Death under a tree in the nearby forest. And when they arrive at the tree, they find not Death, but a huge pile of gold coins. They are ecstatic but decide to wait until dark before carrying the gold back home.

One of the trio is sent to get them food, and he begins to plot to keep the gold for himself. He decides to kill the other two, and he acquires some poison which he pours into two of the three bottles of wine he has bought.

Meanwhile, the other two decide *they* will share the gold themselves. When the third man returns, they engage him in horseplay, so diverting him that he doesn't see one of them draw a dagger. He is killed, and then the other two decide to celebrate. They reach for the wine the third man has brought. Each drinks a bottle quickly, and soon they truly meet Death.

The same quest, the same theme is present here as in *The Treasure of the Sierra Madre*: gold is the foundation of evil; the pursuit of material rewards is not only self-defeating but obnoxious. In effect, when we think we've succeeded, we've failed altogether.

And didn't Traven steal Chaucer's plot?

13. Ambition

Suppose we come across the true story of a simple schoolteacher living in sixteenth-century Germany who teaches in various university cities. The only unusual thing about him is his avocation: in an age of staunch religious worship and influence he likes to do magic tricks, and at times he offers to tell fortunes. He toys with the inexplicable, and in so doing he runs counter to popular belief that man should leave to God and his chosen messenger all things for which there may or may not bean answer.

As our schoolteacher travels about he is dismissed by many as a charlatan, a phony interested only in fattening his private account at the expense of the poor souls he might deceive. But then he appears in Cologne, and the archbishop has a chance to observe him and to witness his magic and his prophecies. Within days, stories of the schoolteacher's supernatural powers burst across the face of Germany, and the archbishop of Cologne becomes his patron. His reputation spreads even as the Protestant Reformation of Martin Luther gathers steam, and in fact Luther himself comes to believe in the supernatural powers of this one-time, little-respected schoolteacher. By the end of the sixteenth century he has assumed almost legendary size as the embodiment of the magic and the pseudoscience that filtered through the medieval period. Tales of what he can do are told and retold across the face of Europe.

Now, what if…we take this true story and create a piece of fiction? What if…our schoolteacher becomes a scholar deeply enmeshed in the meaning of life, aspiring to powers no other mortal possesses? His store of knowledge is vast but he recognizes that man's ability to acquire knowledge is limited. His soul needs release from earthly constraints so he can aspire to the supersensual, where he could learn the very meaning of existence. Now, since the story of the schoolteacher occurs against the background of deep religious upheaval and concern, our scholar—his life updated to a more modern era, of course—might also have to deal with a conflict that bears on religion. But let's not shroud things in dogma or practice. Instead, let's have our scholar become—the pawn in the struggle between the Devil and the Lord. In short, let's reduce the conflict to its barest, most fundamental level...

And for a story we have the famous tale of Faust by Johann Wolfgang von Goethe, written in the early part of the nineteenth century. Goethe's story is, in fact, the retelling of the old legend that surrounded the sixteenth-century magician and schoolteacher who also carried the name of Faust. In Goethe's story the Devil, who takes the name of Mephistopheles, makes a wager with the Lord that Faust can be tempted to renounce his beliefs and his righteous integrity. Both know that the only way this can be done is if Mephistopheles can gain control of Faust's soul. Twice, the Devil tempts Faust, but to no avail. Faust continues to search for the true meaning of life, his ambition now so profound that he renounces most of the things that make life worthwhile. There must be experience so profound, so enduring that it transcends what is available on this earth.

Okay, says Mephistopheles, if this is what you seek, and I am able to provide it, then I claim your soul.

Faust agrees.

Ambition for something unattainable to all other mortals is Faust's desire. It is ambition, without question, on the grandest scale.

Mephistopheles sets to work. First he restores Faust's youth, and then he introduces Faust to Gretchen, a pure and beautiful young woman. At first Faust vows he will not touch her because she is so innocent and unsullied. But the Devil sends her jewels which Gretchen thinks come from Faust, and Faust is then tempted to pursue his love for her, and she surrenders herself to him.

Gretchen's brother convinces her she has done a terrible wrong, and she turns in grief to Faust who decides to kill her brother.

Is his love now so overwhelming and his spirit so fulfilled that he would wish this moment to endure forever? The Devil wonders.

No, says Faust, human love, even enduring love, cannot satisfy my cravings…

Then Mephistopheles creates the living image of the most beautiful woman who has ever lived—Helen of Troy—and in presenting her to Faust hopes that now, finally, Faust will cry for the moment to stay forever.

But Faust doesn't bite. Beauty is but a passing thing, he says, it is no more lasting than any other sensual earthly experience…

And Faust shakes off further ambition for supersensual experience. He sets about producing something useful for mankind. The Devil wipes away the supernatural powers he has granted Faust and retreats, not content to give up his quest.

Many years pass and Faust has now made it possible for large numbers of people to live and work on land he has owned and to produce something useful for themselves and for mankind. At this moment he cries out for everything to stay as it is, that life is worth living and that things, as they are, should endure forever…

And Mephistopheles has him!

Or has he? Faust may have cried for a moment to endure, but has he also renounced his beliefs and righteous integrity? Apparently Goethe didn't think so because in the end the Lord dispatches angels to help Faust ascend to heaven.

Did Goethe steal his plot? Is Faust's overriding ambition so unique that Goethe is the only one who can tell it? Not at all. More than 200 years before Goethe's work, Johann Spiess produced a story *Historia von Dr. Johann Fausten* which had Faust making his deal with the Devil so he could enjoy twenty-four years of pleasure and power before his soul was to be given to the Devil. This Faust even had a sensual experience with Helen of Troy and fathered a child by her. At the end of the twenty-four years he is carried off to Hell and now deeply regrets having bartered his soul for what he claims are transitory pleasures. Then there's Christopher Marlowe's famous drama, *The Tragedy of Dr. Faustus*, written in 1589, as well as a number of other works on the same theme, including symphonies, operas, and other musical works. Did they all steal their storylines and plots?

Certainly, but the legend of Faust and the magician and fortune teller lives on. Anyone can try his hand, it seems.

Shakespeare uses the idea of ambition frequently in his work. In *Julius Caesar*, of course, it is the prime motivating factor for the action. Caesar, by far the most powerful man in Rome, now contemplates accepting the crown which would make him King, his power absolute, his decisions unquestioned. The conspirators gather because they sense an unnerving movement towards dictatorship and unreasonable authoritarianism. They strike!...and Caesar is dead, and the threat of one man's ambition dies as well. What did Shakespeare think of ambition? In the orations of Brutus and Anthony at Caesar's funeral he is quite clear:

Brutus, Caesar's close friend and confidant and one of the assassins, speaks first:

As Caesar loved me, I weep for him; as he was fortunate I rejoice in it; as he was valiant, I honour him; but *as he was ambitious, I slew him.* There is tears for his love; joy for his fortune; honour for his valour; *and death for his ambition...*

Anthony, one of Caesar's generals and a long-time compatriot on the battlefield, then speaks:

The noble Brutus hath told you Caesar was ambitious: if it were so, it was a grevious fault...for Brutus says he was ambitious; and Brutus is an honorable man. He hath brought many captives home to Rome, whose ransoms did the general coffers fill; did this in Caesar seem ambitious? When that the poor have cried, Caesar hath wept; *ambition should be made of sterner stuff...*

The point here is that ambition, to Shakespeare, has pejorative leanings, and when someone is ambitious, that is, when they show strong interest in their own personal advancement, and especially at the expense of someone else, then obviously it is not something to be admired.

Clearly, ambition is the plot motivator for this story. Shakespeare also uses a number of story spicers. Perhaps most prominent is the use of conspiracy, the plotting of Brutus, Cassius, Casca and the others to murder Caesar. We follow the plot from Cassius's first words to Brutus and the disaffection of Casca on through the subterfuge to enlist Brutus's support, the gathering of the weapons and finally the deed itself.

Another story spicer is the use of criminal action—specifically murder—which of course enlivens the plot substantially. By its very nature political conspiracy is a traumatic event because it seeks to replace established power which has already indicated it will not be replaced. Upheaval is the natural result, and violence will follow with certainty. Imagine a political conspiracy without the threat of murder, especially two thousand years ago, and we have a plot that loses much of its tension.

Shakespeare touches on other story spicers in *Julius Caesar*. There's authority in that the conspirators are afraid Caesar wishes to extend his powers; there's deception in that Cassius plays on Brutus's fears to bring him into the conspiratorial circle, and, of course, there's Brutus's deception in turning on his friend and patron and killing him; there's honor and dishonor in the manner of Brutus's approach to the assassination and the fact that he has great respect for Caesar even after killing him. Yet Brutus, too, is held in high honor by those who know him. Note the reaction of Ligarius who encounters Brutus shortly before the assassination. He asks Brutus about his plans and Brutus replies, "A piece of work that will make sick men whole."

Ligarius wonders what that could be, and Brutus tells him he'll explain it if Ligarius wants to come along. Ligarius then says:

Set on your foot, and with a heart new-fired I follow you, to do I know not what; but it sufficeth that Brutus leads me on…

The end product of ambition in political circles is power, and in *MacBeth* Shakespeare has his lead character seeking to become king of Scotland. The plot includes murder, conspiracy, treachery, dishonor—all the items that go along with the concept of political ambition realized to its extreme. Could MacBeth gain his dream of the throne without murdering the king of Scotland? Perhaps, if he had patience, but then once power is tasted, patience is often a casualty. MacBeth, spurred on by his wife, plots to kill the king and his sons, and later when he has assumed the throne and his former friend, MacDuff, has gone away to join those seeking to oust MacBeth, he kills MacDuff's wife and children. MacBeth also murders his friend Banquo in the course of the conspiracy, and then, finally as king, he himself becomes a target of others who wish him removed. It is the story of *Julius Caesar* carried an additional step: now the conspirators themselves have assumed the power they refused to serve.

The ambition of MacBeth is the major plot motivator in Shakespeare's work. The story, in bold outlines, is a blueprint that others have followed through the centuries, and Shakespeare's warning that oversized ambition carries with it the seeds of its own destruction is a thoroughly modern concept. Let's take just one example: a young man with political ambition is county treasurer and he fights against a corrupt building contractor who is constructing the local schoolhouse. The treasurer ends up losing his job over the conflict, but two years later the fire escape on the building collapses during a fire drill and the treasurer is vindicated.

Some years pass and the treasurer is now running for governor, his youthful vigor now replaced by a cynical opportunism. After he is elected, his political maneuvering begins on a grand scale, and his wife retreats to her sister's farm, agreeing to appear in public with him only for the sake of his reputation. He has a mistress, an assortment of strong-armed bodyguards, and an ambition to build a huge medical-center complex carrying his name.

This is the storyline for Robert Penn Warren's fine work, *All The King's Men*, which won the Pulitzer Prize in 1947. Willie Stark, the Governor, is not above blackmail or conspiracy to achieve his ends, and in fact uses and misuses various people in order to maintain and solidify his position. When old Judge Irwin stands in the way of one of Willie's plans, he orders his executive assistant to delve into the judge's past and find a scandal that could be used. When Willie wants a well-respected local surgeon to become chief of the new hospital, and the surgeon turns him down, he has documents shown to the surgeon's sister which prove their father, as governor, had covered up acceptance of a bribe by Judge Irwin. When Willie tries to intimidate Judge Irwin in order to stop one of his political enemies from trying his own form of blackmail, the judge shoots himself after learning that Willie has information about the judge's acceptance of a bribe. When Willie tires of his mistress, he takes up with the sister of the surgeon who heads the new medical center.

And, finally, the surgeon, distraught about the news of his sister and Willie, confronts the governor in the hallway of the state capitol. And he shoots him.

Quite obviously there are wide differences between this work and the Shakespearean tragedies, *Julius Caesar* and *MacBeth*. Yet in each instance it is cynical political ambition turned to self-serving ends that destroys the character. Story spicers fill Robert Penn Warren's work: there's suicide and deception and conspiracy and criminal action that add substance to the basic plot motivator and show, just as Shakespeare does, that ambition provides a fertile arena within which to construct a story. Willie Stark rises to power and maintains himself by opportunism and illegality, and in the end, just as Julius Caesar and MacBeth discover, the people one uses and abuses on the way to the top will have their day.

Modern political ambition on a national scale can also be fruitful for plot motivation, though the only difference with other stories is in the setting. But ever since the late nineteen fifties the somewhat strange and intriguing stage of national politics has become more and more familiar, perhaps starting with Allen Drury's 1959 novel *Advise and Consent*. Ambition always plays a part in these works, and since it's political ambition, we're bound to see story spicers like conspiracy and criminal action and deception fill the pages. Ambition, after all, is pretty dull stuff unless it's spurred by someone doing something he or she shouldn't be doing. A good example is Gore Vidal's *Washington* D. C., published in 1967. Though the action in the story takes place from the late nineteen thirties to the early nineteen fifties, it is a political drama that deals with ideas from any age. U.S. Senator James Burden Day is from a western oil state, and early in his career he had done a favor for an oil speculator interested in buying up Indian lands, a favor which was quite obviously illegal. Now, years later, Day wants to run for the presidency, but then Franklin Roosevelt decides on a third term and Day's ambition is stymied. His assistant, Clay Overbury, also has political ambition, but war intervenes and Overbury serves until the war ends. Then Overbury returns and runs for Congress, and several years later he confronts Senator Day about that little favor he did for the oil speculator some years back. He wants Day's senate seat, and, without being pushed, Day moves aside. At this time Overbury has also married into the Sanford family. Blaise Sanford is the publisher of a very strong and influential Washington newspaper, and he's glad to see his daughter, Enid, marry Overbury. However, Enid slowly succumbs to alcohol and other pleasures of the flesh until she is in danger of becoming a severe embarrassment for Overbury. At this point, Blaise Sanford, who has been beating the drums for Overbury in his newspaper, sees the sorrowful consequences for Overbury if the truth about Enid were made public. So he has her committed to an asylum, and then Clay Overbury is relatively free to begin his real quest—a run for the presidency of the United States.

Here, once again, we have political ambition employing the darker side of human nature to achieve its ends. There's blackmail and conspiracy and deception with but one goal in mind—the top political office. In a general sense Vidal's story mirrors both *Julius Caesar* and *MacBeth*: a conspiracy to gain a position of power, the use of underhanded, illegal, disreputable means and a dangling question of whether the ends sought ever, *ever* justify those means.

Ambition has many faces, though it ultimately translates into power, prestige, wealth, respect in some combination. Can a man aspire to be a good father? Can a tennis professional aspire to win Wimbledon? Can a cook aspire to make a perfect Hollandaise sauce? Can an oil rigger aspire to drill a hole deeper than anyone has done before?

These are the elements of a story, and as we broaden the scope of the ambition that will motivate the story, we create a storyline. Now, can a man aspire to be a good father when his work takes him away most of the week or when he's suddenly confronted by obtaining custody of his children because his ex-wife doesn't want them? Can a tennis professional aspire to win Wimbledon when her marriage has just broken up or her mother is dying or her knees are deteriorating badly?

The point of all this is: how outsized is that ambition? For purposes of a good story, the more outsized the better!

Which brings us to someone whose ambition knew no bounds, none whatsoever. His name is Sammy Glick, and he came from a miserably poor section of New York, his sole aim to "better himself." In Budd Schulberg's *What Makes Sammy Run?* (1941) Sammy starts off as a copyboy on a newspaper in his middle teens, and by the time he is nineteen he has become a radio columnist, even though he has no skill in writing or producing. As the author points out, Sammy's life is a continual "blitzkrieg against his fellow man," yet his ambition never wavers. With the help of a stolen manuscript he moves on to Hollywood and uses ghost writers and collaborators to promote himself. Eventually Sammy Glick— tough, unscrupulous, amoral...and unabashedly ambitious, becomes a Hollywood big-shot writer-producer. But still he can't write a line. Sammy's Hollywood wedding is an unimagined extravaganza and as the book closes Sammy becomes—finally—the head of a major studio.

Even though *What Makes Sammy Run ?* is sometimes called a "Hollywood" novel, it's actually the story of a man's rise in the business world, in this case the business of movie-making. A business setting is a good story forum for ambition as a plot motivator. After all, business and money go together, and if one aspires for wealth, prestige and power, what better way than at the top of the business heap? To be ambitious in the business world is to be expected, it is part of the business ethic. Few business people enter the battle without ambition, and that ambition can form the core of a good story. Sometimes ambition can run amuck, as with Sammy Glick. Sometimes its urgings are more subtle, though the consequences can be equally disagreeable.

In John P. Marquand's *Sincerely Willis Wayde,* published in 1955, we start with a young man, idealistic, interested in the beauty of nature and the outdoors. At age fifteen Willis Wayde and his family move to Clyde, Massachusetts where Willis's father, Alfred Wayde, an itinerant engineer from the western United States, is hired by Henry Harcourt, owner of the Harcourt Mill, to help rejuvenate the mill. This is during the Depression, and with Alfred Wayde's help, the mill and then the town are able to survive the bad years. During this time Willis becomes drawn to Bess Harcourt, Henry Harcourt's granddaughter, and to Henry Harcourt himself. He tries to emulate the old man—his elegant style, his clothes, his knowledge of antiques, the ease with which he manages people.

Willis then goes off to college and finally to Harvard Business School, and we see the idealistic young man slowly become transformed into an ambitious businessman. He becomes very important to the mill itself, and then he gets additional training in New York as an industrial consultant. By this time Henry Harcourt is dead, and his granddaughter, Bess, owns the mill. He asks Bess to sell him the mill, intending to combine it with another business in the first of a series of conglomerates he will create. Bess will sell him the mill, but she assumes, because of their early years together and his love for the mill and the town, that he will protect them and the jobs of those who work there. Two months later, after the mill is his, he closes it down. In short order Willis becomes a wealthy businessman, and by now he is totally devoted to the business way of life. Yet try as he might, he can never recapture the elegance and the style of Henry Harcourt. He wants to become a businessman with social responsibility, but the latter role eludes him completely. "I've tried to be sincere," he tells his wife, Sylvia, "I really have. But sometimes it's a problem, how to be sincere."

As he continues to try and follow in Henry Harcourt's steps, he begins to study up on antiques. But once again he falls on his face. His motivation has no substance. 'The heads of a great many businesses seem to collect antiques," he says, 'They're apt to appreciate someone who knows about them."

In the end it's Bess Harcourt who categorizes Willis Wayde properly. After she learns what he did with the Harcourt Mill once he owned it, she calls him a Uriah Heap.

And who is Uriah Heap? In Charles Dickens's *David Copperfield* he is the despicable little character who starts as a clerk in a law office, worms his way into the confidence of his employer, becomes a partner in the firm, ruins the man who gave him his chance and then embezzles some money—all the time insisting he is a very humble and undeserving person.

Maybe John P. Marquand didn't steal his plot from Charles Dickens, but stealing a character is the next best thing.

Ambition as a plot motivator gives a fertile image to many story ideas. One can be ambitious in politics…in love…in athletics…in business…in war…in science. The settings for a story where ambition plays an important role are as endless as the variety of stories themselves. Ambition as the ardent urge for personal advancement is the key to stories where such craving lifts the character (or characters) from the pack and makes him (or them) outsized, different, memorable.

14. Spicing The Story

Say what you wish about the literary pinnacles achieved by writers such as John O'Hara, Kenneth Roberts, Thomas Costain, Dashiel Hammett, Margaret Mitchell...the appeal of writers such as Rosemary Rogers, Robert Ludlum, Danielle Steele. The literary establishment is prone to scratch its collective head and wonder just what is it that makes people want to read such apparently simpleminded stuff.

But the truth is there in plain view: each of these writers, and hundreds of others who have gone before or will come after, mastered the essence of story writing—*they've learned how to tell a good story!* Convoluted circumstances, two and three-dimensional storylines, lengthy explorations into metaphysical questions may offer the intellectual a comfortable, perhaps an exciting exercise, but for most of us, a good story is a good story is a good story.

What is the writer saying? Critics ask this all the time. Clearly, a book that delves into broader areas than simple entertainment is entitled to be judged by standards appropriate to its aims. If the author wishes to explore the sheer obscenity of war and its consequences, as Dalton Trumbo does in *Johnny Got His Gun*, then his book must be held up against others that have tried to do the same thing. Or if an author wants to show how war and revolution can corrupt even the seemingly incorruptible, as Robert Stone does in *A Flag for Sunrise*, then here, also, a measure can be made.

But every story must have a plot, and it is only after creating it that the author can turn attention to working out what it is he or she wants to say. The literary intellectual may choose books that go beyond basic story telling, such as the various works of William Faulkner portraying the decay and decadence of the South, but even so there is storyline and plot, too. Sometimes a bit frail perhaps, but without plot and storyline all the literary intellectual would be feasting on is a literary essay.

But for a story to be a *good* story, now that's what we're after. Plot motivators will give us the storyline, that much is clear. Whether it's a story about vengeance or betrayal or rivalry, or a combination of all three, we come away with the bare construction. We have the framework put together, but there is no paint, no finish, no landscaping.

That's where story spicers come in. They make a story into a good story, they act with plot motivators to give a richness and fullness not otherwise achieved. A story about vengeance is okay, but what if the story is about vengeance achieved through deception? Or what if the story is about ambition, and we spice it with elements of mistaken identity! It doesn't make things more complicated. Just more interesting.

Think of story spicers as road signs that can guide us on a book-writing journey. Using deception, for example, will turn a story in one direction. Using suspicion may turn it in another direction. And keep in mind that combinations of story spicers may also work. In fact, it is a rare book that doesn't have more than one story spicer.

Here, then, are the story spicers that seem to appear and reappear through the literary ages. Some work better with one plot motivator than another, some work better in one genre than another. (For example, suicide would hardly seem appropriate in a light-hearted romance, but it would most certainly be effective in a mystery.) To the author we leave the question of when and where and what and how to apply…as we would with any accomplished chef de cuisine.

Deception

The literary antecedents here go all the way back to the legend of the Trojan Horse. "I fear Greeks even when they bring gifts," Vergil wrote in *The Aeneid,* and, of course, he was referring to the deception practiced on Troy by the Greeks with their huge wooden horse. Deception as a literary tool has been common for as long as the written word has been used. The Greek legends abound in stories of deception, as with Prometheus in his quarrel with Zeus over the division of sacrificial meats. Prometheus tries to hide the good meat inside skin and the bones inside fat. Zeus, possibly deceived by the outer wrapping of fat, chooses the bones. The legend then proposes that from this time on, men will always keep for themselves the flesh of sacrificial animals, always offering the fat or inedible parts to the Gods. Zeus, however, is aware of the deception, and in his anger begins to hold the gift of fire from mortals.

Deception is trickery; it's double dealing, fraud and cheating. It doesn't have to spring from dark-hearted motivation; there are deceptions clearly justified, such as the actions of Alec Leamas, the protagonist in John Le Carré's *The Spy Who Came In From the Cold*. For most of the book we see him as a case of spook burnout, and only near the end do we realize he's been deceiving the Russians and playing possum. Deception in the name of honor is effective as a story spicer but, of course, it doesn't have to be honorable. Heinous actions such as the commission of a crime (blackmail and extortion, even murder fit pretty well here), character assassination, unbridled ambition, greed and lust also work. Deception is a good springboard for rounding off a story; it carries with it the elements of conflict and tension. The reader wonders whether the deception will succeed, how it will succeed, when it will succeed.

Material Well-Being

Like the plot motivators they work with, story spicers provide movement for a story. They keep things from stagnating. If people are seen either losing or gaining economic worth, the way it happens becomes an important part of the story. As a story spicer, material well-being involves both the increase and the decrease of the things that make a prosperous life. We say *material* because we want to keep everything fairly narrow. Material well-being means an emphasis on things, on creature comforts, as opposed to less tangible effects such as emotional stability. Not that one can't flow naturally from the other, but for purposes of this story spicer we believe the emphasis should be on the physical, on items one can touch.

A classic example of the use of material well-being as a story spicer is Margaret Mitchell's *Gone With the Wind*. It is truly an epic of decline and destruction of the South, a harsh splintering of one family's material well-being. Two major plot motivators are present here—rebellion and survival—and material well-being certainly fits neatly. In fact, whenever the plot motivator is rebellion or survival, the chances are that material well-being will be there, somewhere.

Just as material well-being can go down, it can also go up. In Jeffrey Archer's novel, *Kane and Abel*, we have the story of two men born on the same day, one to a life of comfort and position, the other to poverty and anonymity. How this latter character rises from such mean circumstances to a life of powers and wealth, while carrying on an intense rivalry with someone he has never set eyes on, is the essence of the story. Abel's drive for financial success (translation: material well-being) spices up a story hinged on the plot motivator, rivalry. The wealthier Abel becomes, the more power he acquires in his struggle to outdo Kane. The story is immeasurably strengthened in this way.

Authority

L'état c'est moi! stated Louis XIV almost three hundred years ago, and ever since we have had a measure to gauge absolute power. 'The state is me," and by that Louis meant that he and he alone was the fountain of all authority. He was the living embodiment of everything French. The authority of France started with him and ended with him.

As a story spicer, authority is an artful technique to establish an immediate conflict situation. Either one bows to authority or one challenges. There really is no middle ground.

Shakespeare plays with the pulls of authority in many of his tragedies. In most cases it is an us-versus-them scenario. Either the characters are behind the authority of the ruler or they are against him. In *King Lear* the king's authority is slowly eroding because of his growing senility. In *MacBeth* the king's authority is challenged because of the ambition of MacBeth. In *Hamlet* the king's authority is challenged because he had killed Hamlet's father, the rightful king. The fact that in each story it is a king who is being challenged makes everything so much more intense and serious. The ultimate authority is the king, and this authority is in danger of toppling.

Authority, of course, can appear in many other circumstances. It can be institutionalized as in the armed services, government, church, school, hospitals; it can be morally based as with a parent or a spouse or any other respected person; it can be physically based through fear or terror or simple intimidation. Authority is the power to command through behavior or thoughts or opinion. A plot which is spiced with elements of authority—whether supported or opposed—provides a concrete storyline to follow. Authority is touchable, palpable; we can recognize authority when we see it.

Making Amends

This might be called the guilty-conscience story spicer. We wrong someone, and then we have to decide whether to make it up to them. Do we recompense them, and if so, how?

In Theodore Dreiser's *An American Tragedy*, a young man impregnates a young woman, not out of love but in a moment of lust and passion. Afterwards, he is torn. His true love would be so shocked by what he has done that it would be over between them. Still, he feels something for the other woman, and he is so sorry about what happened. They go out in a small boat in the moonlight, and the young man wants the young woman to try and understand, try to see things from his position. He is so sorry about everything…The young woman goes overboard (helped to an extent by the young man) and is drowned. Eventually the young man is accused and later convicted of murdering her. He wanted to help her. He thought about making amends for getting her pregnant. He tried, he really did.

Sometimes making amends is more successful. In Goethe's Faust it takes a lifetime of orgiastic pleasure-seeking for Faust to realize that helping others and providing for their happiness and contentment is the only true source of joy and fulfillment. After taking, taking, taking, he finally sees that giving is by far the happier alternative. He makes his amends that way.

Amends-making works best with plot motivators which focus

on someone suffering or hurt or otherwise wronged. Betrayal, persecution, vengeance, catastrophe would fall into this category. Of course, the amends-maker need not be the one who did the foul deed. While we may not like it when the sins of the father are visited on the son, human nature is not always so discriminating.

Conspiracy

Two or more people meet, they plot, they plan to do something, they have an end in mind—some definite goal. They *conspire*.

The key is that the entire scheme must result in something wrongful being done. Even if we meet in secret, even if we keep everyone else in the dark, it's not really a conspiracy if what We want to accomplish is perfectly legal and the way we do it is perfectly legal. A conspiracy implies illegality, and that's what makes this story spicer tingle.

Because people doing anything against the law is, in itself, an effective story tool. Conspiracy can be a criminal act, and so it can be linked with criminal action, another story spicer.

But conspiracy doesn't have to be overtly criminal. It can be economically motivated, as with consumers deciding to boycott a certain product or certain business; it can be socially motivated, as with a well-directed snub or shunning.

The great bulk of conspiracy-laden stories, though, are politically motivated. Look at Shakespeare's work: conspiracy after conspiracy in *Othello, Julius Caesar, MacBeth, Richard the Third*—each with some political end. Two or more people get together and they dream of political change, and they act to achieve it. In their actions we see the essential nature of conspiracy; they twist or bend the natural political forces to suit their own ends, they lie, they falsely accuse, they even murder and persecute. The way conspiracy operates, the wrongful aims and the wrongful ends are the necessary ingredients for building tension and conflict. Imagine Julius Caesar, for example, if Brutus had decided to kill Caesar on his own, without being urged by Cassius or anyone else. Brutus's reasons might have been just as sound, but the entire nature of the story would have been changed. Brutus would stand out as a lone assassin and not as personifying the groundswell of public objection to Caesar's ambition. Could Brutus be so sympathetic under these circumstances? Could his character be so evened-off as it is by contrast with the motivations of the other conspirators?

The modern political novel is replete with conspiracy and counter-conspiracy. We need only read Robert Ludlum (*The Holcroft Covenant*, for example) or Steve Shagan (*The Circle*) to see how effective conspiracy can be at spicing up a story. Take any plot motivator, sprinkle a dash of conspiracy and —*viola*! A storyline.

Rescue

Most commonly, this story spicer can be found when the plot involves physical danger or peril. Will he/she make it? Will the rescue work? Plot motivators such as catastrophe, persecution, survival are natural tie-ins with rescue because each can be founded on some element of physical danger. Is there ever a catastrophe without physical danger? When persecution is in the air, isn't there danger all around? When we survive some traumatic event, aren't we rescued?

Typical of this kind of story is Hammond Innes's *The Land God Gave to Cain*, published in 1958. The action takes place in Labrador following an eerie radio message received by a ham operator in London. The message is sent by a man supposedly killed in an airplane crash, and it begins a tale of search and rescue that slogs its way through unbelievably rugged wilderness which compounds the constant physical danger. It is a story of survival with the hope of rescue spurring the characters on.

In most stories involving rescue, the presence of another story spicer—searching—can be found. To rescue someone or something, there first has to be a search. Then comes the rescue. Even where the rescue consumes the story almost in its entirety, a search for some type of final absolution or honor will generally occur. In Walker Percey's fine novel, *The Second Coming*, for instance, the rescue of a schizophrenic girl from her mental strait jacket consumes much of the book, but as the protagonist performs his rescue, he also searches for some divine order in the events as they unfold. The search is there as the rescue takes place. And the rescue, of course, is not so much from physical danger as from emotional turmoil. Danger is no less severe when it is directed in the mind, and a rescue from that kind of circumstance is no less intriguing as a story spicer.

Mistaken Identity

It started with the gods and goddesses in the earliest Greek legends. Zeus and Hera and Apollo and Athena and Aphrodite—all would assume mortal roles for some specific purpose, and then, after they had accomplished their goal, they would return to being gods and goddesses. In the *Odyssey*, Homer writes: "Owl-eyed goddess Athena smiled at (Odysseus's) words and stroked him with her hand; she was in the likeness of a woman fair and tall and accomplished in glorious works, and she spoke winged words to him..."

Or Apollo, taking the shape of a dolphin in *The Hymn to Apollo*, jumps aboard a ship from Crete and diverts it to the bay of Crisa where he finally reveals himself and demands that those around him build a temple in his honor. "I declare to you that I am the son of Zeus; I am Apollo" he says. "I brought you here over the great gulf of the sea with no evil intent, but you shall possess here my rich temple held in much honor among all men, and shall know the counsels of the immortals and by their help be continually honored for all your days..." Thus the Delphic Oracle is born.

Adventure stories seem a natural home for plots which are spiced with mistaken identity. Stories of vengeance, for example, where one of the prime characters is not who the others think he is. Or stories of love and hate where mistaken identity has precipitated such deep feelings. Or stories of a rivalry which might never have existed if there hadn't been a misstep about who was who. In Daphne du Maurier's *The Scapegoat* an Englishman meets a Frenchman by chance in a railroad station in Le Mans. They bear an amazing likeness to one another, and the Englishman is forced to assume the Frenchman's identity and move into his household where he is surrounded by hate and suspicion and rivalry. Mistaken identity is the story spicer that moves this plot along because the Englishman has no choice but to play his role, and the remainder of the household continue in ignorance as the entire story unfolds.

Mistaken identity works from two directions: we see it from the point of view of the one assuming the wrong identity or from the aspect of those relying on the wrong identity. Either way we have a built-in story advantage: will anyone discover the mistaken identity? How will he/she continue to cover up the mistaken identity? What happens when the mistaken identity is revealed?

Unnatural Affection

The Greek legends abound with this type of spicer. From Zeus transforming himself into a bull in order to make love to Danae, the mother of Perseus, to the act of love performed between Pasiphae, wife of Minos, King of Crete, and a bull to the passion of Phaedra, wife of Theseus, for her stepson, Hippolytus (which is further dramatized by Euripides in his play, *Hippolytus*)...to the incest between Oedipus and his mother, Jocasta (also further dramatized by Sophocles in his *Oedipus Tyrranus*).

The point is that any form of passion, whether physical, emotional or both, that steps out of the normal man-woman, adult-adult, non-blood-related framework has a claim to be called "unnatural," and this surely creates an intriguing storyline. It's different, it's unusual, it's interesting. John Irving could have a brother and sister in wild bouts of passion in *Hotel New Hampshire*, and lend a wacky tilt to a story about a family who runs a hotel. Survival, perhaps even discovery, may have been the prime plot motivators, but doesn't it add an air of intrigue and sheer anti-establishment nose thumbing to have a running account of incest?

Of course the ultimate question of what is "natural" and what isn't depends on the lean of the observer. Is homosexuality or lesbianism or even transvestitism natural? To some they are, though it's safe to say that the large majority might not think so.

Yet a work of fiction where homosexuality (see, for example, E.M. Forster's *Maurice)* or lesbianism (see, for example, Marge Piercy's *Small Changes*) plays an important part might shower the reader with aspects of unnatural affection and carry a fairly conventional storyline. In Thomas Mann's *Death in Venice*, we have a story of a renowned author on vacation who gradually falls in love with a young Polish boy, his feelings ultimately consuming him so that he even ignores the threat of an impending cholera epidemic. Survival, discovery, and love and hate are the major plot motivators, and if we erase the unnatural affection, we have a conventional storyline without much passion. But when we add pederasty to the mix, things become not so conventional, then!

Criminal Action

Any act against the law makes a good story. The conflict is built in, the black hats against the white hats. And it doesn't matter from which side one writes the story or which plot motivator we use. They all work here. We sympathize with the bouts of conscience Macbeth suffers even though we know him to be a murderer and a political outlaw. We applaud the unselfishness and higher motives of Brutus even as we read about his plunging his dagger into Caesar's body. On the other hand we find it easy to identify with those intrepid characters who hunt down the criminals— private eyes, police detectives, federal-government spooks —and while genre fiction on this side of the law-enforcement ledger appears to have a monopoly, let's not forget one crucial fact above all—it's a good story we're really after, and we have to be good story tellers! Genre fiction or no, criminal action spices up a story.

Murder, treason, larceny, rape, assassination, extortion, blackmail, counterfeiting, arson—these and many more are the types of events that add body to a story. Imagine a Shakespearean tragedy without at least one murder. Or any of the great adventure novels such as Jules Verne's *Twenty Thousand Leagues Under the Sea*, or Charles Nordhoff's *Mutiny on the Bounty,* or a great political novel such as Robert Penn Warren's *All the King's Men*—without a criminal act taking place. The plot motivators may hinge on ambition or vengeance or self-sacrifice or survival, but when someone plans or commits a criminal act in the course of the story, it means so much more in terms of characterization, plot direction and ultimate story resolution.

Look at it this way. What if…an upstanding citizen of a major city is quietly arrested for shoplifting? There's no police record and no medical record of emotional instability. The shoplifter is successful in business, has a fine, attractive family, is well respected within the community and offers no reason for the crime. Is this not an intriguing plot concept? Would it be less intriguing if there had been no shoplifting? Does it matter which side this story is written from? Don't we want to know why?

You bet we do.

Suspicion

This story spicer occurs in the minds of the characters rather than as an overt event. If we suspect someone of doing or not doing something, the process by which we get there is based on things happening that move us into an area of distrust. Distrust. That's the bottom line with suspicion. If we suspect someone, we distrust them, and if we distrust them, we have a natural conflict to work with.

Obviously, suspicion is always present with the police procedural, the detective stories, the suspense genre. Suspicion—or distrust—is what makes this type of book go because it sets up (as with criminal action) the good guys-bad guys format.

Yet suspicion is really a preliminary step to criminal action. It's in the head, a surmise, a guess, but in no way does it confirm that something criminal or against the law has taken place.

And that's why it has its intellectual side. Is the suspicion justified, we can ask? What *actually* has happened to create the suspicion, and are we seeing those events in their proper perspective? What's the motive for the suspicion? Perhaps the one doing the suspecting is the one we should suspect. There are many variables with suspicion, many levels and approaches we can take. For example, in Daphne du Maurier's *Rebecca,* suspicions abound over just who Rebecca was, what happened to her and why. The story moves from one ominous circumstance to another, leaving behind a growing pile of suspicions with little resolution until the end. Distrust is palpable throughout the book, even though the plot motivator fluctuates between survival and love and hate. Suspicion is what really gives it substance.

For the most part suspicion works best with motivators like betrayal, vengeance, rivalry, survival, rebellion and persecution. That's because these plot motivators demand strong conflict situations, and suspicion is in itself a conflict-laden condition. If we suspect someone of something, we sure don't want to make ourselves vulnerable, do we?

So we step back, button ourselves up and watch our suspicions grow and grow.

Suicide

This is a corollary to the story spicer, criminal action. When we commit a crime, we are doing something unlawful to someone else; when we commit or try to commit suicide, we are doing the same thing to ourselves. (Actually, attempting to commit suicide is, in itself, a crime and a violation of most state statutes. But the law is rarely enforced in this connection.)

The idea of suicide comes in many forms: as a political statement, as the ultimate despair in a failed love affair, as the only release from degradation and horror, as a form of penance, as a compulsive pursuit of unlimited earthly pleasures. Motivations are as varied as the ways we set about killing ourselves, but one thing is clear: the act of suicide conjures up an unsettling barrage of questions. How can someone do that to oneself? What's the *real* reason? Did he/she have to go *that* far?

It seems that the truth of suicide is this: it's embarrassing to family and friends; it's a final clutch at some form of reality; it's rarely without pain; it's an extremely self-centered act; it's the ultimate rebellion.

It's also a fine technique for spicing up a story, and it works best with plot motivators that can strip a storyline to its raw, emotional edge, such as catastrophe, grief and loss, love and hate, persecution, betrayal. Suicide is a catastrophic event, and the feelings it engenders can be equally as substantial.

Suicide, of course, doesn't have to be a single, lone event, happening without warning. There can also be a process to suicide, a slow disintegration that culminates in death. In Gustave Flaubert's *Madame Bovary*, we see moral degeneration taking place, one step after the other, a slow sinking into despair, the result of trying to survive the sheer boredom of provincial life. Joan Didion in *Play It As It Lays* also picks up the theme of a character in the midst of an arid life. In this case Didion has her character indulging herself with pills, drugs, sexual experimentation—anything, in fact, to numb her to the pain of living. Survival is the plot motivator in both these works, but suicide is what is happening. Survival, in fact, fights a losing battle.

Searching

Most often this story spicer should be used in conjunction with rescue. If we search, we hope to find. And if we find, the chances are we're going to be doing some rescuing. Searching implies that something or someone is lost or must be found. Note the difference, though: just because we find something doesn't mean it's been "lost." Some people— such as the waterclerk in Joseph Conrad's *Lord Jim*—don't want to be found. So when we search, it may not be for someone or something that's been lost. Just missing would be better.

Searching works well with plot motivators such as discovery, survival and the chase. Storylines that move the action quite a bit seem natural here because a search implies a series of events that carries us in one direction or another. Of course, we can search not only for someone or something, but for ourselves. That is, we can hope to discover who we are when set against events that are destined to test us. It is one of Hemingway's favorite themes, one he propounds in a variety of works, from Jake Barnes in *A Farewell to Arms* to Robert Jordan in *For Whom the Bell Tolls*. We face a series of tests, and they turn us into a better, stronger human being or they don't. We come to know ourselves and to discover what we can and can't do. Searching for ourselves or for someone or something else, has strong antecedents in Homer's *Odyssey* and *Iliad*. The journey of Odysseus after the fall of Troy is the picture of a massive search, set against a backdrop of survival and discovery. The Lotus-eaters, Polyphemus the Cyclops, Aeolus, king of the winds, the huge Laestrygonians, Circe, Scylla and Charybdis, the cattle of the Sun, Calypso's island—these and more are the tests for Odysseus as he makes his way home in the years following the Trojan War. Odysseus is searching for home and in the process he finds himself.

Honor and Dishonor

This is perhaps the simplest and easiest of the story spicers to use. It works with every plot motivator because it deals with human nature and its changeable form. In a story of betrayal, for example, how the characters act with one another could be hinged on how they honor one another; in a story of grief and loss, is there honor in the aftermath of the mourning? In a story of self-sacrifice, is there dishonor in the ultimate demise?

Honor and dishonor have reference to esteem, both public and private. If we have a sense of honor, it's generally because we have a feeling of self-esteem. We respect ourselves, and thus we can share that respect in our feelings for others. We honor ourselves as we honor others. And the world honors us in return.

Take *Julius Caesar*. Brutus tells Cassius as they converse about Caesar's worrisome ambition that honor is something he holds higher than almost anything else. "For let the gods so speed me as I love the name of honour more than I fear death," Brutus says. And Cassius responds, "I know that virtue to be in you, Brutus…"

It is a story of honor even in the commission of a crime. Brutus remains an honorable man. He is driven to kill Caesar *because* he is an honorable man. He looks for nothing for himself, no rewards of any kind. At the funeral orations, Mark Antony calls Brutus an "honorable man" over and over, implying, of course, just the opposite. But regardless of how the reader ultimately feels, the point is that honor and dishonor have been used as a means to add depth to the story. Suppose, for example, Brutus is not so honorable. What kind of story would there be? little sympathy for the conspirators, much more identification with Caesar…and probably a much less well balanced drama. It is in Brutus's sense of honor that we see Caesar and his ambition unveiled, for if such an honorable man as Brutus is moved to kill, perhaps Caesar deserved such a fate.

The storyline may have been founded on ambition, but it is in the clash between concepts of honor and dishonor that substance and spice have been added. Honor and dishonor…public and private esteem…it's how we feel about ourselves and about others that turns the trick.

Rule Two:
Where Am I?

1. Setting the Story

It is three weeks into the term and my writing students are handing in their first piece of assigned fiction. For some it represents an arduous effort brimming with uncertainty and unexpected reactions—I never thought I'd write about *that*…this is fun! …God, I've led a dull life!…I'm confused . ..

Their faces mirror their sentiments, and as I collect the stories, I say, "Relax, I don't expect publishable material at this stage."

"Mine isn't even readable!" comes an unhappy voice.

There's a ripple of nervous laughter. "How many wrote about something familiar?"

"Something we know, you mean?"

I nod.

"From experience?"

I nod again.

"Books?"

"Stories from my grandmother?" (laughter)

"TV…?'"

"Personal experience is best."

"Is there an alternative?" I ask.

"How about making it all up?"

I've been through this with other classes. There is nothing inherently wrong about writing fiction when it's totally the figment of our imaginations, but sometimes it makes the writing task much more difficult. Everything must be invented, and our level of familiarity—without a good deal of research—is likely limited to clichés and overworked situations.

The initial step in understanding why we should fall back on something familiar is to look at the locale of our story— the picture frame within which we weave the action. It had better be a picture frame we know well.

"Where do you set your story?" I ask a student.

"In a police precinct house."

A mystery story, then?"

"Suspense and murder, drugs and bad guys." A couple of low whistles from other students.

"You ever been in a police precinct house?" I ask.

A slow shake of the head. "I read a lot."

"You ever held a kilo of cocaine?"

"No."

"You ever seen a dead body?"

"No."

"You know what records the police have to keep on confiscated drugs?"

"I can guess."

"Sometimes guessing makes it seem unreal, unauthentic." I smile at the student. "I'm making a point, I think."

"Any chance I could get my story back before you read it?" He's gotten my point. I speak to the entire class. "My point is…?"

A soft response from the front row. "Knowing your setting?" I nod, encouraging more…"Think of capital letters, underlines, exclamation points…"

"KNOW YOUR SETTING!"

'You've got it," I say.

The cardinal principle when we set a story is to be familiar— most familiar—with the locale of what we're writing about. My student had had little contact with the setting of the story and so the clichés, the overworked situations flood the mind and ultimately the storyline. What we know is sometimes not what we are familiar with; an effective scene can best result when what we know and are familiar with become the same thing.

Take my student. Unfamiliarity with the scene might cause the desk sergeant at the precinct house to be described:

…beefy, heavy jowled, slumping behind the thick wooden desk, intent on the sports section of the morning paper…

A portrait of disinterest which tells us the setting will be unappealing. To any reader of police procedurals, this is an overworked description, a cliché-laden scene.

The real situation in the real precinct house is much different. The desk sergeant (who most likely will be behind a glass partition now) must be alert, a commanding figure, because this is often the first exposure to police authority the public has, and it had better set an effective tone. The desk sergeant (or in many cases an assigned patrolman or patrol-woman) is the most visible member of the precinct-house police. Other police officials walk by constantly, the phones are ringing, there is a steady babble. The desk person had better be someone who is both alert and talented enough to handle a myriad of problems, expected and unexpected.

Wouldn't this read better?

…dark-eyed, quiet spoken, a sheaf of reports in her hand, she leaned over the computer terminal and waited for a response to her question…

Knowing our setting means understanding it as well as describing it, and understanding only comes with familiarity. To some writers this means tasting it, smelling it, involving oneself to the point where the setting of a story is as intimate to creator and reader as the birthmark on the buttocks of a character.

Familiarity, deep familiarity.

Here are Robie Macauley and George Lanning, a generation ago, discussing setting as a fiction technique. Things haven't changed:

Writers who stick to familiar ground are less prone to irrelevant detail than those who go afield. When dealing with the unfamiliar, writers respond too often as any tourist does. They carry away masses of what might be called public information—the picture-postcard things that everyone sees...

There was an editor who set a simple standard for good fiction. He believed that four questions had to be answered in the first few pages of a novel, and if they weren't answered, he read no further:

—what happened?
—to whom did it happen?
—when did it happen? (the time boundary)
—where did it happen? (the place boundary)

Each of these bears on the setting of a story, though the latter two have a greater impact. The important thing, however, is to realize that each of these questions must be answered early in the story, in the first few pages, and that the questions all reflect:

Where am I?

See how Booth Tarkington in *The Magnificent Ambersons* answers this question on the first page of the novel:

In that town, in those days, all the women who wore silk or velvet knew all the other women who wore silk or velvet, and when there was a new purchase of sealskin, sick people were taken to windows to see it go by. Trotters were out, in the winter afternoons, racing light sleighs on National Avenue and Tennessee Street; everybody recognized both the trotters and the drivers; and again knew them as well on summer evenings when slim buggies whizzed by in renewals of the snow-time rivalry....

A town small enough so that people with the same tastes and characteristics couldn't hide from one another, a town large enough so there was vivid class-consciousness. From these few lines a reader could gather the atmosphere of the town, as well as its general locale. The reader knows exactly where he/she is.

Details become important because they give the reader a peg to identify with, to fasten on to the action. The setting comes alive when the details evoke a reaction such as "...of course! That's the way it should look or smell or sound..." The reader is a participant, not just an observer. But the use of detail must be carefully apportioned; it cannot overwhelm the other aspects of the story. For example, a room could be described:

...high ceilinged, with rococo molding a foot from the top of the wall, stretching in an unbroken line round the four walls, overseeing seven chairs and one couch spread in a loose square, end tables positioned exactly, the wood highly polished, ashtrays centered on each table, decanters within easy reach, tapestries of rich reds, greens and browns hanging decorously from the thick stone walls...

Or the room could be described:

largish and light-filled, faintly smelling of pipe smoke, thick, country-home chairs and couch well polished, the coldness from the stone walls subdued by rich tapestries...

One half the space to say the same thing, and the reader isn't forced to wade through a bog of detail. The art of scene setting comes not from detail dropping itself but from judicious dropping of *certain* details—those that can portray the scene in the most vivid terms. Here's novelist Mary Stewart on the subject:

A physical setting should never be built up too elaborately... For example, nothing is worse than reading a detailed description of a room. Something of the size and style and color and perhaps three telling details are all that is necessary...Note the above example. Size, style and color (largish, country-home, light-filled), three telling details...smelling of pipe smoke, polished furniture, tapestries on the cold walls.

Do we need much more? Can the action now proceed?

Setting serves a variety of purposes, and the accomplished writer uses and reuses them in order to establish authenticity and a sense of drama in the story. Setting is not a static device that can be fastened on a scene without a close awareness of what its consequences will be. At the same time, though, setting must be utilized thoroughly enough so that a proper sense of *where am I?* can affect the reader. In general, setting should be considered for use in the following ways:

—to add vividness to the story; an unforgettable background will make the characters stand out and be memorable. The sea stories of Joseph Conrad are one example of this, the struggles of poor-white existence in William Faulkner's works are another.

—to influence character; where a person lives, grows up or has telling experiences will often determine the way he/she thinks or acts. F. Scott Fitzgerald's Gatsby is an example of this, as are the urban-oriented novels of Phillip Roth,

—to play a role in the story; where the setting is so powerful it can become an actual character in the story, it can even dominate the characters. Some of Edgar Allan Poe's work—especially *The Fall of the House of Usher*—would come in here, as would William Golding's *Lord of the Flies*.

These uses for setting can be woven and interwoven so that matters never remain stationary. For example, we set a story so the action is played against a harsh environment, man against nature… then, suddenly, the teamwork of the characters dissolves, and one character (or more) becomes a menace to the others because he or she believes the harsh environment will swallow them all:

He watched them through the night, convinced now they would dump him over the side as soon as he sank into an exhausted sleep. Twenty-six feet of floating survival, eight mouths to feed, thousands of ocean miles, empty, unforgiving…he hated them all, uneducated, conniving, cruel, they'd never be rescued…

Setting, then, is the result of the writer's using his or her experience and knowledge to create a locale for the story, and the technique for developing this is through the use of descriptive phrases and details which provide a picture to the reader.

But then there's atmosphere.

Atmosphere goes hand in glove with setting. One without the other is like a painting without a frame or a frame without a painting. Atmosphere (or mood) is what the reader feels as the effect of the setting settles. It is the writer's way of injecting life into the stiff details of the locale. "Atmosphere," according to Peggy Simson Curry, "is the result of presenting the physical details in such a way as to create emotional reaction."

Emotional reaction in the story. Important goal, and the reason is obvious. Emotional reaction is what allows the reader to identify and empathize.

See how Walter Van Tilburg Clark in *The Wind and the Snow of Winter* develops his story atmosphere from a judicious use of setting details. Note, too, how the mood of Mike, an old gold miner heading into town as winter comes, contrasts with the setting itself:

It was getting darker rapidly in the pass. When a gust of wind brought the snow against Mike's face so hard that he noticed the flakes felt larger, he looked up. The light was still there, although the fire was dying out of it, and the snow swarmed across it more thickly. Mike remembered God. He did not think anything exact. He did not think about his own relationship to God. He merely felt the idea as a comforting presence. He'd always had a feeling about God whenever he looked at a sunset, especially a sunset which came through a stormy sky...

In spite of the raging weather and the nearness of winter, Mike feels and projects comfort, as if he is above the tempest. The atmosphere and the mood of the story are generated by Mike's thoughts, and as we see, he is at peace with the elements even though they storm about him. In Peggy Simson Curry's words, the atmosphere of contentment is the result of his slogging through the snow and wind. The rough weather merely affords him a chance to seek calmness—it "creates" the emotional reaction.

We can apply this type of cause and effect in other circumstances: a crowded, bustling street creates torment, perhaps even terror...a moonlit night in balmy weather creates a love-filled heart...a tawdry, run down rooming house creates suspicion, even paranoia…

The point is the physical setting becomes the picture frame within which the emotional reaction blooms. Mood and atmosphere (the terms are really interchangeable, except to a purist, and for our purposes purists are mostly confined behind the walls of academia) are integral to all the parts of a story; they depend on plot, on the characters, on the style the writer uses. Each aspect of the story will influence the mood and atmosphere, each will provide some basis for an emotional reaction. A story set, for example, on a luxury cruise ship could have a plot steeped in mystery and death; the emotional reactions would certainly include fear and terror even in the midst of glorious wealth. The plot itself influences the emotions of the characters, and the plot, in turn, is a creature of the setting—the cruise ship.

It works this way with characterization, too. See how Virginia Woolf, in *Mrs. Dalloway*, portrays segments of the British class system and in doing it also develops a definite story mood:

The crush was terrific for the time of day. Lords, Ascot, Hurlingham, what was it? she wondered, for the street was blocked. The British middle classes sitting sideways on the tops of omnibuses with parcels and umbrellas, yes, even furs on a day like this, were, she thought, more ridiculous, more unlike anything there has ever been than one could conceive; and the Queen herself held up; the Queen herself unable to pass. Clarissa was suspended on one side of Brook Street; Sir John Buckhurst, the old Judge, on the other, with the car between them (Sir John had laid down the law for years and liked a well-dressed woman) when the chauffeur, leaning ever so slightly, said or showed something to the policeman, who saluted and raised his arm and jerked his head and moved the omnibus to the side and the car passed through…

The hauteur of the judge, the silliness of the British middle classes are all part of the setting here, and the fact that the Queen is caught in the traffic jam only lends another dimension to the scene. In fact who would think a Queen could be bottled up in something so ordinary as a traffic jam? The Queen is as mortal as the citizens sitting on top of the omnibus in furs and with their parcels. In this short passage we have a strong portrait of British society painted against the framework of a simple street scene. By setting forth the scene Virginia Woolf portrays a mood of class consciousness and its sillier aspects.

Character build-up can equal mood creation. Try it...

> An imperious financier addresses the board of directors of a company he wishes to take over—the mood is conflict and fury.

> An inept waiter attempts to serve a demanding table. The more he tries, the more disaster looms—the mood is frenzied laughter.

Simple, really.

Suppose we come face to face with nonfiction? Does it affect how we use setting, mood and atmosphere? The clear answer is no...fact or fiction make little difference. The picture frame and the emotional reaction it creates adhere to the same rules. See how Theodor Plievier in his book *Stalingrad*, a recreation of the famous battle, describes what a German lieutenant, Lawkow, sees as he retreats across a plain of darkened snow:

On the following day the peaceful skiing terrain had become a very unpleasant deployment area for Russian tanks; firing blazed on the heights and in the little grove of trees and Lawkow realized again that he was nothing but a grain of dust. But luck was with this grain of dust; he had crossed the Tartar Wall a second time and come again into the familiar chaos—guns, hordes of limping men, and more Russian heavy tanks rolling over trucks and suitcases, over a group of screaming men, cutting off another group. There were five, six tanks on the broad expanse of snow. The hatches flew open and on tanks one, two and three a Russian officer popped up, a submachine gun in his hand....

The setting is a battlefield, the mood and atmosphere death and destruction, all as recorded by the eye of Lieutenant Lawkow. This book is clearly nonfiction (though written in novelistic form), but note the dramatic effect the setting creates. There is tension, drama, ultimate conflict— the same requisites that a good fiction scene demands. The author, himself, provides us with a glimpse of how he went about writing it all, and in so doing shows that good scene-setting can be equally at home in nonfiction or fiction:

I saw the battlefields myself; in my own hands I held those wretched records taken from the dead bodies on the battlefields— the letters and diaries; and I spoke myself with the war prisoners, officers and men; and I undertook to describe what happened on the Volga....

The important thing to note is this: setting, mood and atmosphere arise out of the details in the scene, not out of whether those details are representations of fact or fiction. Good writing can create a word-picture for the reader, and that, after all, is what making a scene is all about.

Where am I?

Sometimes the answer rests not with inanimate objects or with landscape or with character development. Sometimes the answer is in the portrayal of action...what's happening tells us where we are. It's the ultimate melding of plot with setting, mood and atmosphere. And it's a good technique. See how Joyce Carol Oates does it with her novel *You Must Remember This,* the story of a former prize fighter, Felix Stevick, now managing a younger man, Jo-Jo Pearl. Here's Jo-Jo's big fight against a former champion, and Felix is there:

He hadn't seen Jo-Jo fight for nearly two months so it was a relief to note that the boy was at the top of his form; less brash than Felix remembered but still belligerent, pushy, circling his opponent and rushing him with brief volleys that seemed spurred in part by the audience's impatience. In the stark bright overhead lights Jo-Jo's handsome face was carefully without expression, his body quick, urgent, lithe. He was taller than McCord by perhaps two inches and lighter by six pounds though his torso was now well developed with muscle, his neck somewhat thick. By contrast McCord looked paunchy and uncoordinated, swinging crudely, not minding that he missed his target, standing flat-footed and swinging again, head ducked down, knees bent, showing Jo-Jo a dull dogged beady-eyed look of malice…

This is part of a five-page scene, and it is almost devoid of description about the arena, the ring, the spectators—the usual details that spice up a fight scene. But Oates limits herself to the fighters themselves, describing them and the action, including the physical damage each sustains as the fight progresses. In this she is using the action as the setting, allowing us to understand that what is happening really tells us where we are.

The fighters fight, they move and circle and hit and cover up.

Do we need to know the spectators are screaming or the arena is smoke-filled or the beer vendors are doing big business? Do we need to know that a small pocket of gamblers offers ever-changing odds as the fight progresses, or that a big-busted blonde is on her knees searching for a dropped earring as the action in the ring goes on?

Details, details. The fighters are the setting, they are framework of the scene. Anything else would add little.

Where am I?

Fighting in the center of the ring.

2. Creating a Sense of Place

The earliest memory I have is sitting atop a huge dark horse on a cold sunny day somewhere in a city. Years later, my parents show me a photo, tinged with brownish age.

'That's you," my mother says. "In Central Park."

Bare branches and indistinct buildings fill the background. I'm round faced and grinning, swathed in heavy clothes. A sober-faced policeman stands alongside, holding me upright with one hand. The horse stares balefully at the camera, his reins in the policeman's other hand.

"You weren't quite two, then," my mother says. "We moved from the city not long after."

My beginning years as a New Yorker, the earliest memories of what I was and what I became…perhaps. Am I the product of my birth and earliest memories? Is this where I find the grounding to produce what I produce today?

Does my "sense of place" shoot back to the years about which I remember almost nothing?

The answer, I think, has to be yes. We can't escape where we are born, nor where we grow up, any more than we can escape the fact we have blue eyes or large hands. These things influence what we do and how we do it. A New Yorker I am (though I hardly remember the two years we lived there), and somehow I judge other cities, other populations by what I have come to learn about New York. The weakness of my conscious memory has little to do with my sense of my own beginning, and in this I have created my own foundation. It has become the setting for the rest of my life to play out.

This doesn't mean, of course, that I can't settle comfortably in another town or city or dwell in another type of life; what it does mean is that wherever I go and whatever I do, I will take the baggage of my earliest New York impressions with me...streets and odors and crowds and colors and speech ...and somehow they will find their way to influence what I write.

It is my sense of place, my setting.

Every writer has it, and every writer should recognize that the earliest experiences and memories play a part in what is written and how it is written. 'The place of one's birth," according to J. Markus, "becomes as inevitable a fact of one's destiny as one's parents, one's genes."

As a New Yorker I would have difficulty writing about early years on a farm ...but I have little trouble placing myself in the middle of the city and describing a crowded street scene or a rollicking ride on a smelly, screeching subway train.

My sense of place is natural, it's comfortable for me.

And that's the point. Writers develop their sense of place, and they recognize its influence when they create a piece of work. For example:

— Would Philip Roth's novels be so acutely urban if he hadn't been born in Newark, New Jersey?
— Would Nadine Gordimer's work be so poignantly anti-Apartheid if she hadn't been born in South Africa?

For all of us a sense of place is crucial because by developing it, we come to understand what we know best and what it will take for our characters and storyline to stand out.

What then does it take to make up a "sense of place"? Robie Macauley and George Lanning put it this way: "...it is the mountains or hills or plains, the houses people live in, the streets of a town or city, the quality of local life."

True enough, and we can see it in this excerpt from Sherwood Anderson's *Winesburg Ohio*, written many years ago. The book is a compilation of stories about the make-believe town, each one dealing with a different character and different events, though there are a couple of common threads running throughout. Note the sense of place Anderson evokes here as he opens a chapter in the middle of the book:

Snow lay deep in the streets of Winesburg. It had begun to snow about ten o'clock in the morning and a wind sprang up and blew the snow in clouds along Main Street. The frozen mud roads that led into town were fairly smooth and in places ice covered the mud. "There will be good sleighing," said Will Henderson, standing by the bar in Ed Griffith's saloon. Out of the saloon he went and met Sylvester West the druggist stumbling along in the kind of heavy overshoes called arctics. "Snow will bring the people into town on Saturday," said the druggist. The two men stopped and discussed their affairs. Will Henderson, who had on a light overcoat and no overshoes, kicked the heel of his left foot with the toe of the right. "Snow will be good for the wheat," observed the druggist sagely...

A sense of place. From this one excerpt we know a number of things: the time of year (snow on the ground), a small town location (Main Street, mud roads leading to town), rural area (wheat-growing country), quiet atmosphere (major saloon)...It's a setting we can picture in our minds, one with simple virtues and simple truth. What would be more natural than for two citizens to meet in casual conversation along the street, discuss the weather with some gravity and explore its consequences (while one kicks the heel of one shoe with the toe of another)? One imagines the snow will make good sleighing, the other offers it as a boon to wheat growing.

This sense of place puts us right into the story, and when Anderson develops his chapter further we see that it will be about a teacher in the town of Winesburg, Ohio. But now we also know what will be behind the little circumstances that make up the story—the character and the personality of the town. If the writer is able to understand and portray fully his or her own sense of place, the reader has to nod with assurance. "I know where we are, it feels right."

What we are dealing with here is the entire environment of a story, not only its general background or broad sweep. We can write about the mountains or the snow on the street or the cold, brisk air, but to effectively harness a sense of place we have to get specific. As Helen Haukeness suggests, we have to write about"... furniture, weather, people, tools, toys, clutter, lighting, odors..."

The things that make it memorable.

The prison smell assaulted him from the first moment, vaguely sour, distinctly penetrating, reminding him of a man's room that had not been well cleaned. The sharp corridor lights and harsh human noises made him wonder if anyone could retain a sense of comfort here...

Our focus has shifted to the narrowest point. We examine individual traits and circumstances because this will give us clues to where we are. A writer must be concerned about these specific concerns because it is a mosaic we are trying to create—a full, complete picture out of various interconnected parts.

A sense of place is our tool with which to do it.

Watch how Larry McMurtry provides the reader with an unforgettable scene portrayal in his novel, *Texasville*. Here we have the Thalia, Texas Centennial Committee meeting to plan the big pageant. Duane, the story's protagonist, is the chairman of the committee, and the subject of hiring a consultant has come up. Note how McMurtry uses local accents and local characterization to get across the idea of the type of town Thalia represents and what its aspirations are in connection with the centennial celebration:

"I have the name of a man from Brooklyn who directs pageants," Duane said. "He did one down in Throckmorton County and they were real pleased with him."

"Is Brooklyn over near Tyler, or where would it be at?" the Reverend Rawley inquired.

"It's part of New York City," Duane informed him. "He comes with a crew of three, to help him with special effects. We're gonna need a little light show when we're doing the Creation."

"The Lord didn't employ electricity," G.G. pointed out. He saw it as his duty to fend off any skits that might lead to a liberal interpretation of the Bible.

"He employed lightning," Sonny said. "That's electricity."

"He didn't employ nobody from Brooklyn, New York," G.G. said. 'The man might be a Catholic."

Duane sighed. "He's supposed to be real good with fight scenes," he said. "We're doing about ten wars, we need somebody who knows how to stage fight scenes."

"Most people around here already know how to fight," G.G. said...

The characterizations are sharply drawn here, we can imagine the fundamentalist preacher rising indignantly to preserve the pure name of the Lord, we can picture Duane, his patience tried but his determination unflagged. The scene represents a portrayal of small-town politics and small-town prejudices played out in that time-worn setting, the local committee. We don't need to read about the dusty landscape or the boiling summer weather or the tenuous oil-drilling economy to understand the author's sense of place...

We get it from a literal-minded preacher whose world reaches about as far as he can see and whose speech identifies his level of education and tolerance; we get it from a group of citizens who believe their small town is important enough to celebrate a one hundredth birthday and who consider the story of Creation, as well as the replay of every United States war, to be of equal significance as the birth of the town; we get it from Duane whose feelings for his town are stronger than he would like to admit.

A sense of place—a small Texas town preparing for a centennial celebration. The author has been there, and he wants us to feel it with him.

In our modern world, sometimes we need to reach out for a more dramatic reference than a familiar characterization in order to grasp our sense of place. Sometimes we need to utilize mass culture to give us an identity with our readers; sometimes we need to refer to items we have in common. Louise Erdrich, the novelist, believes we are tied to one another through "...the brand names of objects, to symbols like the golden arches, to stories of folk heroes like Ted Turner and Colonel Sanders, to entrepreneurs of comforts that cater to our mobility like Conrad Hilton .... "

In short, she thinks that when we use such signs of modern living with our writing, we give our readers a "context" in which to follow the story. It is a lively, thoroughly familiar picture frame that now projects the story.

Is she right?

Here's a story from John Sayles, the writer and film director. In *Children of the Silver Screen*, see if Sayles's reference to mass culture items give the story greater dimension, more drama. Shine manages a small movie theatre, and on this his last day, he is showing a Humphrey Bogart film, 'The Treasure of Sierra Madre'. His successor has arrived, and it's obvious the theatre is going X-rated. Shine now readies himself to collect tickets for his last show:

They blew in, the Jujyfruits and Almond Joys, Junior Mints and Planters nuts, they grin and wince into bad Bogart impressions, they match wits naming the Magnificent Seven, or the Seven Dwarfs, or even the seven major Golden Age studios. Dopey, they say, Warners and Universal. Steve McQueen and Charles Bronson, they say. Grumpy. A boy who looks like the Spirit of Che Guevara does a soggy soft-shoe in front of the men's room door. The fat girl in the poncho tumbles for a box of popcorn, large, with a nickel's extra butter. A boy in a cape and a girl with a yellow slicker do a brief exchange from a Marx Brothers picture…

Here, then, are the trappings of our mass culture, from familiar movies and familiar characters in those movies to familiar things to eat and familiar people doing the eating, It is the lobby of the theatre just before the doors open, and don't we get a sense of place? Haven't we been here before, somewhere, sometime?

Try and read this passage without brand names, without the movie and movie-character names. Substitute unfamiliar words… does it seem the same? Is the sense of place comfortable, certain?

Probably not.

That's the key. We want to develop our sense of place, and so we must consider a variety of items, from earliest memories to those which are the most familiar trappings of our mass culture.

We must think scenery, structures, streets, speech patterns, the amenities of life, the entire environment...

But it's also important to think brand names, symbols, folk heroes, paranoias, failures...

Then we have our sense of place and the story can proceed.

3. How Many Details?

I read once that the most effective manner to portray setting is to think of myself as a television camera. I would be portable, recordable and focus-changeable. That is, I could fasten on a scene at one angle, and then I could change that angle by the twist of a dial so the scene could be narrowed or widened, closed in or made more remote. The author, finding this imagery appealing, went on to advise me that television camerawork often begins with a wide-angle long shot and then zooms to a close-up in the interest of establishing location and scene.

I remember the author asking…why can't books be written the same way? Why can't we start our setting from a broad perspective and work to a narrow focus? Why can't we begin with a forest and portray a single tree? Or an ocean and a single ship? Or a city and a single street?

The answer is sometimes we can—and do—work things this way. But we don't *have* to, and that's what makes story writing so challenging. We have choices.

Note what happens when the camera begins with a wide angled lens: there are myriad items that seep into our consciousness, regardless of their relevance to the story; if it's a landscape, we see earth and sky, ground contour and growing things, humans and/or animals, vague and fuzzy details that form a part of the broad scene. As the camera moves in, some details take on distinct form, and now we start to feel a sense of where we are because the details themselves grasp us with recognition. We see faces and houses, we hear noises, we feel heat.

But we don't have to start with such a wide-angled lens. Couldn't we begin a story this way?

From a little after two o'clock until almost sundown of the long still hot weary dead September afternoon they sat in what Miss Coldfield still called the office because her father had called it that—a dim hot airless room with the blinds all closed and fastened for forty-three summers because when she was a girl someone had believed that light and moving air carried heat and that dark was always cooler...

This is the opening of William Faulker's *Absalom, Absalom*. Note that Faulkner doesn't begin with a description of the south, or Mississippi or even the town where the action will develop. We are in the office in the heat of the day, and there is tradition and history in what is about to unfold. Faulkner doesn't use a wide-angled lens, he concentrates on what is happening in that room, and we don't need to be brought into the story by proceeding from some broader perspective. We start with the specific.

What about this opening?

His face had the look of dark certainty, but we knew it was a convenient mask. His voice betrayed him as he whispered about the barricades of fire that ringed the cave entrance...

Or this?

The phone rang again, and now he heard it. Shrill destroyer of comfortable sleep, cottony awareness.

"Mayor!" an angry voice,

"Huh?" Metallic mouth taste.

A hushed sob through the earpiece."...police...my son...no reason..."

In either example we have a few details that set out what we need to know to understand where we are. Human emotion portrayed so that where it takes place is evident...in a cave or in a mayor's bedroom. Specific locations with narrow focus.

The idea of using a lot of detail with any description goes back at least as far as Daniel Defoe in the eighteenth century. For Defoe a mass of descriptive detail was a way of adding authenticity to his story, a way of making it more plausible. He came to believe that a relationship between setting and the action was possible, that by including many physical details the story itself could move forward.

Is he right? Here's a passage from Defoe's *Robinson Crusoe*, with the narrator describing how he built a canoe to take him from his shipwreck-island:

I felled a cedar tree, and I question much whether Solomon ever had such a one for the building of the Temple at Jerusalem; it was five feet ten inches in diameter at the lower part next to the stump, and four feet eleven inches diameter at the end of twenty two feet, where it lessened and then parted into branches. It was not without infinite labor that I felled this tree; I was twenty days hacking and hewing at the bottom, and fourteen more getting the branches and limbs, and the vast spreading head of it, cut off...

Don't we get caught up in his effort, in his obsession to survive? Each detail presents us with a quandary—will he overcome it or won't he? Then, as he makes his way, the details themselves become steps along his path to ultimate rescue. He survives, he continues to survive, and we, the readers, share his burdens and his triumphs.

In this sense, then, the mass of details do interact with the plot of the story because the details are, themselves, the story. They make the story.

Substantial detail can still work today, though we must be careful about how we use it. Look to some of the work of Irving Wallace or Arthur Hailey, for example. These authors go to great lengths to present substantial information while weaving all those details through the story.

That, of course, is the key. A strong story where the details, no matter how numerous, are necessary. Could we ever doubt that the details in *Robinson Crusoe* were absolutely essential to the story? If we didn't have those details, what kind of story would we have?

A boring narrative, I suggest, without much tension or excitement.

But be careful when using great amounts of detail. As Robie Macauley and George Lanning suggest, "Excessive detail, like that which is merely picturesque, proves only that the writer has been busy about his homework." The details must mean something to the story, they must do something for the story. Try this: read over some prose with lengthy descriptions, then read it over without the descriptions. Is something missing? Does it read more dramatically with or without the descriptions?

If it can stand without the lengthy descriptions, guess what?

The author overwrote.

One area where there is a tendency to use too much detail is in stories where the writer has no way of knowing the true facts—science fiction, particularly, but also stories that occurred in the far past. We can research some of these items, to be sure, but research takes us only so far, and at some point we have to rely on our imaginations and storytelling talents. The problem is that in attempting to create a realistic setting, we offer so many facts to buttress that make-believe world we are creating. We strive for authenticity, just as Defoe did with *Robinson Crusoe*. But it really isn't necessary. One author advises that the important details, no matter the kind of story we write, involve specific colors, shapes and textures. These, he feels, are the keys.

No question he has a point. Consider the following passage from Ray Bradbury's *Martial Chronicles*. In this opening Bradbury doesn't try to paint an exotic scene; it isn't necessary to make it seem so unusual just because the setting happens to be Mars. He limits his details, and the story might be taking place next door:

It was quiet in the deep morning of Mars, as quiet as a cool black well, with stars shining in the canal waters, and, breathing in every room, the children curled with their spiders in closed hands...

Doesn't he capture our interest because this is a setting with which we could easily become familiar? He mentions colors (black), shapes (waters, canal, curled) and textures (quiet, cool, shining), and this gives us a well-defined flavor of where the story takes place and how matters will proceed.

Just a few well-placed details so we feel comfortable with the story.

The big question remains, though…out of the mass of details where colors, shapes and textures proliferate, what choices should we make? What details are the best ones?

The most effective approach is to imagine ourselves in the scene: it is we who do the looking and the absorbing, and we know what will strike us most forcefully. We seek "key details" with this method, ever mindful that use of detail can overrun us if we aren't careful. No two writers deal with it exactly the same, but there is underlying similarity among the works of accomplished professionals. See, for example, how these novelists handle it:

> …to 'be there' is a tremendous help in [telling my story]. It enables me to pare down descriptive passages to the very minimum, because all I have to do is describe the few key features in any particular room or garden or landscape that strike me the most, just as if I were really there…—*G. Masterton*

The most vivid 'atmospheric' setting is done, not with elaborate description which tires the reader's powers of mental build-up, but with the selection of one or two telling details…—*Mary Stewart*

A few key features, one or two telling details, these are what it takes. Shapes, colors, textures, these are what to choose. Details that matter, details that encourage the plot to move forward without, at the same time, distracting the reader's attention.

See how Graham Greene, an acknowledged master of underplayed detail, does it in his story, *Cheap in August*. Mary Watson, an English woman married to an American professor, is on a summer vacation in Jamaica because her husband is off researching in Europe. She is staying in a large commercial hotel which caters to tour groups, mostly American tour groups, and she is appalled by some of her fellow female guests. Note how each detail adds to the story yet also provides us with a vivid picture of the scene. Note, too, how few details there really are:

Huge buttocks were exposed in their full horror in tight large-patterned Bermuda shorts. Heads were bound in scarves to cover rollers which were not removed even by lunchtime—they stuck out like small mole-hills. Daily she watched the bums lurch by like hippos on the way to the water. Only in the evening would the women change from the monstrous shorts into monstrous cotton frocks, covered with mauve or scarlet flowers in order to take dinner on the terrace where formality was demanded in the book of rules. ..

Don't we get a clear picture of these women, can't we imagine ourselves in a quiet chair watching them? Doesn't this paint a vivid scene, one of tastelessness and over-indulgence? Mary Watson's lack of empathy for her fellow guests is the crux of this story, so Greene's portrayal of her offended sensibilities through physical description works perfectly.

But see how he does it…through what they wear in color and shape. That's all. We don't see the women talk, we have no idea what their faces look like, we don't even know their names. All we know is how they fill their clothes.

A few key features, one or two telling details.

Do we really need more?

4. The Value of an Imperfect Memory

Most of us can remember our first date, at what age it occurred, the person we went with. It was an important event in our young lives, and as the years have moved along, its importance hasn't really diminished. It represented a classic step into young adulthood, the beginning of a long passage that has taken us to where we are today.

Important time, important memory.

But how many of us remember what we wore on that date, whether we really wished we were somewhere else, the month it happened and what we told our friends about it?

In short, do we have total recall?

Suppose we wanted to do a story, and we wanted to weave in a first-date scene…suppose further we had a clear memory of our own first date, and it seemed a good sequence to use in this story. The question then becomes…

Do we wish to *reproduce* the experience?

or

Do we wish to *recreate* it?

Reproducing the experience means we act as a camera, picking out each detail and laying it before the viewer *exactly as it appears to be.*

Recreating the experience means we act as a painter, picking out details but ennobling them with a character and a style that suits the painter and not the truthfulness of the scene.

One is reproduction, the other is creation.

One gives us facts, the other gives us art.

The key is in our memories and what we use of them to form

a piece of writing. We can, of course, jot down everything, missing no detail or circumstance. We can reproduce the event just as it happened...and wonder why it doesn't sing with drama as our memories tell us it should.

I missed nothing, we reassure ourselves. *It happened just this way...didn't it?*

Yes, yes, we answer. Every detail remembered.

But it's not art. It's not creation and it's not fiction. For that to happen we must find drama, and we must use our inventive skills. A story doesn't work just because it happened. Writers know this intuitively, and they also know that a story's freshness is dependent upon the ability to create drama out of unreconstructed facts.

Remembering facts is one thing...but remembering them and then turning them into a good story is something else, "Remote memories, already distorted by the imagination, are most useful for the purposes of scene," said Elizabeth Bowen many years ago. "Unfamiliar or once-seen places yield more than do familiar, often-seen places." The more we come to know a place, the more we see it, the more confined we are by what we have seen or felt. We become prisoners of our own knowledge, and that level of familiarity makes it difficult if not impossible for us to develop anything that is not factually correct.

And as we know, facts don't make a story. Drama does.

An imperfect memory, then, is not a burden to the writer. It is a boon companion in the same way as a reading experience is... they both teach us to think in story terms, to create. Here's Arturo Vivante on the subject of memory:

What is memory? Why do we remember? We remember where our house is so we can find it and go back to it. We remember what happened to us in a certain situation so that we may avoid or seek again that sort of situation. We remember someone who has died and whom we loved, because it is the thing that will come closest to reviving that person for us...that is why we remember—to renew the past, and not, primarily, to recount it...

To *renew* the past, not to *recount* it!

Now, when we write about our first date, we think about those things that made it memorable: what he/she looked like, what pressures or uncertainties existed, whether we ever went out with that person again, what, if anything, happened. We renew the memory, and then we turn it in to a story, changing facts and circumstances to provide tension, a defined plot and a workable setting. It doesn't matter if we can't remember where we went on that first date—make it up! It doesn't matter if we can't remember who else was there, or we can't remember why we went out with that particular person—make it up!

The fact that we had a first date is the memory we want to renew; what we do with that memory is what distinguishes the fiction writer from the reporter.

Eudora Welty has written a wide variety of fiction, much of it set in the south. In *The Optimist's Daughter* she has a major scene set in rural West Virginia with two characters, a mother and daughter, stepping off the train in the early morning. They stand on a steep rock:

...all of the world that they could see in the mist being their rock and its own iron bell on a post with its rope hanging down. Her mother gave the rope a pull and at its sound, almost at the moment of it, large and close to them appeared a gray boat with two of the boys at the oars. At their very feet had been a river. The boat came breasting out of the mist, and in they stepped. All new things in life were meant to come like that.

Bird dogs went streaking the upslanted pasture through the sweet long grass that swept them as high as their noses. While it was still day on top of the mountain, the light still warm on the cheek, the valley was dyed blue under them...

An ethereal setting to be sure! This is the young daughter's first glimpse of the West Virginia that part of her family settled. We can't tell from the words alone whether Eudora Welty is relying on her memory or her imagination, though the description is vivid enough either way. It would be hard to believe that at some point in her life she hadn't experienced the scene she offers...

And, in fact, she had. In an interview a few years ago she had this exchange with her questioner:

Welty: My mother came from West Virginia…[*The Optimist's Daughter*] was literal memory, up on the mountain and the sights and sounds up there.

Interviewer: I've always been curious as to how West Virginia got in that novel so strongly.

Welty: Well, we spent every summer visiting the families. My father was from Ohio and we went to his father's farm down in southern Ohio, and to the home on the mountaintop in West Virginia. That's where all my kinfolks were…

So she was writing from memory, but note it is a selective memory. She doesn't tell us she remembers everything about that mountaintop in West Virginia, only that she was there and that is was familiar country. After a lot of years there had to be things that escaped her recollection, and she doesn't try to recover them.

We're served only those items which provide a dramatic base for the setting, those which touch our senses and give us a feeling of "being there."

But suppose the writer's memory isn't sufficient for the scene she wants to write, suppose the recollection of what happened doesn't fit the scene? What then?

Eudora Welty again, In *Delta Wedding* it is 1923 and she has a young girl from the midwest visit her mother's family in the delta country of Mississippi. It is the girl's first visit, and she will stay seven days—the entire length of the book. It is a story with a number of characters, most of them family, all interacting with the wedding as the focal point. See how Welty sets a family scene through Dabney, the bride-to-be:

It was next afternoon. Dabney came down the stairs vaguely in time to the song Mary Lamar Mackey was rippling out in the music room—"Drink to Me Only With Thine Eyes." "Oh, I'm a wreck," she sighed absently.

"Did you have your breakfast? Then run on to your aunts," said her mother, pausing in the hall below, pointing a silver dinner knife at her. "You're a girl engaged to be married and your aunts want to see you." 'Your aunts" always referred to the two old-maid sisters of her father's who lived at the Grove, the old place on the river, Aunt Primrose and Aunt Jim Allen, and not to Aunt Tempe who had married Uncle Pinck, or Aunt Rowena or Aunt Annie Laurie who were dead...

We know the book will take in a lot of characters, and the question for us is whether Eudora Welty is relying on her memory to set these scenes or whether she is creating them from her imagination. Is this her family she is writing about, the family of someone she knows well, or is it total fiction?

Once again we turn to that same interview a few years back. The interviewer offers a comment:

Interviewer: So you never had the experience that many southern children have of being 'trapped' in a room where all the relatives are talking and telling family stories.

Welty: I've experienced that but only as a treat, you know, in the summer. I had to make all that up for *Delta Wedding*...

The scenes in the book where the family members are vividly interacting come in part from her imagination and in part from her memory. But neither, standing alone, would have been sufficient for the book she wanted to write. She had to go back to her memory for what the characters might have said to one another, but she had to put it all into a new setting, and she had to be creative about putting it all together.

I had to make all that up...

Her memory gave her the key, but her sense of creativity opened the door. See the difference in the way she approached the two books: in *The Optimist's Daughter* she uses her memory to zero in on the action and setting, but in *Delta Wedding* she conjures a new setting and partially fictitious action. Her memory is less effective for one than the other, but in either case she doesn't get trapped into total recall. She remembers, but she doesn't recount.

As writers, we don't want to remember too much because, in the words of Peter Stillman, "...near-total recall would be a cruel handicap. You cannot write imaginatively about past moments if you remember them too clearly. Their details become too burdensome, and hence their essences escape."

That is the value of an imperfect memory. The opportunity it gives us to enlarge upon our recollections, and the challenge it offers to turn out a story other people will want to read.

Make that scene!…and imagine, imagine, imagine!

5. How Much Research?

Years ago I wanted to write a novel set in the coal mining regions of Pennsylvania. I had a general familiarity with the area but that would not be sufficient.

I plunged into it with excitement because I *knew* what I was looking for—I wanted to re-create a town's moral disintegration and set it within a political-social conflict. It would be John O'Hara updated.

Oh, how I researched. Weeks and weeks at the library, careful notes inscribed on a mound of index cards, letters to faraway sources, telephone calls and personal interviews. No one would know his setting better, no one could be more prepared.

After almost six months I was ready to write. No loose ends remained in the research, and I had so many things to tell. Confidence coursed through me.

The writing sped along, and my treasure house of information translated easily to the written page. I had no doubt the reader would experience in vivid fashion the way it was in a Pennsylvania coal-mining town. From the proper construction of a coal sluice to a history of coal-mining extraction techniques to the training procedures of nineteenth century coal miners, the reader would understand and empathize.

When the novel was finished, I presented it to an editor friend for comment.

"It probably needs one more draft," I said. "But I'm pleased so far."

"Coal mining town," he said. "Hasn't that been done?"

"Not like this."

A couple of weeks later we met, and he returned the manuscript. "I've read it," he said.

"I have some changes—they'll refine it some."

He shook his head slowly. "Best advice I can give you— start again. This won't get published."

'The plot's weak," I said. "It needs more story."

He shook his head again. "Start over."

'The characters must be dull."

He tapped the pile of white manuscript pages. "The problem isn't just one thing. It's your approach. What you've done is to tell me more about a Pennsylvania coal-mining town than I want to know. Facts instead of a story. With some changes this might make a pretty good textbook…"

Which was something I certainly didn't want to hear.

My problem? I fell in love with my research, and I couldn't imagine the reader not enjoying the information I found. So I told—everything.

The peculiar circumstances of developing a workable setting mean we have to deal, for the most part, with physical environment. We have to describe things (such as a properly constructed coal sluice), and the risk we run is that we offer too many details, so the story will suffer.

We want our setting to be realistic, but that doesn't mean that the more facts we present, the more realistic it will be. It isn't a case of some being good and more being better. We have to choose and choose carefully, something I didn't do with my ill-fated novel. That doesn't mean, however, that we shouldn't do extensive research. The research is the foundation for whatever comes later, but for the writer the key is this:

—Use enough information so the reader understands and is not overwhelmed by the setting; *make it a judicious sprinkling.*

See how Michael Crichton does it with his novel, *Congo*, about an expedition for diamond exploration in Africa. The team of explorers, led by mathematician Karen Ross, would use the latest technology in their quest. Here, the author explains where the search would be conducted and then has Ross add some further information:

On a map the Great Rift depression was marked by two features: a series of thin vertical lakes—Malawi, Tanganyika, Kivu,
Mobutu—and a series of volcanoes, including the only active volcanoes in Africa at Virunga. These volcanoes in the Virunga chain
were active: Mukenko, Mubuti, and Kanagarawi. They rose 11,000-
15,000 feet above the Rift Valley to the east, and the Congo Basin to
the west. Thus Virunga seemed a good place to look for diamonds.
Her next step was to investigate the ground truth.

"What's ground truth?" Peter asked.

"At ERTS we deal mostly in remote sensing," she explained.
"Satellite photographs, aerial run-bys, radar side scans. We carry
millions of remote images, but there's no substitute for ground
truth, the experience of a team actually on site, finding out what's
there..."

Lots of details and unfamiliar names and designations here,
undoubtedly the product of substantial research. The geological
descriptions in the first paragraph give a scientific explanation to
why the search would be concentrated there, but they are neither
so lengthy nor so esoteric as to numb the reader. What a few se-
lected facts of setting will do is provide authenticity for the action
to follow; it will provide an appropriate background.

And this is what Crichton does. His research must have uncovered much more than what he puts on the page, but then he
wasn't interested in offering a lesson in geography. What he wanted
to do—and succeeded in doing—was to sprinkle enough facts to
keep the story going because the Rift Valley, of course, is where the
search for the diamonds will concentrate.

Then note Ross's speech. A brief survey of the high-tech desig-
nation "ground truth," but here again the details are kept to a mini-
mum, mostly in the form of examples. (Why examples? Because
they tend to create images in the reader's mind, and these are both
more dramatic and more memorable than simple exposition.) To
uncover the essence of "ground truth," Crichton must have had
to do additional research, but he gives us just enough so we un-

derstand without having to wade through a high-tech operating manual.

How much research we do, then, is dependent more on how we want that research to move the story than on insuring the reader understands *everything*. What we as writers may find out through research is one thing; what we should offer to the reader of what we find out is something else.

Just a sprinkling of facts is best.

Suppose we want to write about a world that none of us has ever lived in—it could be in the past or it could be in the future. We know we'll have to research, and the acute question is what should we seek to learn? Historical novelist G. Masterton has some definite ideas: "I undertake an enormous amount of research that I never use; in fact I use as little of my historical research as possible...All I want to be able to do is convey my historical world with the confidence of somebody who happens to know what kind of calendar might be hanging on the wall. What kind of boots that old man sitting in the corner might be wearing, and how much he paid for them."

I undertake an enormous amount of research that I never use... The talents of the writer are directed towards fact gathering, not to be disgorged at the reader but to be picked over and reformed into dramatic prose. Could one suppose that Masterton would uncover the type of calendar on the wall without also uncovering the kind of furniture in the room, the makeup of the house, the size of the floors, the height of the ceiling...?

But he may choose only to describe the calendar because that is sufficient to provide the appropriate dramatic effect. In the same way, novelist Richard Condon presents the products of his research in *A Trembling Upon Rome*, the story of the schism in the Catholic Church during the latter fourteenth and early fifteenth centuries. The Church has two Popes, one sitting in Rome, the other in Avignon, and Condon's story is a dramatization of the split. Major characters appearing in the book include high church, political and military officials. In this passage he shows the corruption that was present in Avignon by listing the prices for church favors.

There was a graduated scale of prices that permitted the laity to choose their confessor outside their regular parish. The pope could change either canon law or divine law; but the divine law was changed only if there was enough money; money could buy anything, deliver any matter of permission to the petitioner.

> For a king to carry his sword on Christmas Day— 150 groschen
> To legitimatize illegitimate children—60 groschen
> For giving a converted Jew permission to visit his parents—40 percent
> To free a bishop from an archbishop—30 groschen
> To divide a dead man and put him into two graves—30 groschen
> To permit a nun to have two maids—20 groschen
> To obtain immunity from excommunication—6 groschen
> To receive stolen goods to the value of 1000 groschen—50 groschen

Does this information help us understand the level of morality in Avignon in the fifteenth century? Do we need to know much more about how the church controlled the lives of the people and what were the important concerns? Does this set the scene for a story of high-level political-sexual-military high jinx?

Condon does give us physical description at other points in the book so we can form a mental image of fifteenth-century Avignon. But his research, undoubtedly, uncovered many more facts than he has placed in the book, and when he wanted to give us a portrayal of the relationship between the church and the people, he doesn't describe beautiful cathedrals, penitent worshipping or high-holy-day processions...

He gives us a laundry list of favors that can be bought.

Doesn't that put things in dramatic perspective?

As we research we will come upon a lot of information that will bear upon our subject but will not interest us. Facts and circumstances—statistics, for example, or tables or overly complicated explanations—that we'll tend to put to one side or to ignore altogether. They don't seem to fit into a scene-setting arrangement.

Here's where we should be careful because it's just such items that might give an undeniable ring of authenticity to our setting.

For example, it would have been easy to understand Richard Condon passing by the laundry list of church favors in order to concentrate on more seemingly dramatic facts to illuminate the moral state of fifteenth-century Avignon. A church trial, for instance, or major speech by the pope or an archbishop., something that could readily catch attention.

But he chose the laundry list. And it worked!

"Not every last bit of essential research is interesting," says novelist Lawrence Block. 'There are things you have to know, matters of fact that will trip you up if you get them demonstrably wrong." He's right. It may not interest us to learn the mating habits of an insect the size of our fingernail, but if our story turns on the bite of that insect then we'd better learn all we can about it. In the same way, our research may turn up facts about how an old building was constructed—materials, dimensions, style and so forth. If that building figures in the story in more than a passing manner, we had better come to grips with those construction facts, even though we think of blueprints as a foreign language. The one thing we don't want to do is make an assumption about the physical characteristics of a setting just because we find the basic facts too uninteresting to pursue.

Nothing will push egg on our faces any quicker than to be caught short by a reader who knows we didn't do our homework… "an oversight"…"overlooked"…"didn't seem important"…might mollify the sharp-eyed reader, but as writers we should have taken the all-important next step and checked it out!

The final goal of research may be to sprinkle facts on our setting, but we've got to be sure they are the right facts. We know when that is because what's interesting and what's not is the question we reserve for the reader, not for our research.

'This could make a good textbook eventually," said my editor friend years ago.

I wrote it as a novel, I wanted to say. Instead, I swallowed and gathered up the manuscript pages. "Start over, you think?"

"Afraid so."

The research had been fun, anyway.

6. Mixing and Matching

Des Moines, Washington…
   St. Louis, Utah…
Baltimore, South Carolina…

The familiar and the unfamiliar, cities we know, states we know, but when we combine them, they don't match. Des Moines isn't in Washington, St. Louis isn't in Utah, Baltimore isn't in South Carolina

But they could be! Write a story and set it anywhere; there's no rule that says we have to follow the geographic plot of our trusty atlas. That is, we can mix up one city with another state, set our story and feel free to develop characterizations and events without the limitations a true-to-the-picture setting would require. It affords us breathing space.

"Why would anyone want to do this?" one of my writing students asks.

"Makes it more creative," another answers.

"Look at William Kennedy's novels," I say, "each one set in Albany, New York. He's writing about a real place."

"Real people, real events," a third student offers.

"Why didn't he mix it up?" I ask. "Set everything in a fictitious place like Albany, Ohio, for example…"

"He knows Albany, New York, so well."

"He could make it sound authentic."

"He wasn't writing about people who are still alive…"

This last pulls a smile from me. "Is that important?"

My original questioner nods with quick certainty. 'There's no one who'd complain if he didn't get it right."

"Anonymity," I say, "Kennedy isn't concerned about it. In fact, the more accurate he is, the more authentic his setting, the more we come to know, understand and empathize with the people in the real Albany."

"He didn't mix his settings, then?"

"He didn't need to..."

But some writers do need to develop an anonymous setting, somewhere that fingers can't point and accusatory voices can't declare to be true to life. One good reason is to avoid legal troubles, even if there's no intention to paint a person or a reputation with venomous colors. The point is that when we use an existing setting, we are limited by what that setting offers us in terms of place, location, name and surroundings, and we run the risk that—fully without intention—we might stomp on extra-sensitive toes in the course of developing our setting.

...it was a hotel made for the ambitious concierge, astride, as it was, the east-west face-offs in Istanbul's old city. A concierge who knew his trade (and they almost always did) could extract hard currency for even the simplest information, and, of course, if some surreptitious photography were needed, he could remain behind his behemoth of a counter, survey and photograph comings and goings through the small lens that poked through his official concierge pin...

Suppose we set this story in a real Istanbul hotel, and we name the hotel, though we avoid naming the concierge...do we have problems?

We could. If there is a concierge at the real hotel, he could certainly complain about the portrayal, even though we don't identify him by name. Other people would know, however, simply because we kept the details authentic.

So what do we do? Use the hotel name, if we wish, but set the story in Oslo, Norway or Athens, Greece. Pick a spot, anywhere but Istanbul.

Then mix and match. Des Moines, Washington...St. Louis, Utah.... Baltimore, South Carolina...

Anonymity is what we're after.

But it's not the only reason to mix and match. In fact, mixing and matching is more than plucking one city or town or location and weaving it into another location, more than simply trying to hide authenticity. Mixing and matching is also a useful stylistic tool when we develop our setting. It can be a way to build drama and reader interest.

Here is the opening to Sinclair Lewis's fine novel, *Babbitt,* set in the town of Zenith in the upper midwestern United States during the 1920s. Lewis sets the broad scene in just two paragraphs:

The towers of Zenith aspired above the morning mist; austere towers of steel and cement and limestone, sturdy as cliffs and delicate as silver rods. They were neither citadels nor churches, but frankly and beautifully fine buildings.

The mist took pity on the fretted structures of earlier generations: the Post Office with its shingle-tortured mansard, the red brick minarets of hulking old houses, factories with stingy and sooted windows, wooden tenements colored like mud. The city was full of such grotesqueries, but the clean towers were thrusting them from the business center, and on the farther hills were the shining new houses, homes— they seemed—for laughter and tranquility...

What we have here is mixing and matching in the stylistic sense—using different, contrasting settings to develop the complete picture. Note the first paragraph: 'The towers...aspired...,'"... delicate as silver rods...,'"...beautifully fine buildings." All of this paints a portrait of serenity, of pleasure for the eye to behold.

But then in the second paragraph: 'The mist took pity...," "... shingle-tortured mansard...,'"...hulking old houses...," "...stingy and sooted windows...," "...tenements colored like mud." No serenity here, no pleasure for the eye to behold. The opposite, in fact. Ugliness and depression, what Lewis calls "grotesqueries." The flip side of the paragraph that precedes it.

These contrasts clearly give an immediate conflict in the narrative, and in so doing, help build the drama. Conflict, tension, these are basic writer's tools, and when we can develop such techniques while simultaneously accomplishing another purpose (such as building our setting) we can consider ourselves fortunate. The truth is, however, that mixing and matching settings in the way

Sinclair Lewis does it is not overly difficult. For example:

> if the setting is a forest, contrast the eeriness of the darkened
> tree shapes to the innocence of young children following a
> narrow, uncertain path.
> if the setting is a cruise ship, contrast the well-appointed
> upper-deck spaces with the over-used, aged engine spaces
> below deck.
> if the setting is a ski area, contrast the beautifully manicured
> ski trails with the diabolical plans of a real-estate developer
> who wants to turn it all into condos...

Contrasts in settings.

It doesn't even need to be on a broad landscape, either. Contrast will work within the framework of any scene—a passenger compartment in a train, a back table in a coffee shop, the floor of the New York Stock Exchange.

Anywhere. See how it works within the walls of a fine old home. These two paragraphs are from *Trinity*, Leon Uris's novel about 3 generations of Irish and English in Northern Ireland during the late nineteenth and early twentieth century. He is describing the interior of Rathweed Hall, the magnificent manor house:

> [The first mistress] established the house's preeminence in white Paonazzetto marble, delicately veined and hued with pink and purple strands, a dazzle that shouted its name and uniqueness to all of Ulster. The main floor, halls, stairs, salons and columns ran heavily to Paonazzetto, then deepened dramatically into darker breccias and verde anticos in the master suite on the upper floors. What might have been a preponderance of marble was broken by twenty thousand square feet of Sasonnerie carpets, each designed to offset its particular area...

And less than one page later, still on the interior: Forays to Venice and Spain burst Hieronymus Bosch and Goya into his life. In bizarre contrast to the clean villa lines of the house and its understatement came a legion of tortured naked bodies, satanists, monsters in the throes of perversions, black masses, grotesque sat-ires of semi-men/semi-beasts....

Such beauty and such grossness all within the same home, all within the same setting. Lovely, quiet colors in conflict with harsh, unsettling figures; subdued marble and woodwork at war with wall hangings that shouted obscenities.

Is this drama? Is this more interesting than reading through a one-dimensional home-furnishings description where every-thing conforms and nothing breaks ranks? Don't we feel an edge of excitement?

The setting contrasts tell us something will happen in that house. It has to. It sets the scene—it *makes* the scene, and the way events occur and characters behave will follow naturally.

The equation is simple...contrast = conflict = drama.

And every story must have drama.

We mix and match to accomplish this, but that's not all we seek to create. Through our use of setting-drama we can build depth and substance in our story, in the characters, and in the overall scene. Using setting-contrasts doesn't mean we stop once we de-velop drama; now we have to mold it and shape it, we have to pro-vide it with substance.

It isn't enough to describe a breathtaking building towering over a filthy, rat-infested garbage dump; we have to show why it is there, what purpose it serves in the story, how it will affect events. Developing the setting-contrast means little unless we plan to use it to bolster the story. Otherwise it's like a leftover stage prop the curtain forgot to hide.

In William Goldman's novel, *Brothers,* note how the setting-contrast provides us with a sense of the importance to the story of the Cafe du Monde. Note, too, how Goldman depicts his setting-contrast in stylistic form, using negatives to imply positives rather than adopting straight narrative.

His protagonist, Scylla, contemplates the Cafe du Monde:

The Cafe du Monde was not a gastronomic palace. And he had dined at many of the world's great bistros. Harry's in Venice, Durgin-Park in Beantown, El Parador's in Manhattan. He adored bistros, Scylla did.

The Cafe du Monde could not even qualify as that.

And since, when you Provided for Division, living was always first-class, no wine list had ever daunted him. So, yes, he'd had the '61 Palmer, many times, and the '47 Cheval Blanc, in magnum, if you please, and the '31 Norval, beyond argument the greatest wine of the century.

The Cafe du Monde didn't have a wine list. It didn't really have a menu. What it served was cafe au lait and beignets. Period. You could have milk if you wanted to. So why had it survived for so long with nothing but chicory coffee and crispy fried rectangular doughnuts, topped with powdered sugar?

Because it had weight. It was a *place...*

Don't we get a sense of the importance of the Cafe du Monde from the fact that Scylla was there for reasons other than the food or the wine list? if he wanted a fine meal, he would be elsewhere—hence there must be something or some-one here he seeks. By using negatives to establish what the cafe is not, we can also sense what it is—a cafe that exists for reasons other than its food and wine. It is subtle contrast, to be sure, but it does the job of establishing a purpose for the cafe, and it provides depth and substance to the scene. Now we know—at least we think we know—that something important will happen.

Why?

Because Scylla is here, and he's not looking for a good meal.

We mix and match to develop drama out of ordinary description, and as we see, there are several ways it can be done. The important thing to remember is this:

Mix and match with a purpose.

When it works, an entire scene can come alive.

7. Using Time to Establish the Setting

Is there something significant about midnight…dawn…noon…dusk? Does an image appear?

Midnight…blackness, eerie sounds, foreboding, shadows, strangers, blowing wind…

or

Midnight…laughter, music, dancing, full moon, excitement, anticipation…

Sometimes we can set our story with the notion that the time of its occurrence should influence where and when the story takes place. For example, our scene is to take place at dawn. Would it be appropriate to have things happen in a corporate boardroom at that time? Or a movie theatre?

Only if the characters are there because they need unrestrained privacy, and they must act without delay.

But we can do better!

Dawn…quiet, cool, streaky sky, shiny, new things, clear thoughts…

The characters need unrestrained privacy. Put them in an automobile on an uncrowded highway, have them explore their thoughts without speaking. Dawn is a good time for all that. See how Alice Adams handles it with the opening of her story, *Molly's*

Dog, and note how the time of day establishes not only where she is (her car) but what's in her mind:

Accustomed to extremes of mood, which she experienced less as "swings" than as plunges, or more rarely as soarings, Molly Harper, a newly retired screenwriter, was nevertheless quite overwhelmed by the blackness—the horror, really, with which, one dark pre-dawn hour, she viewed a minor trip, a jaunt from San Francisco to Carmel, to which she had very much looked forward. It was to be a weekend, simply, at an inn where in fact she had often stayed before, with various lovers (Molly's emotional past had been strenuous). This time she was to travel with Sandy Norris, an old non-lover friend, who owned a bookstore…This trip, she realized, too late, at dawn, was to represent a serious error in judgment, one more in a lifetime of dark mistakes. It would weigh down and quite possibly sink her friendship with Sandy…

Dawn…special truths that seem more easily faced, more honestly explored. At this hour she is able to gauge the staying power of her friendship with Sandy, and she knows it will not last. She sees the trip as "horror," and the pre-dawn blackness gives it substance; then at dawn, when first light comes, she comes to realize that the trip is a mistake. In the blackness of pre-dawn is the emotion ("horror"), and in the light of dawn is the unemotional conclusion.

The time of day establishes what she thinks, how she thinks it and what the outcome will be. The setting—and the time of day—provide the framework for her to do her thinking.

Dawn is a good time for clear thinking, and that's what Alice Adams's character is doing.

Try another. This time we'll use the flashback technique to pinpoint the time of day we want to highlight…*She recalled her father's funeral more than twenty years ago, a strange morning with the snow falling and the sun out, a wisp of spring in the air but thick ice on the porch steps…*

An early spring morning, and we have a setting that fits the time.

See how Lee K. Abbott does it with his story, X, and the recollections of a man about one day in his youth:

I was seventeen then, a recent graduate of our high school (where I now teach mathematics and coach JV football), and on the afternoon in question I had been sitting at the edge of the Club pool, baking myself in the summer sunshine we are famous for. I was thinking—as I suspect all youths do—about the wonder I would become. I had a girlfriend, Pammy Jo (my wife now), a '57 Ford Fairlane 500 (yellow over black), and the knowledge that what lay before me seemed less future than fate—which is what happens when you are raised apart from the big world of horror and cross-heartedness; yet, at the moment I'd glimpsed the prize I would be—and the way it is in the storybooks I read—disaster struck...

It is a summer afternoon in his character's youth, and the flashback pinpoints the time period: a lazy hour, the character quite full of himself, calmness before a sudden storm. Disaster often comes when we least expect it and in a form we least expect (in Abbott's story it is the youth's father who suddenly goes berserk on the golf course, assaulting and menacing others and finally destroying the golf club locker room). This moment, when the young man feasts on himself, is the perfect setting for the intrusion of disaster, a change of pace which makes the disaster all the more poignant because it contrasts so vividly with the moment of self-satisfaction the youth revels in.

Would it be the same if the father went berserk at midnight... or dawn? Probably not, because a flashback to those moments wouldn't have a man on the golf course or a young man at the edge of a pool. And while we could try to create a setting where the young man revels in his own self-image, midnight or dawn are difficult moments for this purpose when he's sitting by the edge of a swimming pool.

But not a hot summer afternoon. That's the time for things like this to happen.

A flashback, a moment, a setting.

Suppose we want to use a transition to establish a *passage* of time instead of a single moment? Suppose we want to jump the action a few moments or hours or days? We need to bring the curtain down on one scene and open it to another:

— "Later we went to…"
— "Next day we decided…"
— "Twenty minutes into the game the rains came…"

The transition serves to move the action along; it also serves to show the movement of time so that we don't get bogged down with nonessentials and irrelevancies. As the transition progresses, we—the readers—get a fix on the new setting, and at the end of the transition, we should be in tune with the writer: "Where are we?" should not be a mystery.

Three hours later the water level had come up to the window ledges on the first floor, and the rains seemed harder than ever. We could imagine everything afloat downstairs, even grandmother's silkscreen cushion that my mother hated so much…

The passage of time shows us that the situation of the characters has become more critical, that the setting for the story has become more dangerous. The characters haven't changed locations during the transition, so the setting itself isn't any different.

But it's not the same, either. Now, things are more suspenseful, and the setting becomes a more important character in the story. What the *passage* of time has done is to change the emphasis of the story, and in doing this it has made the setting ever more crucial.

Of course, transitions can also change the setting:

Three hours later we came to a clearing in the woods…

Later, we took a drive in Uncle Hilly's convertible…

That evening the party had already reached the raucous stage when we arrived…

A transition, a *passage* of time, a change of setting.

The movement of time operates in more than just transitions. Suppose we want to develop a setting out of a broad landscape:

Far off, almost scraping the bottom of the clouds were the sharp peaks of the inner range, their huge slopes shadowed and indistinct. Lines of vegetation crisscrossed the lower levels, and tiny road-trails snaked through the heavy growth. The inner range ran across the horizon, blocking forward progress across a one hundred twenty-degree expanse...

Here, time moves slowly because we are introducing a big, wide setting, and the elements have to come along one by one. As we discover each element of this broad landscape time seems almost to stand still, and the story itself seems on hold—at least until we get through the setting description.

But we can accelerate time within our story by increasing the tempo of our setting description:

A darkened room, a glint in the corner, shadows, neon flashes, the scrape of a chair, a stifled breath, quiet! movement to the door, knife ready, eyes sharp, a bed somewhere on the left, thick chair to the side...

Doesn't time seem to leap forward with this setting? The discovery of each element of the setting at a quickened pace serves to speed the time along, and this, in turn, establishes our setting. That room—and the setting—are full of suspense. We build the suspense by having the characters discover each element in the setting and at a pace which excites and dramatizes. If we didn't want to build suspense in the scene, we might have the setting somewhere else, and we might have the characters discover things in a more leisurely fashion, such as in the example of the broad landscape.

But where we want time to speed up, we do so by having our setting introduced in a more rapid manner. The key is tempo—how fast do we want things to happen?

Slow—a leisurely description of the setting.

Fast—a quick, sometimes jumbled, disorderly description of the setting.

8. Sensory Details, Sensory Images

Is this passage well written?

The woman walked out of the house and stared at the sky. She was distraught because her husband had told her he wanted to leave after twenty-four years of marriage…

There's obvious conflict and the beginning of a plot line, the characters are defined quickly, and we have a general idea of setting. All good and proper technique.

But…somehow the passage doesn't work.

Try this:

The woman stumbled out of the house and stared at the thickening sky, thinking she would be better off dead. Her husband's words throbbed inside her head, she could taste sour bile…*I want out of the marriage*! he had said. *Now! Today!*

The smell of fear confronted her, she could feel her skin burn …

See the difference? In the first passage we are telling our story, and there is little to spark the reader's imagination. If we carried this along for several more paragraphs, the reader would probably lose interest because we haven't given emotions a chance to get activated. We haven't allowed the reader to get inside the story, to live and breathe, feel and smell with the characters.

In short, we haven't allowed the reader to become part of the story.

The second passage, however, does try to do this. Note the use of image-provoking words and phrases:..."stumbled"... "thickening"..."words throbbed"..."taste sour bile"..."smell of fear"..."feel her skin burn"...

These words and phrases are an appeal to our sensory selves, they attempt to make us feel what the characters feel and to become a full partner in the mood and atmosphere that the writer has designed.

In short, again, sensory perceptions are what make up mood and atmosphere:

if we want to show a character in fear, we have him/her taste
sour bile
if we want to show at atmosphere of defiance, we have characters staring one another down

Using sensory techniques is not difficult, but we have to train ourselves to apply them properly. First of all we have to think in sensory details...what are those items in our setting which will appeal to the senses?

A stone wall, perhaps?

Or a pock-marked ridge of gray-black rock with velvety moss?

The last selection works better, doesn't it? It appeals to our imaginations, we can feel the wall's texture, sense its age and sturdiness. From this we develop atmosphere...an air of strength and lonely beauty which will influence the characters and the storyline.

Once we decide upon the sensory details we wish to highlight, then we concentrate on the sensory images we want to invoke. If we wish our readers to feel delight, we use sensory details that will accomplish that (such as a dripping ice cream cone or sparkling sunset or soaring violin solo); if we wish our readers to feel unsettled, we invoke other images (such as a fog-shrouded road or eerie melody or musky, wild-animal scent). Note that these images all appeal to our senses...taste, smell, touch, hearing, seeing. These are where the sensory images are received, and these are what the writer strives to touch.

"Nudging the reader's senses" is the way one novelist portrays it; "the senses must be invoked" is the way another says it; "the writer must deal in sense detail" is what a third believes. Other writers might use slightly different words or phrases, but they would agree that for the reader to have a meaningful reading experience, the writer must make that reader feel what the characters feel and slide right into the middle of the story.

Otherwise, the reader will blink and say, so what? Big deal! Boring...and the book will slam shut.

See how Thomas Mann handles sensory details in this passage from his *Confessions of Felix Krull, Confidence Man*. Mann is describing one single room, but note how he appeals to our senses:

It was a narrow room, with a rather high ceiling, and crowded from floor to ceiling with goodies. There were rows and rows of hams and sausages of all shapes and colors—white, yellow, red and black; fat and lean and round and long—rows of canned preserves, cocoa and tea, bright translucent glass bottles of honey, marmalade and jam...I stood enchanted, straining my ears and breathing in the delightful atmosphere and the mixed fragrance of chocolate and smoked fish and earthy truffles...And my mouth literally began to water like a spring...

There are many, many sensory details here, all relating to the foodstuffs on the shelves, and we get a clear picture of the narrator's delight at what he perceives. The atmosphere, at this moment in the story, is one of sensuous pleasure, and the reader shares that because the senses are "nudged"...the narrator (and the reader) sees...smells...hears...tastes...and what emerges is a pleasurable experience made all the more so because we find ourselves standing in the narrator's shoes. If he stands enchanted, so do we...if he strains his ears, so do we ...if he breathes in the delightful atmosphere, so do we...if his mouth begins to water, so does ours...

Where are we?

In effect, we are in the middle of the story. In a room packed with delectable food, enjoying ourselves immensely.

But...what if the scene takes place in the past, suppose we have to reconstruct something from history? Does it help to make an appeal to the senses?

Here's novelist Mary Stewart:

"...the dynamic use of setting is a weapon that no historical novelist can afford to ignore. To describe scenes, dresses, ways of life of a different age, may make the story move like a pageant in front of us; but to take us alive into another period of time, the senses must be invoked."

The senses must be invoked!

Even when we're writing about times we have no personal experience with, the senses must be invoked. We appeal to sight, sound, touch, taste and smell. History, the future, other worlds, other mindsets, it doesn't matter. The senses make it all come alive..

See how E.L. Doctorow makes a sensory appeal in his novel *Ragtime,* a story set in the first few years of this century. He has Sigmund Freud arriving in New York in 1902 and met by some of his supporters. They show him Central Park, the Metropolitan Museum, Chinatown, and then...

The party went to one of the silent films so popular in stores and nickelodeons around the city. White smoke rose from the barrels of rifles and men wearing lipstick and rouge fell backwards clutching their chests. At least, Freud thought, it is silent. What oppressed him about the New World was its noise. The terrible clatter of horses and wagons, the clanking and screeching of streetcars, the horns of automobiles...

Note the sensory details and sensory images at work here. We have glimpses of silent films and traffic on the streets, but if these details are left uncharacterized, the passage will read more like a report than an imaginative scene:

There were silent films to attend and the streets were filled with horses and wagons, streetcars and automobiles...

Instead. Doctorow appeals to our senses, and by doing this the entire scene comes alive. We see the silent films and the white smoke and men wearing lipstick and rouge...we *hear* the clatter of horses and wagons, the clanking and screeching of the streetcars, the horns of automobiles. Our senses are activated, and now we're in the middle of the scene.

There's something else to note, as well. If our senses are going to be teased, the writer must do more than list the details of the scene. There may be horses and wagons, but what makes them effective as a sensory image-maker is that they clatter! The streetcars are only one dimensional until they clank and screech! The silent films don't live for us unless they show white smoke and men with lipstick and rouge.

In short, the writer must think images even as he or she lists details on the page. Is a chair only a chair or should it be "smoothly finished wine mahogany"? Do horses trot by or do they "snort and give off a hayfield odor"? Is a restaurant interior softly lit and pleasant or does it have "a velvety feel, a scent of jasmine and an appearance of muted elegance"?

These are sensory images, and the reader will thank us for letting him or her take them to heart.

What we strive for is to develop mood and atmosphere so that our story can proceed in a meaningful way. When we create sensory images for the reader, we provide a means for mood and atmosphere to emerge. The more our characters sense and feel, the more the reader will sense and feel; and the more that happens, the easier it will be for mood and atmosphere to prevail.

For example, in James Dickey's novel, *Deliverance,* four men decide to take a canoe trip down a wilderness river, stopping each night on the river banks to pitch camp. Each has his own tent, and on the first night, the narrator is awakened by a flapping noise just outside. He realizes it is an owl:

In the middle of this sound the tent shook; the owl had hold of it in the same place. I knew this before I cut the light on—it was still in my hand, exactly as warm as I was—and saw the feet, with the heel talons now coming in. I pulled one hand out of the sleeping bag and saw it wander frailly up through the thin light until a finger touched the cold reptilian nail of one talon below the leg-scales. I had no idea whether the owl felt me; I thought perhaps it would fly, but it didn't. Instead, it shifted its weight again, and the claws on the foot I was touching loosened again...

It's pitch black, the middle of the night, a wilderness area... how does Dickey develop mood and atmosphere? By appealing to our—and the character's—sense of sight (the owl talons through the tent), a sense of touch (the cold, reptilian nail of the talon), sense of hearing (the tent shakes).

What mood and atmosphere do we get? Eerie uncertainty, a whisper of danger, burgeoning fear. Our senses tell us these things, and the writer can then take it from there.

The senses must be invoked.

Otherwise, what we'll get is a black and white still life.

Instead of a feature-length film.

9. Conflict/Harmony

Once, a student of mine started a story this way:

Lightning flashed through the sky, while thunder rolled across the darkness and rain pelted down in great gobs. The wind howled its fury against the white clapboard house at the edge of the forest, drowning out sounds that might seep from the structure.

"I hate you talking to me like that!"
"Next time you better listen."
"You are a horrible man."
"Just like your mother..."

I reread it a couple of times sensing a problem but unable to pinpoint it. I put it down for a bit, then read it again. Now I saw.

The student had followed story-writing technique well. He had developed his sense of conflict right away, and he had drawn it out sufficiently to grab the reader's attention. After all, a heavy storm raging about a lonely house at the edge of a forest is the stuff of suspense, mystery, horror, gothic, and the reader's sense of anticipation should take it from there.

But...my student overstepped himself when he portrayed the argument inside the house *in the midst* of the furious storm outside. If he wanted to show conflict, the storm itself would have been enough, or the argument inside the house would have done it. He didn't need both, and by using both he threw his entire opening out of balance.

Why?

Call it overkill, I suppose, but there is simply more evidence of conflict than the occasion calls for, and the result has to turn the reader off. Even though conflict is so important to all forms of story writing, it still requires a delicate touch to be most effective, and the mood we want to portray has to intrigue the reader and not desensitize him/her. "Never have the storm outside when there is a storm within," says novelist Sumner Locke Elliot, and how true that is! Keep the conflict localized; don't spread it around.

In my student's story, the mood of anger was portrayed inside as well as outside the house, and there wasn't much purpose in doing it this way. The mood could have been perceived in either instance, and the reader would have been spared a dose of overkill.

This doesn't mean, however, that in some instances similarity—or harmony—of mood and atmosphere can't be portrayed in two or three simultaneous circumstances. This is especially true when the mood or atmosphere is not crucial…as where the narrative relates a series of facts, such as in an historical episode, or dwells on analytical problem-solving. In either case, what mood the narrative depicts and what mood prevails can be similar because it isn't the mood that is so important; rather, it is the circumstances of the narrative that are key.

For example, a narrator could tell a story of treachery where anger and dishonesty flair, while in the very room as the narrator speaks, the overriding emotion—the mood and atmosphere—is also anger. The important thing is what happened, not who felt what.

Usually, however, writers tend to develop conflicts in their portrayals of mood and atmosphere for the simple, yet vital, reason that it makes things more interesting and more dramatic. Take this scene from Leo Tolstoy's *War and Peace*, and note the contrast between the battlefield carnage and the pre-battle serenity:

Several tens of thousands of the slain lay in diverse postures and various uniforms…Over the whole field, previously so gaily beautiful with the glitter of bayonets and cloudlets of smoke in the morning sun, there now spread a mist of damp and smoke and a strange acid smell of saltpeter and blood. Clouds gathered and drops of rain began to fall on the dead and wounded, on the frightened, exhausted and hesitating men, as if to say, "Enough, men!

Enough! Cease…bethink yourselves! What are you doing!"…

Does not the very contrast add vividness to the mood of horror and death? If, a moment before battle, there could be gay beauty, glittering bayonets and cloudlets in the morning sun, doesn't the shattering of that image make the scene which follows it all the more impressive? It's as if we spill a bottle of black ink on a pure white carpet…the stain steps right out and confronts us. If the carpet had been a darker color, the stain would not have been so impressive.

But the sharper the contrast, the more significant the impression. In Tolstoy's epic, it was a case of playing the atmosphere of the physical world (the pre-battle serenity) against the mood of the characters (soldiers ready to kill one another). This is a useful technique and a powerful one, too. Anyone can do it! Watch:

a character bubbling over with joy comes upon a severe auto accident
in an atmosphere of suspicion one character has serenity
in a Buddhist monastery one character has murderous designs
in a super-charged business meeting, one character dreams of his family's vacation

The notion of using conflict in mood and atmosphere follows the idea that readers want to be entertained, and this, in turn, is based upon the fact that underneath it all writers are storytellers.

Storytellers, first!

We use the technique of conflict to add drama to our words, to create a springboard for emotion. It is this emotion-charging that we hope will touch our audience. If they are touched by it, we add substance to the question *Where Are We?*—and to its answer….

Here, in this place, with this mood and this atmosphere.

See how Robert Coover uses conflict between the atmosphere of the physical surroundings and the mood of his characters in *The Gingerbread House*, a story of childhood innocence. Note how with just a couple of well-chosen adjectives he can develop his conflict:

A pine forest in the midafternoon. Two children follow an old man, dropping bread crumbs, singing nursery tunes. Dense earthy greens seep into the darkening distance, flecked and streaked with filtered sunlight. Spots of red, violet, pale blue, gold, burnt orange. The girl carries a basket for gathering flowers. The boy is occupied with the crumbs. Their song tells of God's care for little ones.

The contrast is quite vivid, nothing subtle or hidden. It is the mixing of childhood innocence and the sinister pine forest, of serenity and evil. Note how Coover portrays the innocence of the two children: they drop bread crumbs, sing nursery tunes, the girl carries a basket, she seeks to gather flowers. Even following the old man seems innocent enough, and the colors of the filtered sunlight are happy, too: red, violet, pale blue, gold, burnt orange... these don't present an evil side. (Try gray, black, amber; these have a more sinister effect.)

But then look at his adjectives as he describes the pine forest: dense, earthy greens...darkening...flecked and streaked...These along with the time of day—midafternoon—leave us with the feeling that something sinister will happen. If it is a dense pine forest, we know from experience (and we remember the nursery rhymes from our youth) that the light will slowly recede and that the forest will grow ever more uncertain; something bad is bound to happen there!

The forest is a sinister place; those poor, innocent children are walking into trouble.

And what of the old man? Is he leading them into danger?

This is the atmosphere that the innocence of the children is in conflict with. The mood of innocence and the atmosphere of danger.

Doesn't it make a powerful coupling?

"Most successful atmospheric fiction," writes a current novelist, "achieves a balance of passion and detachment Conrad's sea is beautiful and dangerous; Hemingway's Spain is violent and lovely..."

And Robert Coover's pine forests are serene and sinister.

Sometimes it is possible to have both conflict and harmony

within the same small scene. The purpose would be to add vividness *and* to give substance to what is being portrayed. Conflict provides the emotion and the drama while harmony of mood and atmosphere provides dimension for the action to take place. For example, we could have a character in the depths of depression while moving through the lushness and beauty of a rain forest; suddenly the mood lifts, and the depression becomes manageable and a light touch of euphoria arrives. The mood of the character changes and slides into harmony with the fecund surroundings. The result is to give the new mood greater substance because it *fits* with the lush, beautiful atmosphere.

Marilyn French does this in a passage from her novel *The Bleeding Heart*, a story about an American woman in England who yearns for a permanent love relationship. One day she is on a train leaving London:

…there would be warehouses and factories, sooty row houses, but each with a garden, and each garden held roses. Then suddenly, canals and the river, trees, horses, cows grazing under huge metal power poles. Sometimes a small barge on a canal, which would always make her lean forward, yearn toward it like a plant towards sun. She wanted to be sitting on the deck as the barge slid along the smooth waters, and try to catch sight of small game in the fields, to name the wild flowers. She wanted to be sitting there plump in a heavy, holey sweater saying to the stocky bargeman, "Would you like a cup of tea, luv?" and watch him turn and smile, showing a few gaps in his uppers, and say "I would, old girl." The sex between them still alive despite the years, their pillowed bodies, hair grey and whispy in the light wind.

A dream. He drinks, she nags…

At first we get harmony of the physical atmosphere and the character's mood: the charming countryside (even the sooty row houses have rose gardens) with trees, cows grazing, canals and the river; the settled dream of marital bliss, mellow, fruitful, stable . ..

Then the last line: *he drinks, she nags.* A sudden conflict as the character's mood changes to a less pleasant reality. The charming countryside is still there, the barge still moves along the canal, the small game remains in the fields, the wild flowers are still there to be named, but now there is conflict between the character's mood and the physical atmosphere. She nags (call it anger), he drinks (call it frustration or unhappiness), and we have a blot on the happy, harmonious scene of a moment before.

But the change in mood from harmony to conflict actually heightens our interest in the story because it presents us with a vivid emotional contrast; now we understand the character's cynicism about the opposite sex, and now we appreciate why she could let herself dream about the pastoral scene—it is something she yearns for in spite of her cynicism.

What this does is give us insight into the character beyond a superficial emotional level; now we know what she *really* wants, and this means we come to understand her motivations. Because she can be both in harmony and in conflict with the physical atmosphere, we come to understand her at a deeper level.

Where are we?

On a train through the charming English countryside, dreaming of romantic love but aware that it could never be.

Harmony and conflict, they serve to emphasize both mood and atmosphere.

10. Mood and Atmosphere As Influenced by Physical Description

It is twilight, and a man sits quietly in his horse-drawn buggy in the middle of a street in the middle of a large city. Neither he nor his horse appears to move, even as thick, heavy snow covers them. They are like statues...

Do we have enough to develop an atmosphere, to create a mood? Do we need more description? Do these three sentences convey a sense of what the man must be feeling?

We could stretch a bit and say that the scene, from these three sentences alone, portrays a tableau, a still life of uninvolvement... perhaps. But that doesn't tell us much in terms of mood and atmosphere because we don't know the emotional make-up of the man, and we can't tell what is affecting him.

In short, we don't know—yet—how he fits in his own environment. In the hands of a skillful writer, however, things would be different.

How's this:

Large flakes of wet snow are circling lazily about the street lamps which have just been lighted, setting in a thin soft layer on roofs, horses' backs, people's shoulders, caps. Ione Patapov, the cabby, is all white as a ghost. As hunched as a living body can be, he sits on the box without stirring. If a whole snowdrift were to fall on him, even then, perhaps he would not find it necessary to shake it off. His nag, too is white and motionless. Her immobility, the angularity of her shape, and the sticklike straightness of her legs make her look like a penny gingerbread horse…

Now do we get a feeling for the mood and atmosphere? There's deadness here, isn't there? No spark, no life.

How do we know? Because we can sense the emotions of the cabby, and we see he does not care even if he were buried in the snow. He is a living deadman (the author describes him as "white as a ghost"), and this sets the mood and atmosphere.

The story is *Heartache* by Anton Chekov, and it is a classic example of how physical description can help to develop mood and atmosphere. Could we sense the cabby's despair if the weather was not so cooperative? Note how the cabby's emotions are emphasized by the weather…the heavy wet snow acts as a blanket on everything, it cakes the cabby, his horse and the surroundings into immobility, and this fits with the cabby's mood.

Why? Because a little later on we'll find out the cabby's only son died and there is no one but the cabby to mourn him, no one even to offer condolences.

Chekov sets it all up by having the physical environment produce the deadness the cabby projects. See the individual elements he portrays:

large wet snowflakes setting in a layer over roofs, horses, people
the cabby is white as a ghost
the cabby sits on the box without stirring
the horse is white and motionless
the horse looks like a piece of gingerbread

When all of this comes together, we have a portrayal of lifelessness, and that is precisely the author's intent. The mood and atmosphere is the product of this portrayal, and from it Chekov can develop the other elements of his story— theme, detailed characterizations, plot and so forth—against the background of this mood and atmosphere.

But could Chekov have accomplished the same thing without the physical description? Could he have portrayed the deadness as smoothly?

It would have been difficult without extensive narrative and/ or further character development. I suppose he could have simply written "lone Patapov is filled with despair because his only son has died and there is no one to mourn him," but this clearly lacks drama, and it doesn't grab the reader as neatly.

That's the point with using physical description to influence mood and atmosphere. It *adds* to the emotional buildup, and it envelops the reader in the story.

Mood and atmosphere become more vibrant this way, too.

Why characters do the things they do is often explainable by the mood and atmosphere they find themselves involved in. For example, an atmosphere of emotional liberation might cause people to act with animal instinct...or an atmosphere of total control might cause a character to develop a rich fantasy life...or atmosphere of crass materialism might cause some to be cruel and inhumane to others...

Such moods and atmospheres can be helped by a dose of physical description which, in turn, can be the basis for characters to act in significant ways. Let's look at Leonard Michael's *The Men's Club*, for instance, the story of some men who meet because their women have extolled their own consciousness-raising group. As the evening progresses, the men grow more and more uninhibited until the host brings out a tray of throwing knives and the men take turns whipping the knives around the room marking up door, ceiling and walls. Then, Cavanaugh, one of the men, announces he used to play semipro baseball and after each game won the team members would howl like wolves because that was their nickname:

"Neat," said Canterbury. A white smile cut the gloomy face neatly. He tipped his head back, stretching the slender pipe of his neck and howled as if yearning after Cavanaugh's howl, catching its final note winding it higher, higher and higher toward sublimity. Berliner with lunatic enthusiasm came wailing after Canterbury. The three of them were howling together. Terry joined with a bellowing howl and then Paul started yipping hysterically. Now all five were doing it, harmoniously overlapping, layering the air with howls...

The physical description of the howling is really the effect of an atmosphere of emotional liberation. Why, after all, would a group of sane men act like animals unless their moods were spurred by some stimulus? In this case the stimulus is the gradual unburdening that comes from talking about themselves to the others, and as this occurs, the sense of liberation sets in. They feel freer, more open...so why wouldn't they howl like a bunch of wolves, why wouldn't they throw knives at the door, the ceiling, the walls?

They are, after all, liberated.

And the description of their howling and knife throwing gives us a concrete image of their sense of liberation. It influences the mood and atmosphere we feel.

When we speak of physical description, among the most obvious places to concentrate on is nature or weather or the general out-of-doors. These are so much around us that most writers find it hard to avoid introducing something about them in the majority of scenes. There is some purpose to this because such physical descriptions immediately give writer and reader a grounding in the familiar. We all know something about the weather, about nature and what we encounter outside our doors. It's often easier to describe these conditions than to dwell on the unfamiliar or the just-learned (for example, wouldn't it be simpler to describe a grove of recently picked apple trees than to describe the picking process itself?)

The point is really one we all know: the familiar is easier to describe and it comes off better.

But...there are subtleties to describing even those things we know well, and the influence of these physical descriptions can operate in surprising ways. Here's what Leonard Lutwack says in his book *The Role of Place in Literature.*

Atmospheric conditions of light and weather figure significantly in the tonality of out-of-door places. Night, rain, fog, sunlight change our perception of places...Uncontrollable natural events, such as storms, earthquakes and floods transform civilized functioning environments into places full of chaos and horror. Snow leaves a city intact but strangely without motion, static...

These elements of nature are all about us, and our tendency

is to take them for granted. Yet they can be a useful technique for mood creation, and by describing them with a purpose we can enhance an already existing mood or even create one from scratch.

For example:

It was a fog that seemed to burst from the ocean floor, covering us in steamy nothingness as we entered the forbidden straits. It appeared as if ordered, fuzzy gray, fish-smelling, thick-coated... like an unfriendly tunnel. All visible signs had vaporized, shoreline, sun, clouds...

The mood is one of suspense and disorientation, and the fog helps to establish that. The more we describe the fog, its denseness, its sinister effects, the more we build the mood and develop the atmosphere. We could have written..."fog spread over us, and suddenly we couldn't see anything!" But this doesn't carry the drama that a full-fledged description of the fog would provide— "burst from the ocean floor"; "steamy nothingness", "fuzzy gray, fish-smelling, thick-coated." The more physical description we offer, the more influence that description will have on the mood and atmosphere. If we want to develop suspense and disorientation, the more sinister we make the fog the easier our task will be.

And we make the fog more sinister by adept physical description.

The same thing applies when we want to show character development. As we utilize physical description, this can have an effect on one or more characters, influencing— even controlling—their mood or the general atmosphere. It's especially useful when we do it with nature or weather because the stronger we make our descriptions, the more significant their effect on the characters' moods.

See, for example, a story by O'Henry, *A Matter of Mean Elevation* in which Mademoiselle Giraud, an opera singer, has been performing with a travelling troupe in Venezuela. One day she is kidnapped by a band of Indians who live high in the Andes, and six months later, an American named Armstrong comes upon her— now treated like a princess by the Indians—and rescues her. As they begin their descent to sea level, she removes a leopard-skin robe because it is getting warmer.

It seemed a trifle incongruous now. In the mountains it had appeared fitting and natural. And if Armstrong was not mistaken, she laid aside with it something of the high dignity of her demeanor. As the country became more populous and significant of comfort able life he saw, with a feeling of joy, that the exalted princess and priestess of the Andean peaks was changing to a women—an earth woman, but no less enticing. A little color crept to the surface of her marble cheek. She arranged the conventional dress that the removal of the robe now disclosed with the solicitous touch of one who is conscious of the eyes of others. She smoothed the careless sweep of her hair. A mundane interest, long latent in the chilling atmosphere of the ascetic peaks, showed in her eyes...

The closer they get to sea level the more earthy and crass she becomes, losing the goddess-like demeanor she showed while in the mountains, until finally she becomes the pragmatic performer, now vulgar and gross.

It is her mood that is changing in this story, and the mood changes as the scenery changes. In the mountains she was closer to the stars and away from earthly pursuits...so she acted like a goddess; at sea level she was closer to the center of the earth...so she acted like a flesh peddler.

In this story the physical description controlled the mood of the character, and without such description there simply would not have been a story. The physical environment— and our use of it in our stories—plays a key role in how we want to set up mood and atmosphere. As we describe a scene, remember this:

THINK!

do we want it to affect mood and atmosphere? If so, then:

what mood and atmosphere do we develop?

should the physical description control or simply influence the mood and atmosphere?

what items in our physical description are best suited to develop mood and atmosphere?

Take a deep breath, arrange thoughts and...
Plunge in!

11. The Importance of Tone

Suppose we're Lewis Carroll and we're doing a segment of *Alice's Adventures in Wonderland*:

"I'm sad," says Alice. "I think I'll write a sad story."

"Stories aren't sad," says the Red Queen, "only words are sad."

"No, no," the King of Hearts interrupts. "Sad is what you feel. Mad is what you feel. Sad, mad…stories can't cry, words can't sniffle. Poor things."

"Readers cry and sniffle," Alice says.

"I worry about words. Readers can take care of themselves," the Red Queen huffs. "What is a story but a bunch of words?"

"What's a bunch of words without a shepherd?" the King of Hearts points out. "Someone has to know where the next pasture is."

"The next *grassy* pasture, you mean," says Alice with confidence.

"The next *comfortable* pasture," the King of Hearts corrects. "A bunch of words won't do anything unless they're comfortable."

"What if it's a rainstorm or snowing?"

"Words have no problem with that."

"Is a rainstorm sad, is a snowstorm mad?"

The Red Queen shakes her head. "Words don't feel. Words do."

"Readers feel," says Alice.

"Words *make* readers feel," the Red Queen insists.

"Comfortable words make comfortable readers," the King of Hearts says. "Words must be comfortable. Everyone knows that…"

When we write, our words must do many things, and one of the most important is to develop a level of comfort so the reader isn't jarred or embarrassed by what he or she reads. I don't mean that our words shouldn't push readers into unsettled feelings—if that is our intention—because the comfort level, the writer's professional competence, is still there. But we must avoid stylistic awkwardness which will undo the comfort level we are seeking to maintain. In the passage above, the characters are talking about the comfort level of words and what it means … "Words do" says the Red Queen…"Readers *fee*" Alice answers…

This is the comfort equation. Words will create the comfort, and readers then absorb it. But it must be the words that come first, and we must understand that the underlying principle is this:

Consistency!

Say it aloud…Con…sis…ten… cy!…This is what comfort is all about, this is what style is all about, this is what makes readers feel.

Consistency!

It means not deviating from the general stylistic pattern set early in the story, it means maintaining a steady attitude and weaving it through the work. It means paying attention to the tone of the story…

Tone. This is what consistency influences, this is what every work has, and writers have to be aware that the tone they develop is the tone they want to develop. For example, if we wish to develop a sinister tone (such as Edgar Allan Poe or Stephen King might do), we would not want to minimize its effect by injecting too much explanation or avoiding words and phrases that might spark it. We would want to maintain a consistent, sinister tone.

And as we develop our tone, its basic impact is on mood and atmosphere. If our tone is sinister, certainly the mood and atmosphere would have to reflect that, and we could then use some of the techniques already mentioned to portray it—sensory images, for example, conflict and harmony choices, changing point of view, nostalgia and so forth.

The equation: *if consistency equals tone, tone equals mood and atmosphere*

That's why tone is important.

See how one writer puts it:

"Part of the atmosphere is *tone,* an attitude taken by the narrative voice that can be described, not in terms of time and place, but as a quality— sinister, facetious, formal, solemn and so on..."

It is the quality—the style—of the words that is important. We seek a tone to our work and we develop mood and atmosphere from it.

Tone will take many forms, of course, but one of the most beautiful is when it's touched with poetry...the poetic tone, even with narrative. Here's something from William Faulkner's *The Hamlet*, the story of Frenchman's Bend, a small rural town. Mrs. Armstid, one of the characters, is looking over the town from the gallery of Varner's Store:

After a time Mrs. Armstid raised her head and looked up the road where it went on, mild with spring dust, past Mrs. Littlejohn's, beginning to rise on past the not-yet-bloomed (that would be in June) locust grove across the way, on past the schoolhouse, the weathered roof of which, rising beyond an orchard of peach and pear trees, resembled a hive swarmed about by a cloud of pink-and-white bees, ascending, mounting toward the crest of the hill where the church stood among its sparse gleam of marble headstones in the sombre cedar grove where during the long afternoons of summer the constant mourning doves called back and forth...

Note the images:

— the road (mild with spring dust—past the not-yet-bloomed locust grove)
— the schoolhouse (weathered roof resembling a hive swarmed about by a cloud of pink-and-white bees)
— the church (among its sparse gleam of marble headstone—in the sombre cedar grove)

Read this aloud, and its poetic tone comes alive. It resonates with imagery and sensuous appeal, and it could easily be rearranged into poetic stanzas. The road is "mild with spring dust"... there is an "orchard of peach and pear trees" ... the weathered roof looks like "a cloud of pink-and-white bees"...the sombre cedar grove holds "the constant mourning doves [calling] back and forth"…

A series of clear images emerges in our minds, and we acquire a picture of the town. We can see it, hear it, smell it, feel it. It is poetic in the sense that Faulkner has used his words sparingly (one relatively short paragraph to describe an entire town), he has developed a comfortable rhythm (read this aloud, it has a definite beat), he has sprayed his text with images…

And he has maintained a consistent tone. It is poetic and it is familiar.

How do we maintain that consistency? By careful use of words and phrasing. If the tone is formal, stay away from the informal; it the tone is gloomy, stay away from happy or joyful comments; if the tone is fast paced, stay away from lengthy, analytical narratives; if the tone is studied and somber, stay away from snappy, action-packed scenes with a lot of mirth; if the tone is satire, avoid words and phrases that neutralize the circumstances or characteristics to be satirized.

The point is this: every story has—or should have—tone, and we must be aware of what it is, we must strive to keep it consistent and we must use it to develop our mood and atmosphere.

This is true even if the mood and atmosphere may change. The tone must remain steady and straight. See this selection from Francine Prose's book, *Household Saints*. Lino Falconetti has been playing pinochle with butcher Joseph Santangelo for a long time and losing and finally, one night, half in jest, he bets his daughter, Catherine, on a hand and loses again. Joseph holds him to the wager, even though Lino knows his daughter would never go along. But more to make peace than anything else he invites Joseph to have dinner with them, and he goes home and announces the invitation to Catherine:

"I want this meal to be so good a man would get married to eat like that every night."

Suddenly Catherine remembered Joseph Santangelo telling her to ask her father where he could put his thumb. And now she understood what he'd meant as she imagined it, swollen to monstrous proportions, squashing the Falconettis like ants.

"I've got news for you," she said. "No one gets married for the food."

Catherine awoke at three in the morning with a vague sense of something wrong. She checked back over the previous day, imagined into tomorrow, got as far as Joseph Santangelo and stopped right there. By dawn she was in no shape to cook up a storm. Long before she started cooking, she knew that it was going to be one of those days when everything goes wrong in the kitchen …

Two scenes, back-to-back, two different moods, but a consistent tone. In the first scene the mood from Catherine's point of view is one of defiance…she remembers Joseph and his bullying manner, and she announces to her father that his motives for inviting Joseph aren't going to work. "No one," she says, "gets married for the food"…

Meaning: it isn't going to work, this dinner invitation and what you hope it might accomplish. I don't like Joseph, my cooking isn't going to make a difference.

In the second scene, we have Catherine, no longer defiant, now simply unnerved. She has had a chance to reflect on what her father is trying to do, and while she doesn't like it any better, she now senses her own futility. Even if (a big if!) she went along with her father's plan, the dinner would turn out poorly. Her anger is still there, only now it is directed more at herself than at Joseph. She is uncertain, unhappy and without confidence. The mood is one of minor panic, and we know how this can vibrate through a scene.

But look at the tone. Through two different moods, the tone doesn't change; it is straightforward if a bit understated, snappy and quick paced, informal and pleasantly dramatic. There is no shouting or screaming, no emotion-wracked confrontation, no lengthy narrative to explain feelings, no melodrama in the father-daughter relationship.

In a word, the tone remains…consistent!

If we think of tone as an element of style, it might be easier to understand. In simplest terms, style is "the way" something is presented, and tone, therefore, becomes its voice. A consistent tone is one safeguard to a consistent style, and this is crucial for attaining reader involvement. How effective would a story be if:

— it started out action-packed and withdrew into dreamy stream-of-consciousness after fifty pages?
— it wavered between tongue-in-cheek satire and vicious anger?
— it offered a solemn perspective but without arousing sympathy or empathy?

What tone does is to keep things on path and to set up a framework for mood and atmosphere. Style "speaks" through tone, and tone "speaks" through mood and atmosphere.

Consistency is the key.

Without it the door to mood and atmosphere remains locked.

12. The Nature of Nature

It is dusk on the beach, the end of a summer day, and the colors are changing. There are birds and several die-hard swimmers....

This is the basic scene, the essential elements. Suppose that out of these elements we want to create a mood of joy and contentment. Would we write:

The setting sun bathing in the darkening sea, poured its purple gold rays into the sparkling azure depths. The pelicans soared and glided over the surface, graceful in soundless flight...

Or would we write:

A simple bottle washed up, sparkling with red and orange and purple reflections. A small boy stopped to admire the kaleidoscope before he...

Writing about nature is one of the most valuable tools we have for developing mood and atmosphere. Nature can be personified, made into an actual character and provided with influence—even control—over the storyline. Nature can live!

And it can acquire a mood and develop an atmosphere. Look at how we describe nature:

an *angry* storm
a *raging* river
a *quiet* forest
forbidding mountains
gentle rain

Nature—or its elements—no longer seems remote, untouchable, once we personify and turn it into a character. Think how much easier it is to speak of an "ugly" snowstorm rather than describe a "twenty-two-inch snowfall with the winds blowing heavily and the temperatures hovering around zero..." We call it "ugly" or we describe one of its characteristics such as "the swirling, blowing maelstrom" and we give it life.

How would we apply this to our beach scene at dusk? In the first example we see a number of details grouped together, all of them usual on a beach at dusk. In the second paragraph there are elements which one might not find on most beaches, and there has also been no attempt to overload the passage with details. In short, the second example tries to establish the mood by utilizing one or two key details, leaving the reader free to develop an image that seems most comfortable. In the first example, we paint in all the details, and we don't make it especially interesting because there's nothing unusual, or dramatic, in what we've portrayed.

We'll lose readers quickly if we do this again and again.

It needn't happen, though, if we think in terms of drama, instead of fact-reporting. Anton Chekov, perhaps the most accomplished short-story writer of all, provided a simple formula for using nature with any descriptive passage. "It should be brief and have a character of relevance," he wrote, "one ought to seize upon the little particulars, grouping them in such a way that, in reading, when you shut your eyes, you get a picture...Nature becomes animated if you are not squeamish about employing comparisons of her phenomena with ordinary human activities..."

How about our little boy on the beach? The phenomenon of nature is in the changing colors of the setting sun as reflected by the bottle...and the ordinary human activity would be the boy stopping and examining the phenomenon because little boys are curious. Doesn't this create a mood and isn't this more dramatic than leaving nothing to the reader's imagination?

Once we decide how much nature we intend to use in a particular descriptive passage, we have to think about the mood and atmosphere we want to convey. Will it be gloom or joy or peacefulness or agitation or something else? Do we want to use nature to help set this up? For example, do we want nature to act in harmony with the mood of the scene, or do we want it to act in contrast? In short, how can we use nature to make the most dramatic impact on the reader?

If we use it in harmony with the way the characters are feeling, it has the advantage of emphasizing that mood or atmosphere, of making it more impressive. In some instances this would be important indeed.

Take Ed McBain, the prolific mystery and suspense writer. In his novel, *Rumpelstiltskin,* a woman whom his lawyer-hero had been dating was killed. The lawyer prepares to go to her funeral, and McBain describes the weather and its impact:

Wednesday morning dawned cold and gray and bleak. The temperature on the thermometer outside my kitchen window hovered at the thirty-one degree mark, which meant it was one degree below freezing —point five below zero on the Celsius scale. The cable-television forecast from the National Weather Service in Ruskin, Florida, reported winds from the southeast at twenty-seven knots, seas to twelve feet, and a zero possibility of precipitation. Temperatures in the Tricity Area (which included Tampa, Sarasota and Colusa) were expected to rise no higher than the mid- to upper forties. *It was altogether a rotten day for a funeral...*

The mood in this passage is certainly not happy or joyful. The cold, gray day, the winds, the seas all indicate gloom and bleakness. Temperatures at or below the freezing mark mean discomfort, especially in a sunbelt locale such as Florida, and the prospect for improvement during the day isn't reassuring.

It was altogether a rotten day for a funeral. The author characterizes the mood of the day—a rotten day—and weaves it around the major event, a funeral. A harmony of circumstances, really, the weather and the event. The funeral will be sad and gloomy, and weather accentuates that.

Doesn't that make the funeral even sadder? It's a bleak event made bleaker by the weather. And it has the effect of underscoring the event for the reader.

Something the reader will not forget.

Make the weather-atmosphere harmonize with the event-mood, and the event takes on added importance.

It really does.

But there are times we *don't* want harmony; there are times when we want nature to be in contrast to the event-mood.

Why? Because it adds drama and allows characters and events to be more sharply defined.

Take Herman Melville's *Moby Dick*, for example. We know the story—the search for the white whale, obsession and madness and killing and survival. It is a story of the cruel sea and cruel fate, of nature seeking vengeance, and of men finally overwhelmed. The ship is lost, almost all the men are lost, and the whale triumphs. Nature is not kind to the men of the *Pequod,* but in the beginning of the book that is not the way Melville portrays it:

It was a clear steel blue day. The firmaments of air and sea were hardly separable in that all-pervading azure; only, the pensive air was transparently pure and soft, with a woman's look, and the robust and man-like sea heaved with long, strong, lingering swells, as Samson's chest in his sleep.

Hither and thither, on high, glided snow-white wings of small, unspeckled birds; these were the gentle thoughts of the feminine air; but to and fro in the deeps, far down in the 'bottomless blue', rusted mighty leviathans, sword-fish and sharks; and these were the strong, troubled, murderous thinkings of the masculine sea.

Melville has personified nature—the feminine air and the masculine sea—and this provides a character for the story. Nature becomes all powerful and ultimately destroys men and ship, providing a sharp contrast in mood to the gentler attitude the author takes in the beginning of the story. At first, the sky and the air and the sea are painted in kind tones (the only untoward note is when Melville refers to the sea as having "troubled, murderous thinkings"), and we get the feeling that nature will accentuate and sustain the search for the white whale.

But no. The gentle sea, the kind air, the azure sky become roaring areas of conflict where the mood of the whaling ship —and its sailors—shows suspicion, fury, greed, cruelty, madness. The serenity of nature that Melville depicts in the beginning of the book is in sharp contrast to the atmosphere surrounding the whaling expedition, once things get underway.

Does it help to do it this way? The gentle sea and the urge to kill whales...the balmy air and the cruel obsession for the white whale...the calm sky and the prayers for a successful whale hunt... These contrasts with nature and the mood of the event give the entire story a starker reality than if nature were the personification of evil, because nature becomes a silent, almost disapproving witness to what is happening.

These events are occurring on my gentle sea? They are tearing through my balmy air, my serene sky?

How awful!

How dramatic, we writers would say!

Nature is more than sea and air and sky, of course. It is mountains and rivers and rocks and anything that might be growing in, under or on top of the earth. Nature provides us with a setting that can create a mood or atmosphere that will certainly influence the storyline.

For example, we come upon a natural cave, we enter it and suddenly we're in a huge underground amphitheater; the air is clammy, strange shadows dart across the cave walls, there are unexplained clicking noises from somewhere. Large crystals hang from the ceiling, and a tiny rivulet of water meanders across the powdery floor...

Nature (the cave) has set up a mood or atmosphere (most likely suspenseful), and the story will proceed from here. But note it is nature which has created the setting. From that the mood or atmosphere develops.

All of us can think of nature in many forms, but see the choices Leonard Lutwack offers in his book *The Role of Place in Literature:*

Vegetation has a most important influence on the quality of places. Vegetation is life, and its degree of density indicates the amount of life a place harbors. Places devoid of plant life are associated with deprivation and death, places of abundant vegetation are pleasant and erotic. Deserts and mountain tops present the terrifying aspects of lifeless matter whereas the forest is life in an active, wild state...

What he means, of course, is that the lusher the setting, the livelier the storyline and the livelier the mood and atmosphere. As we saw in the chapter on Mixing and Matching, there are times when we wish to contrast one with the other, but generally he is correct. It is a common technique for the lushness of the setting to influence, if not control, the drama that will take place.

See the following passage from Knut Hamsun's *Growth of the Soil* (which many feel won him the Nobel Prize), the story of Isak who plods the valleys and mountain tops of Norway seeking a place to settle. Isak is alone and one night he settles on a high slope overlooking a valley and goes to sleep.

The morning shows him a range of pasture and woodland. He moves down, and there is a green hillside; far below, a glimpse of the stream, and a hare bounding across. The man nods his head, as it were, approvingly—the stream is not so broad but that a hare may cross it at a bound. A white grouse sitting close upon its nest starts up at his feet with an angry hiss and he nods again; feathered game and fur—a good spot this. Heather, bilberry and cloudberry cover the ground; there are tiny ferns, and the seven-pointed star flowers of the wintergreen. Here and there he stops to dig with an iron tool, and finds good mould, or peaty soil, manured with the rotted wood and fallen leaves of a thousand years. He nods, to say he has found himself a place to stay and live…

And live he does. He develops a homestead, finds a wife, has children and spends the next fifty years farming his land. The theme of the book is…life out of the living earth…and the mood and atmosphere are of a farm family struggling and surviving and building a life.

But note Hamsun's depiction of the land that Isak has found. It is lush and promising and vital—all the things he would need to make his farming and his life a success. The rich land, then, provides a lively background for Isak to build a family and for his family to grow and prosper…

In short, the lush surroundings make it possible for Hamsun to develop Isak and the storyline so that the mood and atmosphere of the book are of life and liveliness, of deep pleasure and strong emotion.

Nature lives!

And so will the story.

13. The Music of Words

From time to time we've mentioned the way words sound, that they tickle the ear as well as the mind, that this is something every writer has to make allowance for. We deal in images, of course, but the words we produce must appeal to a reader's senses, and those senses are what form the images.

We "hear" the words of D.H. Lawrence portray the heavy movements of a team of draught horses in his story, *The Horse Dealer's Daughter:*

They were tied head to tail, four of them, and they heaved along to where a lane branched off from the highroad, planting their great hoofs floutingly in the fine black mud, swinging their great rounded haunches sumptuously, and trotting a few sudden steps as they were led into the lane, round the corner...

Read this aloud...emphasize the image-making words: *heaved...planting...floutingly...swinging...sumptuously...trotting...* Don't we "hear" the crinkle of the leather harnesses, the snorts of the horses, the clop-clop of their hoofs, even the sharp commands of those leading them?

We "hear" the words. Our senses are affected. An atmosphere is created.

And if we take it a step further, we could probably "smell" the musky horse odor and be warmed by the majesty of the horse team as it passed.

But it is the sounds of the words that are key, and we must understand that these word-sounds produce images in our reader's mind. We should strive to establish that these are the images we want the reader to acquire.

These word-sounds are what we call the "music" of words because they do what a violin solo or piano riff or clarinet pizzicato does...they create a sensory reaction whether it's euphoria or gloom or tension. They make us "feel" the sounds, and this provides true involvement in mood and atmosphere.

To some extent we must think as the poet does, using poetic devices such as simile, metaphor, assonance and alliteration. Image-making is what we're after, and these do help:

— "...the simple succor of serenity surprised him..."
— "...he survived as the turtle survives, retreating to an inner fortress and waiting it out..."
— "... she sailed the sea of hope..."

Never forget that what we try to do is establish a mood or atmosphere through the word-sounds we develop. There must be a connection between them...Suppose we wanted to create a scene of euphoria. We certainly wouldn't use words or phrases portraying gloom or sadness:

—...the gray-like walls pulsated with the uneven sounds of happiness...

Doesn't work, does it?

And we wouldn't want harsh word-sounds in an atmosphere of softness and gentleness:

—...she cooed at the baby, clucking her tongue and sucking her teeth...

This doesn't work either.

Now see something that does work. Here's a passage from Doris Lessing's story *A Sunrise on the Veld*. A young fifteen-year-old African boy is getting up to go hunting by himself, and we see how the words fit so nicely in the pre-dawn atmosphere:

The boy stretched his frame full-length, touching the wall at his head with his hands, and the bedfoot with his toes; then he sprang out, like a fish leaping from water. And it was cold, cold.

He always dressed rapidly, so as to try and conserve his night-warmth till the sun rose two hours later; but by the time he had on his clothes his hands were numbed and he could scarcely hold his shoes. These he did not put on for fear of waking his parents, who never came to know how easily he rose.

As soon as he stepped over the lintel, the flesh of his soles contracted on the chilled earth, and his legs began to ache with cold . ..

Think of the hours before dawn. What comes to mind? Darkness, ominous stillness, chill and cold…a variety of unsettling circumstances. Generally, this is a time of watchfulness, of waiting, and if we are going to portray these feelings in a few well-spotted words or phrases, how would it be done?

—…And it was cold, cold
—…his hands were numbed.
—…he could scarcely hold his shoes…
—…the flesh of his soles contracted
—…his legs began to ache with cold . ..

Don't we get the sense of his physical discomfort while we also grasp the broader sweep of an unsettled atmosphere? He's cold and uncomfortable, but out there, in the night, the ominous day awaits. Is he prepared for it?

Cold, numbed, chilled…these are words that produce sounds. Try them aloud…they resonate with discomfort even as they describe the boy's physical condition and provide a clue to the story atmosphere.

Note, too, the poetic simile: "…he sprang out, like a fish leaping from water…"

The music of words. Poetic, sensory, atmospheric.

Sometimes an entire passage can ring with poetic touches, and the words can sweep before us with the broadest musicality. One of these is from a story by Conrad Aiken, Silent Snow, Secret Snow, where the protagonist lies in bed waiting for the postman.

He wanted to hear him come round the corner. And that was precisely the joke—he never did. He never came. He never had come—*round the corner*—again. For when at last the steps were heard, they had already, he was quite sure, come a little down the hill, to the first house; and even so, the steps were curiously different— they were softer, they had a new secrecy about them, they were muffled and indistinct; and while the rhythm of them was the same, it now said a new thing—it said peace, it said remoteness, it said cold, it said sleep…

Notice the rhythm here, the cadence repeated over and over, the same word, the same verb form. All of this phrasing describes the sound of the postman's step so that the reader can form an image which will then establish a mood and atmosphere. See how many ways the sounds come:

—they were softer
—they had a new secrecy about them
—they were muffled and indistinct
—the rhythm of them said peace
—the rhythm of them said remoteness
—the rhythm of them said cold
—the rhythm of them said sleep

What do the sounds mean?

That it snowed during the night. Instead of describing the snow, Aiken has us see it as it affects the steps of the postman. In doing this he creates a much more intense image in our minds because we can visualize the sounds, and from them we can imagine the scene.

The sounds of the postman…are music, really.

The important thing is that the sounds convey an image or put us into a mood or establish an atmosphere. We think of music as a pleasing experience, by and large, because it is supposed to appeal to our senses. But, of course, music doesn't always have to be Lyrical or melodic or even uplifting so long as it moves us in some direction.

The same is true with words. The sounds they convey don't have to establish a pleasurable image or even a respectable one, so long as they establish *something!* Just as with music, word-sounds have to move us in a direction that will create an image which will, in turn, set a mood.

For example, we can use unhappy-sounding words: *gross... sweat-filled...whining...oozed...soured...smog...* and we set up a distasteful image which will then establish an unpleasant mood or atmosphere. *Yet this may be exactly what we intend to do* because our story demands it Don't, therefore, think only in terms of happy sounds or beautiful word-music. Use the sounds to establish a mood or an atmosphere consistent with the story.

Just as Tom Wolfe does in his novel *The Bonfire of the Vanities.* The setting is a chi-chi dinner party in midtown Manhattan, and the host is giving a little talk to the dinner guests about his pleasure in their company. He mentions one of the guests, Bobby Shaflett, known as the "Golden Hillbilly," an opera star of some renown. The host continues:

"I mean, sometimes we ask Bobby to come over just so we can listen to his *laugh*. Bobby's laugh is music, far as I'm concerned— besides, we never get him to sing for us, even when Inez plays the piano!"

Hack hack hack hack hack hack hack hack went Inez Bavardage. Haw haw haw haw haw haw haw haw, the Golden Hillbilly drowned her out with a laugh of his own. It was an amazing laugh, this one. *Haw haw haww hawww hawwww hawwwww hawwwwww,* it rose and rose and rose, and then it broke into a sob. The room froze—dead silence—for that instant it took the diners, or most of them, to realize they had just heard the famous laughing sob of "Vesti la giubba" aria from *Pagliacci...*

These word-sounds aren't particularly pretty—at least until we get to the aria—but they do ring through our ears, don't they? Wolfe is describing a laugh, not with adjectives (such as "loud" or "harsh" or "squeaky") but by the way it hits our ears. "Haw haw" brings it to us in its most natural, direct manner, it is not the characterization of the sound but the sound itself. "Haw haw haw…" may not be musical in the conventional sense but it produces the word-wound that will establish the mood and the atmosphere for the story.

Read this passage aloud. The sounds give a clear image of the person—whether Inez or the Golden Hillbilly. Inez doesn't sound attractive does she? Is this the image Wolfe wants to produce? If it isn't, why then, let us "hear" her laugh?

The mood and the atmosphere of the dinner party, of course, are what Wolfe is trying to portray, and by appealing to our sense of hearing, he shows us that some dinner parties are sillier than others, that some people for all their worldly goods and veneer of sophistication remain unattractive, even ridiculous. He uses the actual sounds of words to make us see things that other writers attempt to portray with adjectives and adverbs.

It is the music of the solo instrument rather than the symphony of an orchestra.

Does it work?

Mmmmmmmmmmmmmmmmmm…

Sure does.

Rule Three: Who Am I?

1. Dialogue is...

A friend called one day. "Someone I've known for thirty years sent me a manuscript," he said. "A fascinating story. You'll love the plot."

"A published writer?" I asked.

"She sets the story in Charleston, South Carolina, at the turn of the century—the old South embracing the Industrial Revolution, black-white love interests...."My friend paused. "She's always wanted to write."

Unpublished, I thought. "You want me to look it over."

"I know you're busy."

"Did you enjoy reading it?"

"She's a social worker—she understands people."

"You think it might go?"

"I'd really appreciate your thoughts...."

The manuscript arrived two days later, neatly bundled, with the barest note from my friend. Three hundred and forty typewritten pages, centered properly; a prefatory statement and a brief background on the author. I began reading.

And by page fifteen I knew the manuscript had no hope. The storyline was interesting, the characters richly endowed, the historical perspective clear and accurate.

What happened?

This happened: on page four the young hero's superior says to him,

"Talk to Harrison, show him what's here, then call me."

"Yes sir."

"You know *what's* here?"

"Yes sir, I think so."

"Are you sure?"

"Yes sir."

On page six:

"Good morning, Mr. Harrison."

"Good morning."

"Would you like to see some samples?"

"Yes."

'They are over here, sir."

"Oh, they are, are they?"

"Yes sir."

On page fifteen:

"Is Harrison here?"

'Yes sir."

"Good morning, Mr. Harrison, have you seen the samples?"

"Your young man has been showing them to me—what's your name again, son…"

And so forth.

Dialogue. This is what tripped the author and turned what could have been an interesting story into one that barely plods. *Dialogue must move a story*, Peggy Simson Curry wrote more than 20 years ago, and when it doesn't, everything— storyline, character development, mood enhancement-grinds to a halt. Let's be clear about one thing, though: dialogue is one of the most difficult skills for any writer to master. The sense of reality to be conveyed is often misunderstood because we're dealing with an essential sleight-of-hand. What is, is often not enough, just as what passes as fact is not the same as truth. Dialogue must not only be factual, it must be *dramatically* factual, and in this way the writer must convey not so much what is said as the sense of reality, spiced dramatically.

In the passages of dialogue by the social worker-author, we can't deny the evident conscientiousness. She has faithfully record-ed each conversation.

The reader's reaction is—so what?

The writer will probably respond:

—That's the way people talk.
—Those are his exact words.
—That's the way it happened.

Maybe, but it doesn't make a story. Here's Samuel Johnson, more than two hundred years ago:

Tom Birch is as brisk as a bee in conversation, but no sooner does he take a pen in hand, than it becomes a torpedo to him, and benumbs all his faculties.

Conversation, then, is not dialogue. And when we insert conversation on the written page assuming it is good, realistic dialogue, it's like throwing cold water on whatever drama we are building. Conversation is…conversation; dialogue is dialogue. They are easy to mix up and hard to separate.

But the diligent writer perseveres. He or she knows what will crackle on the written page, and what will die.

"Where do you live?"

"230 State Street."

That's conversation.

'You live around here?"

"If you want to call it living."

That's dialogue.

In some respects good dialogue-writing is a mirage. It *seems* to be realistic, it seems to portray actual people doing actual things.

But it doesn't. Not really.

Here's Geoffrey Bocca from his book, *You Can Write a Novel*:

Of all aspects of novel writing, none plays a greater con job on the reader than dialogue. The art of dialogue lies in leading the reader to think that the characters are speaking as they do in everyday life, when they are doing nothing of the sort. What people speak in normal life is conversation, not dialogue. Conversation is exchange of information: 'What's the time? 'Six o'clock'. That's conversation, but it is not dialogue.

Then what is dialogue? Perhaps the answer is more elusive than we might think. We can say what it is not, and that might be a good deal easier than artificial rules to define what it is. But we do know certain things: we recognize good dialogue when we read it, we're grabbed and shaken by its veracity. Is there any doubt that the following passage from John O'Hara's *Ten North Frederick* sparkles as dialogue?

"What do you think I've had you in my office for? To talk about baseball?"

"No sir."

"Then answer my question."

"*Which* question, sir? Gosh, you ask me a thousand questions, and I don't know which I'm supposed to answer."

"There's only one question. Are you guilty of smoking cigarettes in the toilet and endangering the property, the lives and property of this school?"

"I smoked. You know that, sir. I was caught."

Perhaps like a beautiful woman or a mystical experience, good dialogue is easier to recognize than it is to define. But there are certain guides we can follow: good dialogue will do each of the following:

—characterize the speaker;
—establish the setting;
—build conflict;
—foreshadow;
—explain.

For example, suppose we want to show a character's cynical nature. A physical description will hardly do it, and if we call the person cynical, it certainly loses something in dramatic effect. So we put words in the character's mouth:

"Life's a bitch, man."

or

"I never trust a man who parts his name to the left. He's hiding something."

Here's John O'Hara again. A judge and lawyer are talking informally, and the judge suggests that a recently widowed female friend hire a young, bright, fresh lawyer, set him up in practice, and use him as a stud. The judge continues:

"…I'm telling you, it's a fair bargain. All she does is support him till he gets established. Why is it so much worse for a young guy to sleep with an elderly woman than a young girl to go to bed with an elderly man? You look around this club. You know yourself, half the members of this club are giving money to young girls for some kind of satisfaction."

'"Half? That's pretty high."

"Arthur, your own friends are doing it, and you know it."

"No, I *don't* know it," said McHenry. "I suppose there are two or three…"

Now there's a cynical man, and O'Hara paints him through the use of his own words. The essence of his cynicism is furthered by the contrast with the other speaker who is certainly more forgiving. The two sides of the equation demonstrate character traits in both men, and we get to know them each a little better.

Dialogue in a vacuum, however, serves little purpose. A character saying something for no reason or without adding to the story wastes the reader's time and patience. It's like inserting an unwanted ingredient into a carefully orchestrated meal—it can have the effect of contaminating everything. Anthony Trollope said that dialogue must contribute to the telling of the story and that when extraneous matter is added the reader feels cheated. Arturo Vivante agrees. 'There should be a nexus, link or connection between one line and another. The dialogue should make a point. The gist of it, its purport, should come through."

Suppose two characters are discussing a matter of importance, and in the course of their discussion they become increasingly agitated with one another. The tension between them is palpable. At this point the author has a choice: the verbal tension can result in physical action—one could strike the other, or simply walk away in disgust. Or the verbal parrying could be diffused by words that neutralize the conflict quickly. In each case, though, the author has to be on top of the characters' reactions. Nothing should interfere to misdirect the reader's attention. Otherwise the effect of the scene is lost, and so are the significance of the disagreement and its aftermath. For example, if the author interrupts the dialogue with a descriptive passage about the weather or about some third party not involved in the scene, or if the dialogue has little relation to what the characters are speaking about, the reader will just be confused. Trollope would ask: does it contribute to the telling of the story?

Characters greet each other and say good-bye in all phases of literature. They ask questions of and learn about one another repeatedly. *But they don't do it the way it's done in real life!*

> "Hello, Bob."
> "Hi Jane."
> "When were you born?"
> "What's your address?"
> "How old are you?"
> "What kind of work do you do?"
> "Good-bye, Bob."
> "Bye, Jane."

Real life is questions and comments like these. Good written dialogue ignores such phrases. Comings and goings don't need to be marked so assiduously; they can be implied by a descriptive passage indicating that so-and-so came in or left. In addition, one character might begin a statement with a declarative sentence:

> "Glad you could make it..."

> or

"I'll stop at Harry's on my way home…"

Arturo Vivante calls questions such as "when were you born?" and "how old are you?" irrelevant and pointless. In his mind they are *passport questions*, the type of drama-free interrogation we go through when we apply for a passport. Sure, they identify us, and if the reader would sit still for a word-report on who we are, a clear picture would emerge. The problem is … passport questions are just a report, they are not dramatic (unless the scene itself is dramatic, such as in a courtroom or a police interrogation), they don't make a story. Take age, for example. The only time it is important in dialogue is when it contributes to the telling of the story. If one of the characters lies about his/her age, then we have the tip of a curtain raised on characterization as well as on plot line. The story will move forward because the reader knows something at least one of the characters doesn't know. And perhaps the misstated age will affect the actions of other characters. Thus the plot is influenced. Otherwise, age and similar passport questions are best left to descriptive passages where they can be disposed of with a broader sweep.

What about this passage of dialogue?

'T-t-t-thank you, Henry."

"Aaaargh…" He sputtered, downing the milk.

"Um…you-ah-still t-t-think we…um…should do it…um…t-t-the people downstairs…um…aren't so sure."

"Aaaargh…"

"T-t-t-that milk doesn't look fresh."

In real life we all hem and haw, sometimes uncertain how to phrase words or uncertain even whether they should be said. And I don't think there's anyone who hasn't sputtered when drinking something that went down the wrong way. Nor do I believe that at some point in our lives each of us hasn't stuttered out of embarrassment, nervousness, or simple uncertainty.

But do these things add to the telling of the story? The question is a key one. Are these mannerisms helpful in pushing the drama along? There's no doubt that such things occur in real life—we've all been exposed to them. Yet they have a tendency to distract the reader, to deflect attention from the unfolding story. It's really the same distinction we made between conversation and dialogue. One is fact, the other is art. We can draw characters with life-like mannerisms, and we've achieved a realistic portrait. But what does it do to the drama of our story?

It slows it down and neutralizes it.

Then we have a story going nowhere.

This doesn't mean, however, that we can't have characters who will sputter or stutter or hem and haw, but the key is that we needn't portray these things incessantly. A stutterer, especially if this characteristic is important to how the story unfolds, can show this affliction once, twice at the outset and then rarely again. Respect the reader's ability to chronicle such a trait and fit it into a mental image of the character. A character who sputters can be presumed to act this way whenever the stimulus that brought on the initial sputtering reappears. It isn't necessary to show it repeatedly, even if such a trait does add to the telling of the story.

Let's examine sputtering a bit. When might it occur? Perhaps from indignation or pomposity or overindulgence…it's a mannerism that indicates dissatisfaction and explosive release. Now, we might describe a character sputtering, as in: "I can't believe it!" he sputtered…, but to attempt a word description of the sound, such as aaargh, and to write it repeatedly to define a character's reaction is a bit much. Use the character's own words to portray the sputtering, not the sounds he/she makes.

Even though we've all heard the real-life noise.

But sometimes we put our words on the written page, we follow ail the rules, and it still isn't right. We know what we want our characters to say, we think we have them saying those things and in the way we'd like them said, but it just doesn't flow. We restudy what we've written, we even walk away and focus on something else, thinking this might break the pattern.

Even that doesn't work. What, then, can we do?

Here's John Sayles: "I always read my dialogue out loud, give it what actors call a 'cold reading' without dramatics or a great deal of inflection. Typewritten words have a lot of power-they look very official and convincing even though you know you just made them up. Your ear may catch what your eye is fooled by."

Consider this:

"I don't want to go, you can't make me go, no one can make me go."

'The problem isn't you, it's me. I'm the problem, just me. I want you to go, I really do."

On the written page it reads as two people in an intense disagreement. Clearly they are at an emotional pitch. But read it aloud, give the words no inflection…and we see it is overwritten. The repetitiveness doesn't add to the high level of the emotions, it makes the exchange melodramatic. Would this read better?

"I don't want to go, you can't make me," she said.

'The problem isn't you, it's me." His voice was tired.

A cold reading means a tight reading, it means dialogue that has no fat and fully contributes to the telling of the story. Try it.

But remember…no inflections, no drama. Avoid characterizing anything, even though the urge may be overpowering.

Perhaps the most important aim of dialogue writing is to fashion every speech so it doesn't bring the story to a dead stop. When we have characters meeting one another and the dialogue appears this way:

"How are you, Bob?"

"I'm fine, thank you. How are you?"

"Good!"

The story hasn't moved a bit. As we've seen, such exchanges may mirror real life, but they really have no place in fiction. Now suppose we carry the exchange a bit further to where the characters are seated comfortably:

"Did you notice the Wedgewood plate hanging in Sarah's house?"

"No, I didn't."

"I would have thought you'd seen it."

"I never looked at it."

"Why didn't you look at it?"

"Because I didn't."

"If you had looked, you might have seen something."

"Such as?"

"Whether Sarah had moved it the past 24 hours."

"Is that important?"

"Yes, it's important..."

This dialogue isn't bad, really, it's just dull. Questions and answers, each passage responding directly to the one immediately preceding. A symmetry that could lull us to sleep.

Most good dialogue, however, doesn't work this way. The questions and answers don't follow one another; in fact, some questions are never answered, and in any event good dialogue passages are not simple declarations or tidy examinations. They are what generally goes on between people when they're talking: uneven, sometimes unresponsive, often unprepared comments that provide a glimpse into the character of each speaker and into the relationship between the speakers. Good dialogue evokes drama, even though what the characters say may not be in neat order with each passage directly responsive to the one preceding it.

"This ship barely answers her helm."

"Maybe we better think about pumping the forward tanks."

The second passage is not directly responsive to the first. Yet the story does move forward.

Compare this:

"This ship barely answers her helm."

"Yeah, I know what you mean."

Ford Madox Ford, a prolific writer and contemporary of Hemingway, Fitzgerald, and Conrad, puts the approach to responsive dialogue in perspective: "'One unalterable rule we had," he writes, "for the rendering of conversations, for genuine conversations that are an exchange of thought, not interrogatories or statements of fact—was that no speech of one character could ever answer the speech that goes before it. This is almost invariably the case in real life where few people listen, because they are always preparing their own next speeches…"

We'll see in the succeeding chapters how authors through the ages have utilized the technique Ford Madox Ford describes. But here's a sampling:

Ernest Hemingway in *A Farewell to Arms*:

"Tell me," he said, "what is happening at the front?"
"I would not know about the front."
"I saw you come down the wall. You came off the train."
"There is a big retreat."
"I read the papers. What happens? Is it over?"
"I don't think so…"

F. Scott Fitzgerald in *The Beautiful and the Damned*:

"When we have a baby," she began one day—this, had already been decided, was to be after three years—"I want it to look like you."
"Except its legs," he insinuated slyly.
"Oh, except his legs. He's got to have my legs. But the rest of him can be you."
"My nose?"
Gloria hesitated…

Joseph Conrad in *The Rescue*.

"How unnaturally quiet! It is like a desert of land and water without a living soul."
"One man at least dwells in it," said d'Alcacer, lightly, "and if he

is to be believed there are other men, full of evil intentions."

"Do you think it is true?" Mrs. Travers asked.

Before answering d'Alcacer tried to see the expression on her face but the obscurity was too profound already.

"How can one see a dark truth on such a dark night?" he said, evasively. "But it is easy to believe in evil, here or anywhere else..."

Dialogue writing is dramatic writing, and the techniques are there for us to follow. More than sixty years ago—about the time Ford Madox Ford was describing his approach to dialogue-writing—an obscure teacher of English set forth some ideas which expanded Ford's concept. Glenn Clark, the teacher, listed techniques any writer of fiction could— and should—follow:

1. Make your speeches short. No one in real life talks in long sentences, and no one except on platforms makes ten-minute speeches.
2. Do not hesitate to have one speaker break in on another. Interruptions and rapidity in "taking one's cues" keep the dialogue lively.
3. Instead of answering a question, have the character addressed ask another.
4. Instead of a character answering a question with a statement of what was done, have him tell why it was done.
5. Have a character ignore the question and anticipate the next and answer that instead.
6. Have a different character answer a question by using different words from the questioner.

Put it together, what do we have? One simple rule, really. Trollope's dictum: *dialogue should contribute to the telling of the story!* How it's done and the specific instances in which it is done are what we'll explore in the chapters to come.

2. Connecting the Dots

A character walks into a room, but, while in a cartoon the dialogue bubble and the character's appearance sit in the same panel, a writer has to deal with the way that character looks at first to others in the room! A heavy-set man, an elegant woman, a child in a clown suit—these are the first impressions those in the room may have. Now, it's true that dialogue and a character's entry may happen simultaneously, but usually there's a small beat between the effect of someone's *appearance* and the ensuing dialogue. For example:

She looked up from her book, and there was Ben in the doorway, tall and angular, like his father. "I've been thinking of you," she said...

Note it's the way he looks that first touches the reader, even before the dialogue. And because of this, a character's appearance can be a major clue as to who a person is—not only to the other characters in the story but to the reader, as well. Novelist Janet Burroway puts it this way: "...it is appearance that prompts our first reaction to people, and everything they wear and own bodies forth some aspect of their inner selves."

Take the way a character wears his hair. Short and bristled, perhaps with scalp pinkness showing. He runs a brush through it perfunctorily. This is someone little interested in style, other than for the purpose of neatness. We can build on this and develop a character with clear-cut points of view, a "you're with me or against me" attitude.

Or how about a character with blown-dry and dyed hair? Right away we form an opinion because we see how important his appearance is to him. He doesn't have to open his mouth. Unlike our bristled hair character, this one may present a less clear portrayal because character inconsistencies such as a streak of cruelty might go with his finely groomed exterior. Janet Burroway again: "…it is often in the contradiction between appearance and reality that the truth comes out," and obviously, we want our characters to be interesting enough so the reader seeks to know the truth.

It's external factors—the way someone looks, speaks, carries him or herself, dresses, moves—that provide the first inquiry for us. Dialogue, of course, fleshes out a character because it gives us something to listen to, but even before we get to dialogue, we must form some opinion on how a person looks when the writer introduces him or her to the story. "Yon Cassius has a lean and hungry look," says Caesar in Act I of *Julius Caesar*, and we know how that translates later on in the play. It is Cassius's appearance that offers a glimpse of his character, and the later action confirms it.

Sometimes it is these external factors that actually control or become crucial for the unrolling of the story. In Tobias Wolff's story, *Hunters in the Snow*, three men are hunting in late fall, and it's obvious that one of them, Tub, is the butt of most jokes, mainly because he is overweight and insecure. The other two, Kenny and Frank, keep after him:

"He looks just like a beach ball with a hat on, doesn't he?" [Kenny]
"All I can say is, it's the first diet I ever heard of where you gain weight from it." [Kenny]
"You fat moron…you aren't good for diddly." [Frank]

Tub seethes inside, and while we get tiny glimpses of his anger, we aren't ready when it explodes…yet we find it perfectly understandable, given the mean way the other two characters treat him. But it is Tub's *appearance* that provides the first clue to his character. In fact, Tub's name, itself, is a clue (Tub, Tubby = Fat, Fatty), and what we have is an application of the idea that no one enjoys being overweight because our society is inclined to denigrate it. We tend to make value judgments: the overweight person is lazy, self indulgent, weak…the overweight person is unattractive, ungainly, unstylish…the overweight person is slowfooted, clumsy, soft muscled…and so forth. All of these judgments are applied to Tub by Kenny and Frank, and of course they color each other's attitudes and end up controlling the story.

As we, the readers, note Tub's physical appearance (helped along by Kenny and Frank's jibes) we form an image. Then midway through the story when Tub has had enough and grabs Frank, pushes him back against a fence and shakes him, we comprehend why he would say:

"What do you understand about fat…what do you know about glands…what do you know about me."

Frank acknowledges Tub's words, offering no resistance.
Then Tub says: "No more."
And we know he really means it.

Here, then, is character developed from appearance, from the way someone looks. It is Tub's appearance that moves this story along and provides adequate motivation for what ultimately happens. The dialogue illuminates the motivation and shows how physical appearance will influence not only what is said but how it is said.

Think of it this way: would you feel as comfortable with a waiter who smiled as with a waiter who scowled? Would you speak more sharply to the scowling waiter, would you feel a touch of anger? Would your words be different with the scowler?

The experienced writer knows that external effects are the result of internal causes. Hence, the scowling waiter may be wresting with a major financial or romantic problem or may be suffering physical pain or may have taken a dislike to the customer or maybe playing some type of role. The point is that characterization influences these external factors, and a writer can paint a pretty complete canvas with them.

Look at Tub in Tobias Wolff's story. His physical appearance and what he says about it tell us so much about him that we empathize with his pain and understand his anger. Externally, we've come to know him.

But we need not stop with external disclosures. Suppose we

speak of a character's style: the Gucci shoes, the Rolex watch, the Armani luggage, the Donna Karan outfit, the Zuni silver/turquoise bracelet, the Countess Mara tie…on one level we know the character is financially well fixed and clearly style conscious. Externally, the character's appearance tells us certain things.

But what of the internal character, what's going on behind the array of stylish clothes and jewelry? Here, now, we have a chance to get to know the character *on the inside*, to develop what fiction writer Arturo Vivante calls "inward characterization." What's he mean? "Characterizing people by how and by what they feel, think, say and do…" he says, and he goes on to illustrate. We can describe a character's eyes as blue and "run the risk—as in a poor painting—of not transfiguring inert pigment into live color." In short, we can touch on the external factor—the blue eyes—and if we leave it there, we just might have a ball of mush because we haven't tried to add life and verve. "One has to do more," Vivante says, "to tell about the light in those eyes, their expression, the way they look, what they see, how they see it…"

We need to get *inside* the character so those blue eyes come alive! See how external and internal factors can work together:

thick fingers —hates to feel clumsy
gravel voice —knows he scares people
large feet —enjoys surfing

The internal character provides us with feelings—wishes, joys, embarrassments. Each of these offers a clue to character motivation (for example: self-anger when one drops a delicate piece of porcelain; embarrassment when told to speak more softly). But without knowing the external character trait, we might not understand why there's anger or embarrassment.

So we speak of the clumsy fingers, the loud, crude voice, the wide, thick feet, and now we tie the external and the internal together. Once we describe the character externally —his or her appearance—we can write about the anger, embarrassment, joy and the tie-in is clear. It's his *thick fingers* that make him clumsy with delicate things and it frustrates him; it's his *gravel voice* that makes him sound scary and it embarrasses him when he's around children; it's his *large feet* that allow him to surf well, and he's proud of what he can do. The emotions he feels are the internal character, the way he appears are the external character. Combine them and we answer the question—at least partially—Who Am I?

In the hands of a strong writer the external and the internal can dovetail, sometimes in the same passage or paragraph. The writer can develop the character's feelings and at the same time refer to how those feelings make the character appear to others. For example:

"You should have consulted me."

"I don't answer to you, not anymore." It made me feel so good to say that!

"I'm your father."

A biological slip-up, I thought. "You have a union card, or something?"

His face darkened. "I won't stand you smirking at me. You think this is a game?"

"Why not?"

"Look at you! Earring, eye liner, shaved head. .A snort from his diaphragm. "What are you, son?"

A lot different from you, thank God, I thought…

Note the melding of internal and external character here: the son's anger, resentment and determination to strike back coupled with his bizarre appearance. When this happens, we get the well-rounded character, one who shows us both sides and allows us to develop a substantial image.

How's it work so easily? Dialogue is one way (though not the only way, as we'll see directly ahead), and a character can express feelings by means of speech ("I hate you!" or "I think I'm falling in love with you!"). Then, as above, the other character or characters mention the way that person looks, his or her appearance ("Your eyes scare me!" or "I love your voice when you say that"), and so the package is complete. Obviously, the second character can mention other aspects of appearance—the hair, clothes, way one sits or stands and so forth, and the external character is drawn even more broadly.

The point, however, is just this: when we bring out both sides of a character, we can do so through dialogue simply and easily. Even if we use two or more characters and provide dialogue in succeeding passages, should we wish it.

Then there are occasions when external and internal characterization can co-exist within the same narrative passage. (It would be hard to do it within a single dialogue passage because a character rarely speaks of the way he/she feels while also describing his or her own appearance.) It's done in narrative form because here the narrator's eye can take in more, can range further, than can a character who is offering dialogue. In Louise Erdrich's novel, *Tracks*, Pauline, a young Chippewa-French adolescent, is taken in by distant relatives after her mother has run off. Bernadette, one of the relatives, is the local mortician, and one day Pauline and Bernadette share a death watch over a local woman. Pauline realizes she finds another's death "liberating" and "as a form of grace". So she latches on to Bernadette and absorbs all she can about the mortician's work. Normally, we'd expect a presentation of internal characterization, items about how she felt touching a cadaver's skin, on the nauseating odors from the embalming room, on how much she respected Bernadette and enjoyed working with her. All of these may, in fact, be true, but for Louise Erdrich there was more than just internal characterization to present. Note how, in one simple paragraph, Erdrich is able to combine internal and external characterization for a more complete picture of Pauline:

"I became devious and holy, dangerously meek and mild. I wore the nun's castoffs, followed in Bernadette's tracks, entered each house where death was about to come, and then made death welcome...I learned, from Bernadette, the way to arrange the body, the washing and combing and stopping of its passages, the careful dressing, the final weave of a rosary around the knuckles. I handled the dead until the cold feel of their skin was a comfort, until I no longer bothered to bathe once I left the cabin but touched others, passed death on..."

She tells us what Pauline looks like and what she learns— the external character (wears nuns' castoffs, doesn't bathe, knows how to prepare a body), and she describes what Pauline feels—the internal character (became devious and holy, meek and mild, made death welcome, cold skin of the dead a comfort). The obvious benefit is to achieve a fuller depiction of the character, but a less obvious benefit is to allow Pauline (who remains narrator throughout the story) a broader canvas to tell her story. Not only does she speak of what she learns, but she also provides insight into those things which will contribute to and in fact motivate acts and thoughts at future moments. In other words we're offered the total character, however briefly, in this one paragraph.

It's important, though, to de the external with the internal, to present them so they dovetail or support one another. That doesn't mean we can't offer apparent contradictions that make a character more interesting. We have the "inside-outside" contradiction where the way a person appears may be at odds with the way they *are*. Think of a beautiful woman, a handsome man, and then depict them with meanness or cowardice or cruelty, and we have the contradiction. How about an ugly physical presence covering a warm, sensitive heart? Or a blind, deaf person with a genius mind? All of these contradictions don't change basic character, nor do they interrupt the external-internal connection; what they do is make a character memorable. And isn't that what we hope to accomplish?

But there must also be some support *inside the character* for the appearance the character presents. Suppose, for example, we have this dialogue:

"Why do you say things like that?" she whispered.
"No sense of humor?" he grinned.
"I hate it when you're like this!"
He brushed off a lapel, his eyes scanning the room. "I want this appointment, you know I do."
She swallowed, closed her eyes. "I won't cry, I swear I won't."
"That'll help," he said coldly...

Here's what we know: she is on the verge of tears, he's said something that's hurt her, she's trying to preserve her decorum, he's angry. If we were in the room with these people and observed them, what would we see?

She: face tightened up, eyes shut, perhaps the glint of a tear, skin flushed

He: face composed, eyes hard, well-fitted clothes, measuring the crowd

These are the external signs of character, and they tell us a good deal.

But not all. For the complete picture we need to look at the internal character, and when we do that we can see why the woman and the man look the way they do. Internally, the woman feels embarrassed and hurt, while the man feels annoyance and ambition and determination. If we write about their *feelings*, then we can use their *appearance* to solidify their character. The woman: feels hurt, so a tear may come and her skin may flush; the man: feels angry so his eyes grow hard, is determined so he measures the crowd. "We all lead inner lives that run parallel to what we are actually doing or saying," write Anne Bernays and Pamela Painter in their book, *What If?*...In our imaginations we run through a wide array of feelings and emotions which can be translated to the way we appear:

hope
fear
wonder
yearn
dread
suspect
project
grieve
plan
judge
plot
envy
lie
repress

pray
relive
regret
dream
fantasize
compose
associate
brood
doubt
feel guilt
speculate
worry
wish
analyze

Who Am I? I'm someone who has a feeling like one of these, and my outward appearance—what I say, how I move —reflects that feeling.

As we settle on characters and the way we wish to depict them, savvy writers know that the most vivid portrayals happen when we have our main characters change as the story goes along. The person we meet on page one is not the same person we'll meet on page two hundred and one. The reason's fairly obvious: a rigid character means a rigid storyline, and that means a dwindling audience. Characters change because that makes them interesting, and the reader wants to understand how and why certain events or circumstances influence the major characters. How, for example, the outsized ambition of Julius Caesar in Shakespeare's play caused Brutus, his most trusted supporter, to join the plot to assassinate him. Or why Ebeneezer Scrooge in Charles Dickens' *A Christmas Carol* could move from "Bah! Humbug!" to a total embrace of the Christmas message by story's end. The change is what's important because then there's no story bog-down, no character rigidity. We like a character who challenges us, who will grow and develop, and good story writing feeds off this approach.

Take a look at John Cheever's story, *An Educated American Woman* which opens with external character portrayal and ends with a revelation about the inner substance of that same character. The story begins:

"I remain joined in holy matrimony to my unintellectual 190-pound halfback, and keep myself busy chauffeuring my son Bibber to and from a local private school that I helped organize..."

A few lines later we realize this is a report for her college alumni magazine from Jill Chidchester Madison, and we see her living—not too happily—the life of a suburban matron. She is filled with energy while her husband leads a more passive, less frenetic existence. As the story goes along they grow farther and farther apart with Jill throwing herself into civic work and her husband finally having an affair. At this point the Jill Madison of the opening page, the suburban matron, is now a respected local political/civic leader, and one day she finds a letter about the affair that her husband thought he'd destroyed. She confronts him and he admits the affair. But she refuses to believe him, and he is stunned:

"You don't believe me."
"I do not, and if I did I wouldn't be jealous, My sort of woman is never jealous. I have more important things to do..."

The change in Jill is clear: from a suburban mom who spoke of chauffeuring her young son as a highlight of her life to a strong-willed feminist who can't be bothered with her husband's peccadillos. She can't even bring herself to acknowledge her husband's need for another woman, and so we see how jaundiced she has become in her quest for some sort of self-affirmation.

If Cheever had kept Jill at the suburban Mom stage throughout the story, things would have grown dull rapidly. Without any change, Jill would project as one dimensional and boring. But by changing, becoming someone different at the end than at the beginning, she is more interesting and we follow her progress as she proceeds to gain public approval and experience personal disaster.

Who Am I? I'm a feminist, strong, competent, self-reliant, successful and divorced...but I wasn't always this way!

We know two things about dialogue: it must contribute to the telling of the story and it can develop character. In this latter sense it shows us how a person says things, why they say them and what they may be thinking. If we were inexperienced writers, we might use dialogue passages only to move the story along, never realizing how important it may be to rely on character development. In effect we won't connect the dots between what a person says and why they say it. It's certainly true that dialogue must move the story, otherwise we stay in the rut of story bogdown. But understanding how external characterization works and how it connects to internal characterization creates a more vivid opportunity for story development. The dots are there for us to see: external characterization, the way we appear…internal characterization, the way we feel. Connect them, and the story grows and grows.

Who Am I? I'm someone to build a strong story around.

3. Suppose We Want to Create Tension

What do these situations have in common?

A man and woman are walking hand in hand. The man is in love with the woman and wants to tell her so. There is no way of knowing how the woman will respond.

It is a hot, tropic evening and a man and woman have just finished making love. They are close together on the bed, their attention on one another. A black widow spider crawls under the sheets.

A woman has been abducted, but she has fought off her kidnappers. She finds herself alone, on a dirt road, in an unknown place with the temperature dropping. She has had little experience with the outdoors.

As storylines, the three situations tend to catch the eye. There is uncertainty and mystery and danger. The characters are not plodding along in relative tranquility. Something is troubling them. Matters are not under absolute control.

Tension is the answer. Each of the storylines has tension or conflict built into the circumstances. Tension is the basic molder of a story; it's what catches the reader's eye and holds the reader's attention. Tension is the key that turns dull material into something we all want to read.

Tension is appropriately portrayed through dialogue; in fact, dialogue without tension has little going for it. Consider the following two exchanges:

"I think we should walk to the restaurant," he said.

"I-I don't know," she responded.

"I think we should walk to the restaurant," he said.

"Sure," she responded.

It's the woman's answer that determines the level of tension. In the first example, her uncertainty projects to the reader. Why is she uncertain, what's she afraid of? In the second example, she's agreeing but there's no drama in it. Hence, no tension. It's like a report. There's no mystery here, no unanswered questions .

Dialogue must create tension to be effective, and there are a variety of ways this can be done. The first and most obvious, of course, is by argument or disagreement. Two or more people not seeing eye to eye. This doesn't need to be a screaming match, nor a basic "yes-no" standoff. The disagreement can be portrayed subtly yet distinctly. In *The Cider House Rules*, John Irving has his protagonist Homer Wells in conversation with Candy Kendall alongside the conveyor belt at the packing house. They are talking about Candy's pregnancy, which Homer was responsible for:

"If I work as hard as I can," Candy told him, "it's possible that I'll miscarry."

It was not possible, Homer Wells knew.

'What if I don't want you to miscarry?" Homer asked her.

"What if?" Candy asked.

"What if I want you to marry me, and to have the baby?" Homer asked.

They stood at one end of the conveyor belt in the packing house; Candy was at the head of the line of women who sized and sorted the apples—who either packaged them or banished them to cider. Candy was retching even though she had chosen the head of the line because that put her nearest the open door.

"We have to wait and see," Candy said between retches.

"We don't have long to wait," said Homer Wells. "We don't have long to see"...

What Irving is doing is using questions and declarative statements. "What if...?" is really another way of saying "I don't..." and by doing this he is developing the disagreement between Candy and Homer. The subtlety of the disagreement is apparent in the fact that neither Homer nor Candy provides a direct, stiff resounding "No!" to the other's suggestions, yet is there any doubt about who feels which way?

And by having Candy retch during the conversation, Irving is underlining her feelings about having the baby and about the immediacy of having to make a decision. These uncertainties, coupled with the disagreement, are what build tension into this exchange.

Sometimes, however, disagreement can rise beyond the subtleties and become blatant anger. This disagreement has escalated into sheer fury. Though examples in literature abound, suppose we look at one by a writer whose masterful portrayals have entertained us through the centuries. In William Shakespeare's *Romeo and Juliet* we have Juliet's father, Capulet, just informed that Juliet will not marry Paris, the suitor her father has chosen. The tension in the scene is evident from the intensity of Capulet's wrath:

Capulet: But fettle your fine joints against Thursday next, go with Paris to Saint Peter's Church, or I will drag thee on a hurdle thither. Out, you green-sickness carrion! Out, you baggage! You tallow face!

Lady Capulet: Fie, fie! What, are you mad!

Juliet: Good father, I beseech you on my knees, hear me with patience but to speak a word.

Capulet: Hang thee, young baggage! Disobedient wretch! I tell thee what: get thee to church o' Thursday, or never after look me in the face; speak not, reply not, do not answer me; my fingers itch. Wife, we   scarce thought us blest that God had lent us but this only child; but now I see this one is one too much, and that we have a curse in

Note how Capulet exhibits his fury: name calling, threats, disgust, even a refusal to listen. The anger is not on both sides—only from Capulet, yet tension is certainly created. A disagreement does not have to show anger reflected from each of the parties. It's enough if one of them is angry and the anger is sharp and loud. The fact that others in the scene try to calm Capulet, even appease him, does not limit the tension. It is the anger, itself, which creates the tension.

Sometimes, it isn't even necessary to produce give-and-take dialogue when there is anger. An appropriate monologue can do the trick, the words themselves conveying the depth of feeling by virtue of the subject matter. Suppose we have a young man at his father's grave side, swearing vengeance on those he believes killed his father? Or suppose we have a young woman who has suffered much and who yearns for the release of death? Her solitary plea for the courage of suicide is certainly tension-provoking.

Or suppose we have a man whose family had sworn allegiance to one of the claimants to a European throne and had suffered grievously for it. Now suppose that allegiance is to be renounced. It can be a spine-tingling moment if it is done with high theatricality. In William Thackeray's 19th-century work, *Henry Esmond*, this is what takes place as Colonel Esmond revokes his allegiance to the Pretender:

"You will please, sir, to remember," he continued, "that my family hath ruined itself by fidelity to yours; that my grandfather spent his estate and gave his blood and his son to die in your service; that my dear lord's grandfather…died for the same cause; that my poor kinswoman, my father's second wife, after giving away her honor to your wicked perjured race, sent all her wealth to the King; and got in return that precious title that lies in ashes, and this inestimable yard of blue ribbon. I lay this at your feet and stamp upon it: I draw this sword and break it and deny you; and had you completed the wrong you designed us, by Heaven, I would have driven it through your heart…"

This is threat and anger, unmodified by other dialogue, yet establishing the scene and motivation. There is no need for another character to speak, there is no need to break up the speech for any other purpose. Esmond tells us why he feels the way he does, he tells us what he intends to do about it, he tells who he believes wronged him. The disagreement is there, of course, in the nature of Esmond's words, yet it's all done by monologue.

Is there any doubt we have tension? The anger's there, the disagreement is plain, and we certainly want to know what will happen next.

And it's obvious, to echo Trollope's words, that this dialogue contributes to the telling of the story. The storyline is certainly moved forward.

Sometimes, the most effective tension-building comes not so much from what the characters say to one another as from what they *don't* say. What they hold back, what they hide, brings the reader directly into the scene, assuming the reader knows what is being held back. The reader becomes a partner with the author, watching and judging reactions. Suppose, for example, one brother suspects another brother of a crime, but he knows he'll be lied to if he asks. He has to know, yet he can't come right out and ask:

"You got home late last night."
"Lousy driving, fog, the roads were slick."
"See the paper this morning?"
"Something I should know?"
"You ought to get home earlier. You look shot."
He laughs. "Ease up on the booze, you mean."
"I guess."
"Hey." He taps him on the shoulder. 'Who's got the old man's booze talent in this family?"
"Look..."
"Gotta go," he says, rummaging in the closet for his coat. "What about the paper, anyway?"...

This is tension of the unsaid thought, which can be a powerful story-mover. Note how nothing was said about the crime or about the suspicion. Yet we feel the uncertainty.

Raymond Carver does this beautifully. In his short story, *What Is It?*, he has Leo on the phone with his wife whom he sent downtown to sell their convertible for cash. Leo needs the money desperately because he is bankrupt, and his wife calls him from a downtown restaurant. She is having dinner with a sales manager from a used car lot to whom she has sold the car, and the sales manager will drive her home. Leo is jealous and upset, but he doesn't want to show it:

"Honey?" he says. He holds the receiver against his ear and rocks back and forth, eyes closed.

"Honey?"

"I have to go," she says. "I wanted to call. Anyway, guess how much?"

"Honey?" he says.

"Six and a quarter," she says. "I have it in my purse. He said there's no market for convertibles. I guess we're born lucky," she says and laughs. "I told him everything I think I had to."

"Honey?" he says.

"What?" she says.

"Please honey," Leo says.

"He said he sympathized," she says. "But he would have said anything." She laughs again. "He said personally he'd rather be classified a robber or a rapist than a bankrupt. He's nice enough, though," she says.

"Come home," he says. "Take a cab and come home."

Does Leo shout or cry or scream? Does he warn his wife that the sales manager may be a threat to her or to both of them? Does Carver show Leo tight lipped with anger?

He has him plead, he has him suppress his feelings into one plaintive word—*honey*—and we know what he must be feeling. We squirm with his discomfort, yet how different it would be if Leo had shouted out his anger.

Which of the two methods produces the greater tension? In Carver's story Leo's struggle is really a double battle-he battles his wife, who seems not to be responding to his urgings, and he battles himself as he tries to suppress his true feelings. If he had shouted out his anger, then the battle would be limited to his wife, and a layer of tension would be wiped off.

But note the artistry—one word, *honey*, can accomplish so much.

The underplayed scene is a useful device for provoking tension because there is that double battle, and often the bigger struggle is the one of restraint. But underplaying a scene can be just as effective when nothing is held back. The tension of underplaying comes in the calmness of players against the exploding intensity of the atmosphere. The dangers lurk, but the characters don't back away from them. It is the tension of two conflicting circumstances.

Take Elmore Leonard, for example. His dialogue is well recognized for its brutal realism, its absorbing style. In *City Primeval*, he has his detective, Raymond, standing across a table from Clement, a vicious criminal who has challenged Raymond to an old-time shooting match—basically a quick draw. They are in a high-rise apartment, and they each have pistols, though Raymond has taken Clement's away from him and has it resting in the middle of the table. Notice the seeming rationality with which Raymond discusses the issue with Clement; notice, too, that Clement is not so calm:

"...This is fair, isn't it? You said, why don't we have a shooting match. Okay we're doing it."

"Just grab for the guns, huh?"

"Wait a minute," Raymond said. "No. I think the way we ought to do it—pick up the gun and hold it at your side. Go ahead. I think that'll be better." Raymond brought the Colt toward him and held it pointing down, the barrel extending below the edge of the desk. "Yeah, that's better. See, then when you bring it up, you have to clear the desk and there's less chance of getting shot in the balls."

"Come on," Clement said, "cut the shit."

"All right, then you reach for yours and I raise mine," Raymond said, "it's up to you." He waited...

It's a murderous scene, and at the least there should be sweat, heavy breathing, and the beginnings of terror. Someone is going to die.

But Raymond talks as if he's directing a bake sale. The calmness in the midst of excruciating uncertainty. The tension of opposite circumstances.

Try these examples:

— anger in the midst of peaceful tolerance;

— giddiness in the midst of unsmiling gravity;

— unscrupulousness in the midst of trusting acceptance.

We could develop dialogue for each of these situations, and we'd have a mirror image of what Elmore Leonard does. At least one of the characters reflects a point of view or a posture directly opposite to the general atmosphere. The tension of opposite circumstances.

The reader remains a key player in dialogue tension, and as with the Raymond Carver story, if the reader knows something one of the characters doesn't know, there's an element of suspense. This is especially true when what is unsaid becomes a reason for something happening. It becomes motivation, but only one of the characters knows it. The dialogue becomes an exchange between people on different levels, basically unresponsive.

Deborah Singmaster shows this well in her story, *The Burial,* set in Ireland. Pat and Maureen have been engaged to be married for four years. Pat meets an exciting young woman on the beach and follows her into the dunes where they make love. Father Sullivan, newly arrived in the parish, comes upon them, but says nothing. Two weeks later Pat and Maureen are married, and then, years later, Father Sullivan dies and Pat drives the hearse containing the body. Somehow the hearse goes off the road and the coffin plunges into the sea with all the mourners watching. It is a few moments later…

Maureen looked at him, trying to catch his eye. Pat avoided her gaze, he was staring down at the mud one moment and up at the sky the next, blinking as if there were sunlight pouring down on him.

"Look at me," she said, keeping her voice low. Pat looked at her. He was grinning. Behind him the men were heaving the hearse back on the track. Maureen said, "That was no accident, was it? You did it on purpose, didn't you?"

"And why would I do a thing like that?"

"God alone knows, for what harm did he ever do you, Pat Riordan?"

"What indeed."

Maureen turned her back on her husband and walked up the hill to join the other mourners...

The only thing Maureen really knows is that things aren't quite right. She doesn't know why, and she doesn't know how. Just that her husband allowed the priest's body to find a watery grave, clearly a violation of ordered civility.

But Pat knows. And the reader knows. The why of it is simple retribution. Would he have married Maureen if the priest hadn't spotted him in the dunes? Was his short leap for freedom aborted? Has he blamed the priest for his dull, conventional life with Maureen?

Especially when he had tasted what life *could* be like, however briefly?

Sing-master doesn't spell it out for us. But the inferences are clear. And so is the motivation. Singmaster has Pat playing dumb to his wife's inquisition, but we, the readers, know that he has collected a debt.

Unsaid, unmentioned.

The essence of dialogue tension, of course, is in the words we use. Certain words or phrases create tension, such as he *barked*, *she screamed, he shouted, she slapped*...verbs, in other words, that signify action or anger or some aspect of conflict. There are nouns, too, that get the job done When we talk about *hate, fear, death, bully, winner* and *loser, criminal,* we are setting a certain mark on the page that must be countered. For example, if someone is a bully, there must be someone else to push around, and the very nature of the relationship leads to tension and conflict. Or if we call someone a criminal, then something unlawful—perhaps even terrible—must have happened. An automatic two-sides question, the good guys and the bad guys. The word "criminal" implies this from its very appearance on the page.

The importance of careful selection of words and phrases that promote tension and conflict must be emphasized. The words, themselves, set up the scene and carry it forward. The words are the foundation blocks. If we have one character call another "pleasant, delightful, enjoyable" we have no tension; if we have the same character growl that the other is a "yellow-spined coward, mean spirited and a thief," we have tension, for sure.

Take John Updike. Many of his scenes are set in mannered circumstances. There is general politeness, and usually an air of civility. How does he create tension without at the same time dissolving the entire scene into chaos? He uses tension-producing words, and he lays emphasis in certain places. Words and emphasis, a good combination.

In his story, *Marry Me*, he has two couples in a showdown over the affair between Jerry (married to Ruth) and Sally (married to Richard). Sally and Ruth are having it out with husbands looking on. Sally is speaking…

"…I've cried plenty on your account. I feel sorry for anybody who's so selfish, who's so weak she won't let a man go when he wants to go."

"I tried to hold my children's father with them. Was that so contemptible?"

"Yes!"

"You can say that because you treat your own children like, like baggage, like little trinkets to set you off when it suits you."

"I love my children, but I have respect for my husband, too, enough respect that if he made up his mind I'd let him do what he decided."

"Jerry never decided anything."

"He's too *kind*. You abused that kindness. You used it. You can't give him what I can give him, you don't love him."…

"Girls, girls," Richard said…

Sally cries…feels sorry…she accuses Ruth of selfishness, weakness, of abusing kindness, of using it…she can give Jerry more…

Ruth accuses Sally of treating her children like baggage…like trinkets…she puts Jerry down because he never decided anything…

Simple words and phrases, but they carry the seeds of conflict. Updike pits the women against each other, not in any violent manner but with sharp, civilized thrusts. Note that he emphasizes the word "affair," giving it a greater significance thereby. The fact of it might have been missed, if he hadn't emphasized it. So he uses it as an additional epithet, as a highly charged tension-producer. "Affair" is not only a description here, it is also a characterization. That "affair" means an immoral event only an especially immoral person would undertake. It's the same as criticizing someone who treats children like baggage.

Words and emphasis, they can accomplish the same thing.

And dialogue tension can be substantially enhanced along the way.

4. Would He/She Say That?

"Her voice is full of money," Jay Gatsby says, describing Daisy Buchanan in F. Scott Fitzgerald's *The Great Gatsby*. Does that build an image for us, can we picture what Fitzgerald means? *Her voice is full of money!* When Daisy speaks, it tells us things about her, she becomes more than a walk-on character, she has a distinction we remember.

It tells us she is rich, it tells us she doesn't hide the fact she is rich.

And if she's rich, other characteristics flow: self-confidence, good taste, easy gratification.

Her voice is full of money!

Dialogue is an essential ingredient for the portrayal and development of character. Narrative describes a character but dialogue humanizes and personifies the character. It gives dimension and substance and individuality. "We all sound different, use different words, expressions, euphemisms, dialects, speech styles and varied inflections," wrote Robyn Carr some years ago. "What we say, how we say it, when we choose to speak reflects who we really are."

Dialogue, then, must be fashioned in the manner of a sculptor molding a piece of clay. It must individualize the speaker, and it must be something that speaker would say. For example, we wouldn't have a character with a limited education hold forth on highly technical matters, nor would we have an elderly person speak in the jargon of a teenager. These, of course, are extreme examples, and the real dilemma a writer faces is to draw more subtle distinctions such as:

— the reaction of a single mother to criticism of her child by her new lover; would it be anger, excuse-making, guilt?

— the reaction of a quiet, studious young man to unexpected
honors; would it be boastfulness, modesty, withdrawal?

Would she/he say that? An important thing to remember. In
the case of the single mother, her first reaction might be to defend
her child, without thinking of the divisive effect it could have on
the relationship with her lover. "He didn't mean it like that!" is one
thing she could say. "He's tried to do things the way you want!" is
another way. Make her defensive, make her uneasy with her lover's
criticism, especially directed at her child. The mother stays in character, and the story moves.

As for the young man, his reaction would seem to be more consistent with modesty or withdrawal. "Why couldn't they mail the
plaque and check? I hate speeches," is one reaction he could have.
His withdrawal might be silence or unavailability or tearful avoid-
ance. He could say or do these things and still remain in character.

Would she/he say that?

One of the more useful techniques for dialogue is to have one
character talk about another, give us clues to that other's personality. Remember Jay Gatsby's description of Daisy Buchanan? *Her
voice* is *full of money…*when Daisy speaks we remember what
Gatsby says.

David Kranes does the same thing in his story, *Dealer,* about
a man, Hatch, an expert dealer of cards at a Nevada gaming club.
Hatch rarely loses, and like the gunfighter of the Old West, he has
a reputation that attracts people who try to beat him. One night a
woman comes to his table to play, and later Hatch runs into her at
the bar:

"You're very good," she said.
Hatch nodded.
"Buy me a drink?"
Hatch held his hand up. The bartender came. Hatch pointed at
the bartender for the girl.
"I'll have a whiskey sour, please," she said.
The bartender moved off.
"I'll bet you're a very cruel man," she said, her voice uneven.

'The way you deal. There's something very..."

"I just deal," Hatch told her.

"No you don't." Something approached a smile on her lips. "No you don't. No."

Three things happen here, each brought out in the woman's words. *You're very good*, she says, and this reaffirms the fact that he is good. Hatch is a very good dealer, and the woman says so. Then she says, *I'll bet you're a very cruel man.* This is a new thought, barely hinted at up to now. Would a hot dealer be a cruel man? We could make a case for it...unemotional, opportunistic, unkind, strongly competitive. It takes all of these things—and more—to make a successful card dealer. One ounce of compassion and the dealer loses the edge.

So when the woman calls him cruel, we can be pretty sure she's got him pegged.

The third thing the woman does is to disagree with his "aw, shucks" self-description. *No you don't*, she says, *No you don't. No.*

This reinforces her description of him as cruel. In repeating her statement, she is adding something else: when he said *I just deal*, and she disagrees, the sense of it is much more significant. The woman is tipping us off, even though she doesn't offer anything more, and it encourages us to read on and find out.

One short passage is all it takes. One character describing another, and a solid mental image emerges.

Hatch is a very good dealer; he's cruel, and he's more, much more, than his self-effacing self-description tells us.

Sometimes, the character being described does not even have to be present. "Let me tell you what I found out about Henry..." a conversation can go. "He's the man with the puffy red cheeks and the lopsided grin. You can't miss him..."

Men get together and talk about women, women talk about men, even though the opposite sexes are not present. We can call it gossip or a bull session, but it does develop character, it can describe and illuminate. And once in a while we meet a descriptive passage of dialogue that lifts us beyond the usual. It is uncommon enough to set an example.

Such is *Mrs. Bathurst*, a story by Rudyard Kipling set at the turn of the century. British army enlisted personnel are talking about their favorite subject—women—and as they talk, the name of Mrs. Bathurst comes up. Note how her character is portrayed, especially in contrast to the men's attitude toward other women:

Said Pyecroft suddenly: "How many women have you been intimate with all over the world, Pritch?"

Pritchard blushed plum color to the short hairs of his seventeen-inch neck. "'Undreds," said Pyecroft. "So've I. How many of 'em can you remember in your own mind, settin' aside the first—and perhaps the last—*and one more?*"

"Few, wonderful few, now I tax myself," said Sergeant Pritchard, relieved.

"An' how many times might you've been at Auckland?"

"One-two," he began. "Why, I can't make it more than three times in ten years. But I can remember every time I saw Mrs. B."

"So can I—and I've only been in Auckland twice— how she stood an' what she was sayin', an' what she looked like. That's the secret. 'Tisn't beauty, so to speak, nor good talk necessarily. It's just It. Some women'll stay in a man's memory if they once walked down the street..."

The curious thing about this story is that Mrs. Bathurst never appears. She remains a vivid memory to all, nothing more. She has "It," and Kipling is smart enough not to get more specific. "It" can mean what each of us wants it to mean, something important, something sexy, something desirable. "It" is personal and individual, though no less effective. "It" is significant and Mrs. Bathurst materializes in our minds, doesn't she?

And when she is contrasted with the other women—who clearly don't have "It"—she becomes even more significant.

Mrs. Bathurst isn't the only one being developed here; the soldiers, themselves, are portrayed. By learning what they feel is important in a woman, we learn what they might be like. What they find attractive, in other words, is what gives us clues to their characters.

Suppose, though, we turn it around and look at attraction from the woman's perspective. What is it that a woman finds attractive in a man, and how does the woman say it? If the soldiers in Kipling's story look for "It," what might a woman look for?

In *The Moon and Sixpence*, W. Somerset Maugham's lengthy saga of the trials of club-footed Philip Carey and his barely requited love for the elusive Mildred, we see a portrayal of a different kind. Mildred is talking with Philip about herself and she lets us glimpse her in provocative fashion. We learn a bit of her background and her standards for judging men:

"I was not fifteen when my father found that I had a lover," she said. "He was third mate on the Tropic Bird. A good-looking boy."

She sighed a little. They say a woman always remembers her first lover with affection; but perhaps she does not always remember him.

"My father was a sensible man."

'What did he do?" I asked.

"He thrashed me within an inch of my life, and then he made me marry Captain Johnson. I did not mind. He was older, of course, but he was good-looking, too."

For Mildred "good-looking" is the operative phrase. It became sufficient motivation for her to enter a teenaged marriage without resentment. What can this tell us about her?

Three things at least:

she was a sexually precocious fifteen-year-old;
superficial good looks were sufficient justification for almost anything;
she held no anger towards her father for forcing the marriage.

When we translate this into how the adult Mildred speaks and behaves, we see her as experienced, confident with men, and still highly charged with sexuality. When Maugham gives us a portrait of Mildred as a fifteen-year-old, he's providing reasons why, later in life, she might treat the bumbling, uncertain attentions of Philip with disdain. Mildred has been *around,* and her words and manner of speaking mirror this. What she says as an adult we expect, from the way she described herself as a teenager.

"A "good-looking" man turned her on when she was young. Would it be any different now that she is older?

An important consideration with most fiction is that the characters—or at least the main characters—grow or change as the story moves along. If characters remain static, they become dull, and page after page the reader can only look forward to more of the same. Character *rigor mortis* has set in.

Lively dialogue, however, can bring on character development and show changes happening right before the reader. Characters may grow kinder, wiser, angrier, meaner, healthier ... and they provide the evidence through their own words. We don't have to tell the reader these things happen, we can show them taking place:

"I don't think I want to sell my uncle's drawings."
"Two months ago you begged me to buy them."
"My mother died last week. I've no family now."

A character changing before our eyes, becoming something different, acquiring different values. The reader has to be interested because the story will change. The expected is now the unexpected, and the other characters will have to adjust.

A recent literary example of this is a conversation between father and son in Louis Auchincloss's novel, Honorable Men. Chip Benedict, the son, is about to enter law school and he has decided he wants more control over his financial affairs. He has directed the bank trust officer to send him whatever money is due from family trusts and not to pay it over to his father as has been done. His father invites him to the Yale Club to discuss it:

"...But are you sure, my boy, that you're acting in your own best interests? I thought you and I had agreed that I should handle any money settled on you for tax reasons while you were busy being educated."

"I've changed my mind. That is, if I ever really made it up. From now on, I'll be my own boss."

'You don't consider that you may hold money that your mother and I gave you in a kind of moral trust?"

"I don't see how a money trust can be moral. But of course I understand what you're driving at. You'd be entirely justified in disinheriting me. Go ahead..."

Chip Benedict is making a strike for independence, he is changing, he is no longer the dutiful son. He is challenging his father, offering to take the consequences if his father picks up the challenge. This is not the same young man who went about his days contentedly aware that Daddy would take care of things. Chip Benedict has become a different character, and the writer's task now becomes to portray him in this manner.

Two questions must be dealt with:

— How does he react with the other characters—what changes in their relationships take place?
—How will the story itself be changed—what will happen now?

One thing only can we be confident about: an independent Chip Benedict will have a pervasive influence in both areas.

All because a character changed. Doesn't it fit Trollope's words: *dialogue should contribute to the telling of the story!*

From rational, gentlemanly behavior, dialogue can certainly produce highly-charged circumstances. Neither Chip Benedict nor his father raises his voice. Their manners are most civilized, yet Chip offers a profound alternative—disinheritance. The passions are there—they are only subdued.

But the passion need not be hidden. Dialogue can show changes in character in the midst of electric emotion. Ernest Hemingway portrays this well in The Sun Also Rises, his story of American expatriates in Europe following World War I. Jake Barnes, the sexually impotent hero, is speaking with Brett Ashley about a young bullfighter both have come to know. Jake is clearly in love with Brett who is compulsive, neurotic, and obviously in an agitated frame of mind.

> "Do you still love me, Jake?"
> "Yes," I said.
> "Because I'm a goner," Brett said.
> "How?"
> "I'm a goner. I'm mad about the Romero boy. I'm in love with him, I think."
> "I wouldn't be if I were you."
> "I can't help it. I'm a goner. It's tearing me all up inside."
> "Don't do it."
> "I can't help it. I've never been able to help anything."
> "You ought to stop it."
> "How can I stop it? I can't stop things. Feel that."
> Her hand was trembling.
> "I'm like that all through."
> "You oughtn't to do it."
> "I can't help it. I'm a goner anyway..."

Brett is changing here. Through her own words we see her admitting a weakness and an inability to cope. She is asking for help, yet saying at the same time that she is beyond help. Note her words: *I'm a goner*...she says it four times, and we see that now she is a different person than she was before she fell for the bullfighter.

The character's own words tell us the change is taking place.

The passion and the excruciating discomfort of the event keep us interested.

Dialogue is the key. The characters come to life.

Keep these items in mind:

— *know the characters* (their habits, backgrounds, points of view);
— *understand the characters' motivations* (why they say what they say);
— *make the characters consistent* (don't have them saying uncharacteristic things).

Dialogue writing must illuminate character development, not suppress it. Consider the following:

"I would hardly expect you to understand my reasons," he said.
"I'm not going to listen," she said.
"Slut!" He backhanded her across the room.

Does the man stay in character? Is there motivation for his striking the woman? Do we know why he gets angry?

Doesn't his response really hide the fact that there might be cogent explanations for why he has no faith in her understanding? If the man were allowed to remain consistent, we might learn more about him and more about the story.

Wouldn't a better response from him be:

"Ever since we were ten years old, you've believed that crazy story Aunt Minerva spread…"

What crazy story, we ask? How does it bear on this incident, and what will happen next?

This is character development, not suppression, and the story moves along.

Suppose we have a scene with more than two characters, and each is different enough so that individual dialogue passages have to be distinctive. We have to write so that readers will be able to identify who is speaking, even if there are no modifiers or descriptive aids.

Ken Kesey performs this sort of thing with his story of life in a mental institution, *One Flew Over the Cuckoo's Nest*. Note in the following passage how he sticks to the rules about knowing his characters and their motivations. Note, too, that by their words we know who is speaking at any moment.

We have three characters: McMurphy, the irrepressible, con-man rebel; Harding the defeated intellectual; and Billy, the wishy-washy good boy. The issue is whether they will badger Nurse Ratched to turn on the World Series even though it will change the routine in the ward.

"I tell ya, I can't figure it out. Harding, what's wrong with you for crying out loud? You afraid if you raise your hand that old buzzard'll cut it off?"

Harding lifts one thin eyebrow. "Perhaps I am perhaps I am afraid she'll cut it off if I raise it."

"What about you, Billy? Is that what you're scared of?"

"No, I don't think she'd d-d-do anything, but"—he shrugs and sighs and climbs up on the big panel that controls the nozzles on the shower. Perches up there like a monkey—"but I just don't think a vote wu-wu-would do any good. Not in the l-long run. It's just no use, M-mack."

"Do any *good?* Hooee! It'd do you birds some good just to get the exercise lifting that arm."

"It's still a risk, my friend. She always has the capacity to make things worse for us. A baseball game isn't worth the risk," Harding says.

"Who the hell says so? Jesus: I haven't missed a World Series in years…"

Even if Kesey had left off the descriptive modifier in each passage, we would know who was speaking. McMurphy is clearly defined, as are Harding and Billy. Each one shows us a side of himself consistent with the general portrait already put together. We see McMurphy trying to rally the inmates, and his rebellious con-man instincts shine through; we see Harding, admitting fear of Nurse Ratched, showing defeat even before the battle is started; we see Billy, unable to muster any strong enthusiasm even though he might give the project some personal support. His stutter adds to his uncertainty.

It comes back, then, to one simple phrase. *Would she/he say that?*

If the answer is yes, character development flows.

If the answer is no, the dialogue lessons haven't been well learned.

5. Do I Show, Do I Tell?

In Vladimir Nabokov's novel, *Lolita,* a character rushes in with the words:

"Mrs. Humbert, sir, has been run over and you'd better come quick."

To the protagonist, Humbert Humbert, this is news with a joyful twist; now he can have his young stepdaughter to himself, now he can shuck the pretense of the dutiful husband.

It is this event which allows Humbert to begin a cross-country sexual odyssey with his nymphet, Lolita. A key passage and a key transition.

Note that Nabokov accomplishes all of this with one simple sentence of dialogue. He could, of course, have described Mrs. Humbert's death, and the plot itself would not have been affected. Mrs. Humbert would still die, and Humbert would still go on his sexual odyssey.

But Nabokov chose dialogue instead of narration, and somehow it seems proper.

The key thing with dialogue is its immediacy. What is being said is happening now, what the characters talk about is occurring now! In the passage above, Humbert is conversing with others when the news of his wife's accident is brought. The immediacy of the news is underscored by the abrupt change in the conversational pattern it produces. Think of it...we're discussing a new book or someone's latest allergy when the word flashes: your spouse has met with an accident?

The immediacy of the news is apparent—it has just happened *now, this minute!*

Narration doesn't accomplish this sort of thing as well. It takes a longer-range view of events, more concerned with the fullness of description than with the rush of instant action. Narration gives us a tool to paint time and space in broader perspectives than does dialogue, yet both should work together.

Generally, dialogue is best used when we:

—wish to focus on a specific event and need the reactions of the participants;
—want to break up lengthy narrative passages, gain a change of pace;
—want to develop a shortcut to characterizations;
—wish to inject a sense of life into the scene.

Narrative, on the other hand, takes us further and can show us more. It is description and summary and scene-business rolled together. It is expository writing with the purpose of moving the story along. William Sloane gives us a pretty good handle on the elements of narration:

Narration is not an easy thing to define. One way of getting at it is to say that it is all that part of a manuscript that answers three basic questions. What has happened? What is happening? What is going to happen?

If dialogue shows us immediacy, then narrative tells us what is happening.

Note how the two can work together. A.B. Guthrie uses elements of each in *The Way West,* his story of people pushing westward during the nineteenth century. The narrative portion describes the landscape, and the dialogue characterizes the speakers.

Lije whoaed his oxen when he came to the top of the hill. Rebecca walked up to him and saw the train winding down and, below it, Fort Laramie, white as fresh wash, with trees waving and shade dark on the grass and the river fringed with woods. More to herself than to Lije she said, "I never thought to be so glad just to see a building."

"It's Fort Laramie. Sure."

"Not because it's a fort. Just because it's a building."

"It's Fort Laramie all the same."

"You reckon they've got chairs there, Lije? Real chairs?"

There was a light in his eyes. He said, "Sure," and cut a little caper with his feet and sang out:

"To the far-off Pacific sea,

Will you go, will you go, old

girl with me?"

She said, "I just want to sit in a chair..."

We learn much more about the surrounding terrain than about Lije and Rebecca through the narrative. We see the Fort and the river and hill and the woods. The narrative provides us, as it is supposed to, a sense of what is going on. In this case it is Lije and Rebecca cresting the hill and reaching their objective, Fort Laramie. It also tells us what the countryside is like and how Lije and Rebecca hope to fit in.

The dialogue shows us the relief the couple feel on reaching their objective, and it's obvious they are both tired. We should be able to *feel* their fatigue if the dialogue contains a sense of immediacy.

And the feel is there...Rebecca wants to sit in a chair. Haven't we all had that feeling at some time? Just a chair, any chair. A place to rest weary bones.

What Guthrie has done here is give us the broader picture with his narrative and then focus on the dialogue for close-ups of Lije and Rebecca. It is a classic use of the two techniques and, as we see, it works well.

Suppose we want to describe a street scene, and we want to establish an atmosphere of menace. We can do it either way:

The shadows curved away and evaporated into blackness, vague lights muted the curb edges, and a fine dust seemed to hang in the air. Rough brick walls towered over them, following the shadows into the night, and the stillness was palpable...

or

"It's too quiet," he said.

"Who's walking the streets at 3 A.M., anyway?"

"Wonder what's behind those brick walls."

"C'mon. let's move it."

"Wish we had a moon to go by."

"Watch it! The curb…"

"Why didn't we wait till it was light out for God's sake!"

Which of these two passages is more dramatic? Which provides the reader with a greater sense of immediacy, which is more alive? The chances are it's the dialogue passage. The conflict between the two characters and the environment is easily portrayed in just a few lines. For the narrative passage to work it would take more time and even then would we have the immediacy we seek?

This doesn't mean, of course, that a narrative passage can't paint a scene of conflict or menace—in fact, we have a good start on one right here. But what dialogue can accomplish with just a few lines might take narrative several paragraphs to do.

So we have to ask ourselves when we have the choice between narrative and dialogue—do we want it short and lively, or do we want it longer and more sedate?

The question hangs there for each of us.

Generally, though, dialogue and narrative work together, as a team. There's a place for each one in a piece of written work, and it is the writer's task to blend them well.

Consider change of pace. Narrative proceeds for a couple of pages, then we inject some dialogue, then we go back to narrative. It can work in the reverse, of course…dialogue, then narrative, then dialogue…but it seems less important to break up the flow of dialogue than it does to break up the flow of narrative. What we seek to do is never allow the reader's attention to flag; we keep the pace of the written work ebbing and flowing so the reader must stay on top of things.

Dialogue as a change of pace works well. See how Judith Rossner does it with *Attachments*, her novel of a young woman, Nadine, who has a passionate crush on a pair of Siamese twins, Amos and Eddie. She conspires to live with them in California where they have a large house and pool. One day Nadine swims in the nude while they watch. Just before the dialogue passage below, there are two long narrative paragraphs describing how she slowly removes her clothes, tests the water, languidly dives in and swims a few laps. She climbs out, towels off in front of them, then drops to the grass...

"How do we go about this?" I asked.

"Tell us what you want us to do," Eddie asked.

"I want to get in between you," I told him.

Obligingly, they went back to their lying down, facing-each-other position. I climbed over Eddie's legs and inched up on my belly until my nose was touching their joint, which was closer to the ground than I'd hoped. Too close for me to crawl under.

"You're making this very difficult," I told the joint.

"Here," Eddie said. "Lie down over there." He pointed to the grass near their feet. Obediently I lay flat on my back on the grass, sexual desire temporarily smothered by anxiety. But it was too late to turn back. My heart beat wildly. They squirmed onto their knees.

"Now lie on your side," Eddie said...

Then, for the next two pages it's all narration. In almost four pages the only dialogue is what we have above. Rossner could have described everything without dialogue, but doesn't it make things more interesting if we have the characters doing some talking? We get glimpses of their character, and we can find ourselves identifying with them easily.

Rossner has changed the pace with her dialogue, breaking up a lengthy passage on the sexual antics of one neurotic woman and a pair of Siamese twins. The reader is bound to pay more attention when the characters are talking because it's interesting to see reactions and counter-reactions. Narrative can't really give us that.

But then dialogue can't give us the long-range view of events either. Dialogue is for close-ups, for immediacy, for breathing a sense of life into a scene.

Remember that, and the blend between dialogue and narrative will be smooth, indeed.

6. He Says…Or Does He?

I recall reading one of James Thurber's works dealing with reminiscences of Harold Ross, the highly praised, unpredictable, somewhat zany editor of *The New Yorker*. Ross and his editorial staff—especially Wolcott Gibbs—developed some editorial rules for manuscripts, and that was that.

One of the rules, according to Thurber, was that a passage of dialogue is best followed by "said." Anything else— "shouts" or "exclaims" or "retorts," for example—is just wasted motion. No verb, in other words, should substitute for "said."

It got me thinking…"Stuff it in your ear!" he…*said?* Wouldn't "retorted" be better?

Or…"My God!" he…*said?* It seemed to me "exclaimed" would fit more easily.

I thought further. The sense of Ross's rule began to dawn. A writer should be able to phrase dialogue so the impact of the words would be clear. "Go to Hell!" he shouted—could be a redundancy. "Go to Hell!" itself is a strongly worded statement, and why do we need "he shouted"?

Of course, maybe we don't need any modifying phrase at all. "Go to Hell!" could stand by itself. No "shout," no "said," no nothing. The reader's imagination could probably conjure a fitting modifier.

Today, even *The New Yorker* allows substitutions for "said." Yet the rule shouldn't be dismissed because what Ross and his editors were trying to accomplish had considerable merit. A writer *should* be able to create dialogue that doesn't rely on the descriptive modifier; the words a character speaks should carry the emotion in which the words are spoken:

"You—you aren't my dead uncle's long-lost great-great grandson!"...

"Oh Everett, I love these children so..."

In the first sentence do we need modifiers like *he gasped,* or *he blurted out...*? Wouldn't he said work as well? Perhaps we don't need to say anything-maybe that would work even better.

In the second sentence, do we need *she purred, she whispered—*? We could insert *she said,* and it wouldn't detract from the impact of the dialogue. Then, too, perhaps nothing at all would be even better.

There are no precise rules on when to use "he said," when to use a substitute, and when to use nothing. It's a matter of feel and an understanding that the reader doesn't want to be overwhelmed by a rush of descriptive modifiers. Generally, however, we can say this:

— "he/she said" is the basic modifier, and it should be used at least three-quarters   of the time any modifier is used;
— a page of dialogue should not go by without a couple of "he/she saids";
— when in doubt, leave the "said" out—add nothing; —in dialogue between two people, use "he/she said" with only one of the characters—nothing with the other.

In the cleanest writing, of course, we don't use anything at all. We let the dialogue passages stand for themselves. But if we have to use a descriptive modifier, the important thing to remember is that "he/she said" serves two purposes: it is an identification device (letting the reader know who is speaking and what the speaker is feeling), and it can change the pace of the dialogue, allowing the reader a slight respite from one unmodified dialogue passage after another. It can give breathing room.

Dialogue without any "saids" is as close as we'll get to script writing, and there are writers who feel that this is the art toward which we should strive. "The more nearly a novel resembles a play in prose form" wrote Lawrence Block some years ago, "the simpler it is for the average reader to come to grips with it." I think what he meant was that readers fasten on dialogue passages, enabling themselves to gain a better understanding of the story.

Note how Thomas McGuane develops a storyline without using any "said." In *Nobody's Angel* he has Patrick, his protagonist, meet up with his dead sister's lover, who happens to be an Indian. They have never laid eyes on one another before:

> "Do you need to see me?" Patrick asks.
> "If there is something between us."
> "What's that supposed to mean? Is that Indian talk?"
> "I don't know."
> "What's your name?"
> "David Catches."
> "Well, they're going to bury my sister. Will you be going?"
> "You'll make another speech. I don't want to hear that kind of thing."
> "Then why don't you come to the house tonight?"

Except for the first line, every passage is without modifier. We know who is talking, don't we? The emotions of the characters are clear from the words they use—we don't need any help. This reads almost like a script.

Note one thing, however: McGuane uses a question-and-answer technique, and this is one way of avoiding any "saids." If we know the identity of the questioner, then we also know the identity of the responder (assuming there are only two people in the scene), and one of the reasons—that of identification—for using "he/she said" doesn't apply. Note, too, that the nature of the question-and-answer exchange tends to be conflict-producing, and so the tension between the two characters doesn't really need further depiction through descriptive modifiers.

But what if we don't feel comfortable unless we use "he/she said"? A lengthy passage without a "said" might not be to our liking.

My rule is this: always use "said" unless you must characterize the action further by telling *how* something is said...It is best to remember that *what* is said in any page of dialogue is at least three times as important as *how* it is said…

Marjorie Franco wrote that a while ago, and it still works. Suppose we want a character to show disagreement. He can say:

"No! I won't buy that!"
But, suppose we want anger to be demonstrated, as well. Then we write:
"No! I won't buy that!" *He slammed his fist on the table…*

The dialogue passage tells us what is said—that there is disagreement—and the modifier tells us how it is said—in anger.

"I love you," he said, stroking the back of her neck. (Intimate.)
"I love you," he confessed. (Vulnerable.)
"I love you," he shouted. (Prideful.)

The words of each dialogue passage are the same, but the way the words are said differs. How the dialogue is uttered becomes important when we want to underline the dialogue words themselves.

Call it characterizing the dialogue, perhaps, and we wouldn't be far off. We are actually giving some personality to the dialogue. But there is more than one way to characterize the dialogue; we won't have to be limited to synonyms for the "saids." In the hands of an accomplished writer the personality of the dialogue can blossom through the use of interior monologue—that is, by having the actor think of the words he/she has just used and *characterize* them. The "saids" then take on added substance.

See how Eudora Welty does it with.her story, *Death of a Traveling Salesman*. Bowman, a shoe salesman, traveling in the remote farm country of Mississippi, has a car accident, and he approaches a lone farmhouse. He is tired, unwell, and discouraged. He is met at the door by a suspicious elderly woman who allows him into the house:

"I have a nice line of women's low priced shoes…" he said.
But the woman answered, "Sonny'll be here. He's strong. Sonny'll move your car."

"Where is he now?"

"Farms for Mr. Redmond."

Mr. Redmond. Mr. Redmond. That was someone he would never have to encounter, and he was glad. Somehow the name did not appeal to him…In a flare of touchiness and anxiety, Bowman wished to avoid even mention of unknown men and their unknown farms.

"Do you live here alone?" He was surprised to hear his old voice chatty, confidential, inflected for selling shoes, asking a question like that—a thing he did not even want to know.

"Yes. We are alone."

Instead of the "saids" and the modifying phrase that would give further meaning to the dialogue, Welty has gone inside Bowman's head. The way he feels, his despair and even his surprise come off better through the interior monologue than they would have if she had substituted a word or two for the "saids."

"Do you live here alone?" he said despairing…

"Do you live here alone?" His voice sounded with a mixture of despair and surprise…

Doesn't Welty do it better? The interior-monologue technique, taken up later in this section, is useful, and it can graphically depict a passage of dialogue.

The rules change a bit, however, when we have more than two characters in the scene, and all of them speak. Two persons are fairly easy to keep straight, but three or more mean we have to use "saids" or their equivalents fairly regularly. The main purpose has to be for identification.

In Jimmy Breslin's novel, *Table Money*, we have Owney, in the army and getting ready to ship out for Viet Nam. He's home in Queens, and he's at a soda fountain with his friend, Glenn, and Delores, a woman he has just met (and who is destined to become his wife). It's a three-way conversation, and the "saids" appear at the appropriate times:

Owney looked at Delores. "What do you think?"

"I'd hide him in my house."

"Is he your boy friend?"

"No, I'd hide you, too."

"I don't want anybody to hide me," Owney said.

"Then I won't hide you." "Do you think Glenn is scared?" she asked him.

"I don't talk like that. Glenn is my friend. He can do anything he wants. Run, hide, fight. Whatever he does is fine with me. We're cool."

"The only reason I won't hide is I'd get bored staying under the bed," Glenn said. "I'll, go up where there's tundra."

"All right with me," Owney said.

"I'll send you letters."

"Where from?"

"Where there's ice."

"Who wants to hear about some glacier? I want her to write to me." Owney was looking at Delores.

"I'll write," Delores said…

We have no doubt who is saying what at any given moment No confusion, no uncertainty. The "saids" are dispersed economically throughout the passage, and Breslin allows the dialogue itself to characterize the speaker.

This is the way it should be done.

A writer in complete control of his material.

7. Should He Gesture, Too?

Question: Are there times when fiction and nonfiction writing are barely distinguishable from play writing?

Answer: Absolutely. Stage business, for one thing, must be considered in both cases.

Stage business?

The non-playwright calls it gesturing.

"Thank you," he said, *smiling.*

"Why not?" he said, *with a grin.*

"No way!" he said, *his eyes fierce.*

"Certainly," he said, *handing over the documents.*

D.C. Fontana, former story editor of *Star Trek,* says stage business, or gesturing, includes "a look, or move, a facial expression, a tone of voice, a mood, a pause in speech…" It means that the writer wants to couple some physical action with the dialogue. On the stage this is called "business," as when an actor delivers lines and does something physical at the same time. "Business" is crucial to performance in a play and it is no less crucial on the written page. "Business" is the bridge that ties lines of dialogue together.

For example, if we want to show mild rebuke, we could write:

"You're home late," he said, tapping the pencil on the counter…

The gesture—tapping the pencil—characterizes the dialogue passage and, in fact, underscores it. The tapping pencil is a sign of agitation, and that, in turn, must flow from some element of distress.

There are, basically, four reasons why we use gestures in conjunction with our dialogue:

to portray character (as in: "I'm leaving now," he said, *kicking in the glass door panels with a vicious swipe);*

to develop mood (as in: "I won't hurt you" he said, *running a finger across her cheek and neck…*);

to emphasize a crucial moment in the story (as in: "Leave me alone!" she said, *the tears streaming down her face…*);

to allow a pause between dialogue passages (as in: "Let's go," he said, *struggling into his leather jacket.* "I mean now!"…).

Gesturing or stage business implies that we want our characters to do more than simply utter unadorned dialogue. We want to inject some form of movement in the scene so things won't—or can't—bog down. On the stage, characters rarely speak their lines without doing *something*—sitting or walking or drinking or making a face—a host of physical mannerisms that complement the spoken word.

The situation should be the same on the written page. Gestures-business—must complement the dialogue.

See how Jayne Ann Phillips does it in her story, Souvenir, which is about the relationship between Kate, who is studying for her doctorate, and her mother, who remains in the family home. Kate has just gotten word her mother is in the hospital for tests. She thinks back to the prior summer when the two of them were in the kitchen and her mother was stirring gravy and they were arguing. Her mother speaks:

"Think of what you put yourself through. And how can you feel right about it? You were born here. I don't care what you say." Her voice broke and she looked, perplexed, at the broth in the pan.

"But hypothetically," Kate continued, her own voice unaccountably shaking, "if I'm willing to endure whatever I have to, do you have a right to object? You're my mother. You're supposed to defend my choices."

"You'll have enough troubles without choosing more for yourself. Using birth control that'll ruin your insides, moving from one place to another. I can't defend your choices. I can't even defend myself against you." She wiped her eyes on a napkin.

"Why do you have to make me feel so guilty?" Kate said, fighting tears of frustration…

Note the gesturing the author uses here: the mother looks at the broth, perplexed...Kate's voice is shaking...the mother wipes her eyes on a napkin...Kate fights tears of frustration. Each of these points of business serves a basic story purpose.

They emphasize the dialogue itself.

Mother and daughter are arguing; there is conflict and tension in the scene. Essentially, their argument is about style of life, an ages-old generational conflict. It is certainly a crucial point in the story. The gesturing, then, highlights the disagreement between the two characters; it gives it substance and importance.

Take the final dialogue passage, for instance. "Why do you make me feel guilty?" Kate said...Do we know the precise frame of mind Kate is in when she says those words? If Jayne Ann Phillips had not added the phrase, *fighting tears of frustration,* we might assume Kate was asking the question at a lower emotional pitch. The words challenge her mother, of course, but there are different levels of challenge, and this one could be less conflict-laden, more like a recurring complaint.

Except when we read the tag line—*fighting tears of frustration.* Then we know. This is a highly emotional moment. If frustration brings tears to one's eyes, there is deep feeling, and the event is underscored for us.

Suppose we want to create an atmosphere that will amplify and explain our dialogue. Gesturing is an easy way to do it, and it can serve to develop the character of the speakers, as well. If we want to show contentment, for example, we can have a character say:

"Such a meal," he said, *stretching back in the chair*...Or if it's uncertainty we want to show:

"My goodness!" she said, *reaching out to touch the scarf but drawing her fingers back*...

See how Joseph Conrad does it in his novel, Under Western Eyes, the story of Russian exiles in Geneva, Switzerland, during the time of the Tsars. Razumov is a student who has come from Russia to help plot some type of government overthrow in his native land. He and others are at a small meeting in an apartment when the subject of phantoms and apparitions comes up. The atmosphere turns gritty and uncertain:

The tenseness of Madame de S's stare had relaxed and now she looked at Razumov in a silence that had become disconcerting.

"I myself have had an experience," he stammered out, as if compelled. "I've seen a phantom once."

The unnaturally red lips moved to frame a question harshly.

"Of a dead person?"

"No. Living."

"A friend?"

"No. I hated him."

"Ah! It was not a woman, then?"

"A woman!" repeated Razumov, his eyes looking straight into the eyes of Madame de S. "Why should it have been a woman? And why this conclusion? Why should I not have been able to hate a woman?"...

The gesturing here all contributes to making the atmosphere challenging and uncertain...the silence is disconcerting...Razumov stammers, as if compelled...unnaturally red lips frame a question *harshly*...Razumov looking straight into the eyes of Madame de S...All of these things buttress the words the characters speak, and when Razumov and Madame de S parry questions and answers we know it is not a pleasant, friendly conversation. Both are on guard.

Could we have known this if there had been no gesturing? Try reading the dialogue without the stage business; read it out loud and see how it sounds.

Try it, go ahead.

It doesn't seem the same, does it? We need Conrad's gestures in order to get the particular flavor of this scene. Without the gesturing, the uncertainty and the tenseness between the characters don't seem so significant.

And if they're not significant, then what purpose does the scene, itself, have? Not much, really.

Atmosphere, then, and with it elements of characterization, is an important by-product of stage business. Its influence and use should not be ignored.

Still another reason for gesturing is to inject a pause between dialogue passages. Why do we need a pause? We don't want to overwhelm the reader with an avalanche of "he says," "she says," nor do we want to trivialize the dialogue itself. By that we mean offering so much dialogue it just runs together and no passage carries any special significance. Breaking up dialogue by gesturing serves to change the pace and keep the reader's attention.

Take a look at this passage from T. Coraghessan Boyle's novel, *Budding Prospects*, the story of Felix and his friends who have been tending a huge marijuana plot in the uninhabited country north of San Francisco. Their hopes for a major financial killing have been done in by a variety of factors, and Felix now wishes for satisfaction from Vogelsang who put up the money for the land and the cultivating equipment in the first place. Felix suspects Vogelsang has twisted things so he, Vogelsang, will come out ahead.

Suddenly he was on his feet, catty, clonic, the old Vogelsang. He paced to the end of the table and swung around. "I bought that property in February, like I told you. But not this February. February two years ago. You know what I paid?"

I knew nothing. I was a loser.

"Ninety-two.'"

Chink doom, went the goatherd, *doom-doom*.

"You know what I'm getting—what I got? Already?" The cords stood out in his neck like stitches in a sweater. "I signed over the title yesterday—the deal's been cooking for months. Months." He was twitching, jerking, dancing in place like an Indian whooping over the corpse of an enemy. "One-seventy. And do you know why? Because you improved the place for me."

I sat down. Hard...

The pieces of stage business between the dialogue passages are important because they not only emphasize Vogelsang's self-satisfaction and Felix's despair, but because they make the words even more significant Vogelsang's coup on the price of the land is all the more galling and triumphant when we see him showing high excitement—he's won, he's won big. By stringing out the revelation, the author has made the triumph even more substantial, and the dialogue passages become the highlights that reveal the triumph. It is simply a more dramatic way of showing the circumstances than it might have been if no gestures were used.

Try the test. Read the dialogue without gestures.

It's not the same, is it?

Several generalities can be drawn about the use of gestures with dialogue. Earlier in the chapter we saw why gestures are used, their application and their value. Now we need to know *how* they should be used.

Gestures and dialogue should match. (Note the title of my book: *"Shut Up!" He Explained.* This is not a match, and Ring Lardner, the writer from whom the exhortation was borrowed, knew it).

Too many gestures should be avoided. (The best rule is to limit gesturing to one piece of business per dialogue passage.)

Gestures should be believable. (The person doing the gesturing must be the kind of person who would do such things. For example, a grief-stricken character would probably not break into a broad smile.)

The gesture should have a purpose. (The writer must ask himself/herself why this gesture, why not something else or nothing at all?)

8. What About Transitions and Flashbacks ?

What do all of these have in common?

"You better be there tomorrow where I can see you. .."
"Guess how far we've come these past two weeks…"
Two days later he said…

They imply *change*. There has been or will be disruption in the storyline. A period of time has passed or will pass between events.

Phrases like this are known as transitions, and they are a common technique for highlighting the passage of time. Most stories pass through events in such a way that periods of time must be accounted for as unobtrusively as possible. These time periods may have only peripheral influence on the storyline, yet if they are ignored, the reader could be confused.

So, we employ a transitional device to alert the reader that a period of time will be passing. The most usual vehicle for this is the standard time-passing phrases: *The next day…One month later…It was six months before*…And dialogue is a handy adjunct to all of this. *One month later he said*…We can even begin the transitional passage with dialogue:

"You didn't act this way two weeks ago when…"

The point is that we must highlight the change, and dialogue, by virtue of its dramatic effect, can do this easily. It doesn't matter whether the change takes place in hours, days, weeks, months, or years, dialogue will bring the flavor of immediacy to the act of transition. In doing this it will lend credibility to the fact that there has been a change and that things have occurred during that change which probably have little effect on our storyline. What the characters are saying now is the important thing. The transition has given us a leap through time.

Generally, however, dialogue has a difficult time if it is in both ends of the transition. It's hard to mesh properly two different stages of dialogue without some device for intervention. The reason should be apparent: because dialogue carries such a strong sense of immediacy, two passages, one right after the other, must have something inserted so their time-relevance can be distinguished.

There are two ways, at least, to do this:

use a narrative insertion, such as *One month later…*;
skip several lines, leaving space in the manuscript, separating the two sections so that different periods of time are apparent.

There is, also, a third technique which can—though it doesn't have to—combine the two above. Dialogue is especially helpful here: simply allow our dialogue passage to provide a clue or an insight about the coming transition. If we do this, we don't have to use a narrative insertion defining the passage of time, nor do we have to separate our text or mark out a different scene. This is what W. Somerset Maugham does with his story, *The Colonel's Lady*. One of his lead characters, a well-known British author, is complaining about a publisher's promotion efforts for his latest book. A cocktail party has been arranged, and the author is attempting to convince a friend to attend:

"I expect it'll be very dull, but they're making rather a point of it. And the day after, the American publisher who's taken my book is giving a cocktail party at Claridge's. I'd like you to come to that, if you wouldn't mind."

"Sounds like a crashing bore, but if you really want me to come I'll come."

"It would be sweet of you."

George Peregrine was dazed by the cocktail party...

Note how the dialogue anticipates the transition. The conversation speaks of the cocktail party that's to come in the future, and so the reader is alerted that a time period is about to pass. Maugham doesn't bother skipping lines when he *writes: George Peregrine was dazed...*nor does he need to insert: *Two days later George Peregrine was dazed...*The clues in the dialogue made all that unnecessary. The time change has occurred simply, easily, with the reader in step.

Flashbacks, like transitions, also call for change, and similar techniques can be used. It's important to understand, though, that while all flashbacks are transitions, the reverse is not true; all transitions are not flashbacks, or put another way, flashbacks are but one form of transition.

All writers use flashbacks, and they are a most useful device. They can give body to a story, provide motivation, flesh out characterization, even offer a moral imperative which can become a central theme. But flashbacks need to be handled properly, and, when dialogue is involved, that means understanding the sense of immediacy that will be injected into the story.

We've all gone to the most usual flashback techniques ...*I heard the music and it reminded me...That nasal telephone voice took me back to* ... "*Tell me about the time that...*" I call these "memory lane" devices, and they are perfectly appropriate for a story.

In using them—or any other method—there are some general principles we should keep in mind.

Flashbacks require careful use of tenses; it may be necessary to start with a past tense, but things should be brought to the present tense as quickly as possible to preserve the sense of immediacy.

Flashbacks must be relevant to the action; they must play an integral part in the story.

Flashbacks should occasion no break in the story flow; if the reader has to go back and forth to understand where he/she is in the story, the flashback isn't of much use.

Flashbacks need not be provided in just one segment; portions can be applied throughout the story, if it contributes to the telling of the story.

Let's look at one of the twentieth century's finest pieces of literature, Robert Penn Warren's *All the King's Men*. The story takes place in Louisiana. Jack Burden, the narrator, is assistant to Willie Stark, the Governor. Burden has been told by Stark to go to Mason City and find something derogatory about Judge Irwin who has become a political obstacle. As the next chapter opens, Burden remembers the last time he had been sent to Mason City, seventeen years before...

The managing editor of the *Chronicle* called me in and said, 'Jake get in your car and go up to Mason City and see who the hell that fellow Stark is who thinks he is Jesus Christ scourging the moneychangers out of the shinplaster courthouse up there.'

"He married a school teacher," I said.

"Well, it must have gone to his head," Jim Madison, who was managing editor of the *Chronicle*, said. "Does he think he is the first one ever popped a schoolteacher?"

'The bond issue was for building a schoolhouse," I said, "and it looks like Lucy figures they might keep some of it for that purpose."

"Who the hell is Lucy?"

"Lucy is the schoolteacher," I said.

The key here is the immediacy of the dialogue. This conversation is taking place *now*, even though Warren made it plain it actually occurred seventeen years before. The immediacy, however, comes from the verb tenses Warren uses...*I said...Jim Madison said*...rather than I had said, etc. In this way Warren makes us understand that Burden and Madison are speaking in a contemporary frame. See how the technique works: going to Mason City makes Burden remember (the "memory lane" device); the first passage of dialogue uses "said" and from that point we have the sense of the present tense; and everything spoken is taking place as we read. Our awareness is not of a past event but of a current conversation. Then, when Warren wants to pull Burden back to the real present, he simply has him stop remembering. An important thing to catch here is the insight this flashback scene also provides into the character of Willie Stark. We find out his wife was a schoolteacher, we find out who gave him the information about construction defects in the school building, and we find out how he used this information. By preserving the sense of immediacy in the dialogue, Warren has made the revelation about Stark's character more dramatic-and more interesting.

Suppose we write:

Thirty years ago I *had had* the same experience. My father had been there to see it. "Look?" he *had* said. "A cloud in the shape of the devil!"

"Does it mean bad luck?" I *had* asked.

"Your mother would call it a sign of evil," he *had* scoffed...

All of this is in the past tense, and the element of immediacy is certainly reduced. It may still read dramatically, but it probably would read more dramatically if we got into the present as quickly as possible. The opening line of the flashback could remain: *Thirty years ago I had had*...but after that we could write...*I said...I asked...he scoffed*...and have immediacy back again.

This is the way John Steinbeck does it in a scene from his book *The Winter of Our Discontent*. Ethan Allen Hawley lives in New England and is beset by pressures from his wife and family to live a better life, one that would require him to compromise some of his moral values. He recalls the death of his brother-in-law the year before, a death he witnessed, and the sudden horrifying apparition that appeared before him, and his urge to bite out the apparition's throat:

When it was over, in panic quiet, I confessed what I *had* felt to old Doc Peele, who signed the death certificate.

"I don't think it's unusual," he said. "I've seen it on people's faces, but few admit it."

"But what causes it? I liked him."

"Might be an old memory," he said. "Maybe a return to the time of the pack when a sick or hurt member was in danger. Some animals and most fish tear down and eat a weakened brother."

"But I'm not an animal—or a fish."

"No, you're not. And perhaps that's why you find it foreign. But it's there. It's all there."

He's a good man, Doc Peele, a tired old man. *He's birthed and buried us for years...*

Note that Steinbeck uses the past tense to get us into the flashback ...what I had felt...but after this it's all the present tense. As Doc Peele and Ethan discuss the apparition and its normal occurrence, they might as well be speaking in front of us. There is no indication—except for the original flash back entry—that the conversation took place one year before. The drama in the passage bursts upon us because it is immediate. It's as if we're spectators at a live production, and we're hearing every word.

Then when Steinbeck wants to take us out of the flashback, he moves away from the dialogue into a narrative of Doc Peele and gradually, easily, we are brought back to the present...He's birthed and buried us for years. The next sentence could begin with dialogue or narrative, but we can be back in the present without anything further. Steinbeck has given us a bridge, and with a word like *now*, or a phrase to indicate contemporaneity such as *All of that was a year ago*, we're out of the flashback.

As with any story device, we have to make sure the flashback fits in well with the story we are writing. The flashback must serve a purpose; it must highlight character, advance the plot or develop the story theme in some way. It must, in other words, *fit in.*

Dialogue without good purpose is, as we've seen in an earlier chapter, static writing. Nothing moves, nothing lives.

So, in our flashback, the dialogue must do something to the story.

See how Mary Lee Settle does it with *The Killing Ground*. Hannah, now a famous author, has returned to her West Virginia home, and an old friend, Kitty Puss, has just called her with a drunken outpouring of invective at how Hannah embarrassed everyone during the 1960s with her liberal, civil rights views. Notice, in the following passage, how Settle uses the "memory lane" flashback device:

Kitty Puss had called up an old trial and I was back within it. A headline in the morning paper. "Local writer leads march…" My father was striking the paper against his hand while he stood at the door of my apartment at seven o'clock in the morning. He strode into the room without looking at me. How did he begin? I only heard again "…Some consideration for our place in the community…under no circumstances are you ever to humiliate us again…" as if I were sixteen instead of thirty-eight years old…

In this passage, we have only snatches of the dialogue, but it is enough to give us the flavor of the scene. The flashback erupts because of a conflict ("the old trial") and continues into conflict between Hannah and her father.

But the real key is what it tells us about the relationship between Hannah and her parents and about Hannah's political views. This is character development in the primary sense because we learn things we never knew before, not only about Hannah and her parents but about Kitty Puss. The characters come to life.

The storyline develops.

The flashback is…relevant.

9. Suppose I Want to Talk to Myself?

"**Y**ou are the one who writes, and the one who is written." Edmond Jabes offered that a number of years ago in his *The Book of Questions*. He is referring to a writing technique where we talk to ourselves about ourselves in the privacy of our own psychic pastures.

It is dialogue with only one talker and one listener, a stage with only one performer.

People call it stream of consciousness or interior monologue (essentially they are the same thing), and it is the process of entering the mind of a character and witnessing the psychic life cycle of a portion of that character's existence.

Bruce Kawin puts it well. Stream of consciousness, he says:

...has come to refer to a method of presenting, as if directly and without mediation, the flowing or jagged sequence of the thoughts, perceptions, preconscious association, memories, half realized impressions, and so on, of one or more characters—the attempt, in fiction, to imitate the complete mental life as it manifests itself in the ongoing present.

In simplest terms, it means we have characters thinking and talking to themselves about what they are thinking.

Stream of consciousness has been used for many years by some of the finest writers: Virginia Woolf, Marcel Proust, Gertrude Stein, Samuel Beckett, Manuel Puig, among others. It is a way of delving into characterization far beyond the limits of objective portrayal. We can get to know the characters so much better.

Think of it...Usual dialogue is limited by what people actually say to one another. Not so with stream of consciousness. We can have the characters thinking much more broadly, much more deeply than would be shown by what we could have them say out loud.

"I hate you!" she said.

We might know why she hates from what she has said earlier, or we might figure it out from things that have happened to her in the course of the story. But if we use stream of consciousness, we would know, not only why she hates, but what effect it might have on her moral balance, whether she's ever hated before, how it might affect her behavior towards others, what philosophical give-and-take she has encountered or will encounter, what role hating can play in her life as well as in the lives of others, and so forth.

We read it from her perspective, and when we're finished, there isn't much about her we don't know.

James Joyce was one of the foremost practitioners of the stream-of-consciousness technique, and in his novel, *Ulysses*, he employs it over and over. Joyce, however, isn't content with simple declarative phrasing: he offers a sometimes-poetic, sometimes-obtuse, sometimes-unfinished thought style which could reflect the true psychic process in motion.

See how he handles his lead character, Stephan Dedalus, and his impressions of the moment of awareness. Does Dedalus see things first or does he feel them?

Ineluctable modality of the visible: at least that if no more, thought through my eyes. Signature of all things I am here to read, seapawn and seawrack, the nearing tide, that rusty boat. Snotgreen, bluesilver, rust: coloured signs, Limits of the diaphone. But he adds: in bodies, then he was aware of them bodies before of them coloured. How? By knocking his sconce against them, sure. Go easy...

These are seemingly disjointed thoughts, but there is an actual pattern to them. Joyce is showing that the eye can take in only so much, that the other senses have to take over in order to make a complete picture. This is what is going through Dedalus's head; the thoughts are flying around like electrons inside the atom. Yet the process produces the desired result; don't we know Stephan Dedalus better than if Joyce had written:

"Tell me what you see."
"What I feel, you mean. Seeing comes later."

Objective dialogue may give us the message, but stream of consciousness gives the message substance and flavor. When we talk to ourselves, we are simply less inhibited. Note how Joyce is not bound by pronoun conventions. He uses "I" and "my" interchangeably with "he." It's all the same person. As the mind flicks from concept to concept, phrase to phrase, isn't the change of pronoun perfectly logical?

What Joyce's style says is this: the mind itself is not subject to an editor's blue pencil. It can't be and remain in psychic freedom. If it is truly stream of consciousness, it must be allowed to flow unimpeded.

Most writers use this technique only sparingly, and even then, they avoid the total free flow that Joyce gives us. Sentences are more conventional, vocabulary more everyday, but the purpose is still the same: to probe the limits of the mind through the free association of thoughts.

When we talk to ourselves, we seek answers, or at least partial answers. We want to know something, we want to understand something. Stream of consciousness is a way of letting us learn more.

Answers, we want answers.

So, we ask questions.

It's a most appropriate stream-of-consciousness technique. Questions and answers.

See how Gail Godwin does it with her novel, *A Mother and Two Daughters*. Nell is in her garden, remembering times long past. A widow, she is entering a comfortable old age, content in her relationship with her daughters and the close family ties.

...If only we were not mortal, she thought; if only we were not personal, there would be so much less pain. But how do I know that? This flower is not mortal, it is not personal. But if I wrenched off its taut, prim petals, if I snatched the bulb from its hole and left it lying to bake in the sun, to die, it would feel its own kind of pain and betrayal. Would I prefer to be this crocus and take my chances on suffering its kind of pain? Even if I could live longer than the human being who planted me, even if I could be spared the human pains of memory, or anxiety about the future?...

Nell explores her own feelings about mortality, and she does it by asking herself—how and what if? *How do I know that?...what if I snatched the bulb...what if I could be the crocus ?...*

She answers these questions with one simple word:

No.

The question approach is hardly new, yet it remains a most useful way of handling stream of consciousness. We talk to ourselves, we ask and we answer, and in this way we explore the psychic realm. Many people refer to the question technique as "Socratic dialogue," meaning that the true answers come only after we question, question, question. The first answer, even the tenth answer, might not be sufficient, but with each question and answer, we come closer and closer to what we seek.

The point is that stream of consciousness (or interior monologue) probes the reaches of the psyche in an effort to show us the truest nature of the character. Edouard Desjardin wrote that interior monologue is "the speech of a character in a scene, having for its object to introduce us directly into the interior life of that character, without author intervention through explanation or commentaries."

The interior life of the character.

Doesn't the question technique operate well here? How better to expose a character's interior life than to have him or her ask themselves personal questions and then answer them?

Desjardin goes on, "...it is an expression of the most intimate thought that lies nearest the unconscious..."

The most intimate thought ?

But did I...?

Suppose I...?

How can I...?

Why should I...?

Sometimes, stream of consciousness comes off better when we stay away from the first person—I or we—and use the second person—you. Then, it's—you think...you don't...you will...you can't...and the feeling comes across that it's just the teeniest less intimate because things are more declarative and less conversational.

Isn't this what it seems like in Ernest Hemingway's *For Whom The Bell Tolls?* Robert Jordan, an American fighting with the Republican forces in the Spanish Civil War, is part of a guerilla band planning to blow up a key bridge. He thinks about his responsibilities to the other members of the group:

So you say that it is not that which will happen to yourself but that which may happen to the woman and the girl and to the others that you think of. All right. What would have happened to them if you had not come? What happened to them and what passed with them before you were ever here? You must not think in that way. You have no responsibility for them except action. The orders do not come from you. They come from Golz. And who is Golz? A good general. The best you've served under. But should a man carry out impossible orders knowing what they lead to?...

Obviously, here too, Hemingway uses the question technique, but note he stays with "you." It's as if he wants Jordan to square his shoulders and stop thinking and acting in some less acceptable way. Hemingway has Jordan rap himself across the psychic knuckles—*you must not think...you have no responsibility...*

Try it in the first person. *I must not think...I have no responsibility...*it doesn't feel the same, it doesn't command the same attention.

Using the second person gives the explanation strength, as if another individual is inside the character's head, wagging a finger and giving encouragement. It's hard to visualize the same thing when we use the first person.

Stream of consciousness presents a rich canvas upon which to portray a story. As we talk to ourselves, we can develop a number of themes, all of which lend substance and variety. We should not make the mistake of assuming that just because stream-of-consciousness writing seems to mirror narration, it can't be flexible enough to do what objective dialogue does best—give a sense of immediacy and drama to the script.

Objective dialogue can show characters with all their warts; it can present them as caricatures or as heroes; it can turn them into objects of derision and ridicule as well as into instruments of mockery and irony.

But so can stream of consciousness.

See how Jerzy Kozinski does it in his novel, *Pinball*. It is the story of Goddard, a highly acclaimed rock musician whom no one has ever seen. Domostroy is a famous composer, and he has fallen for Andrea, who is using him to find Goddard. Domostroy has just received an offer in the mail to join a vasectomy club:

Domostroy stopped to think. If he should ever undergo a vasectomy—although he could imagine nothing less likely—what right would he have to proselytize? Furthermore, if in search of external identity—again, a concept quite foreign to him—he should decide to define himself as an American Vasectomite, where would he feel confident wearing the National Vasectomy Club lapel pin or the tie tack? To cocktails? To dinner with a date? To church? And what about the membership card? Why and where would he need it? To whom could he show it? He imagined being stopped by the highway patrol for speeding and saw himself producing, in addition to his driver's license, his National Vasectomy card...

This, of course, is satire, and it's done as Domostroy talks with himself. The question technique is apparent and useful, and note how the questions take us further and further from the reality of a simple vasectomy. Kozinski is skewering mailorder club memberships, the American penchant for club joining, the inclination to proselytize, the urge for self-confession and self-expression... Kozinski seems to be saying: *is it really necessary to tell the world everything? Must J share it all?*

The point is that by portraying the ridiculous lengths to which such a thing can go, he shows us its essential flaws. This is fine satire.

It also shows us ingredients of Domostroy's character. We see the level of his modesty, as well as the sardonic cut of his wit. We come to know him better.

And it's because we can see him talk to himself!

10. How Do I Handle Questions and Answers?

"**. . . W**hen he swerved across the white line and just missed an oncoming car . . the professor said. He waited while the sixty law students stirred uncomfortably. Incomprehension was general.

He leaned forward, his words clipped. "…about opposite the schoolyard…"

Again, incomprehension.

"C'mon, folks," he urged.

"Give us a clue," a voice from the back said.

The professor waited another moment, then he shrugged. "What course is this?"

"Evidence!" came a small chorus.

He held his palms up, arms apart. "So?"

More incomprehension. Then, from the back, a hand shot up.

The professor nodded.

"Questions," came the reply. "You want questions. Finding evidence is asking good questions."

A smile creased the professor's face. "What were the statements I gave you?"

"Answers."

"So give me the questions," the professor said, and the students did. When they were finished, the professor told them, 'The lesson is simple. We've got to ask the right question to get the right answer. If we want the right answer, *be sure to ask the right question.*"

Questions and answers, they do not spin in separate worlds, independent of one another. They work with one another as a team, and when we write dialogue that includes questions and answers, we must be aware, not only why we are using them, but how effective they will be. I'm not referring to one or two questions and answers in the course of other dialogue; this use is fairly easy to control. What we want to look at here are circumstances where the bulk of dialogue in a series of passages is heavily weighted with questions and answers.

Such as in a courtroom or an interrogation.

How do we handle this kind of thing? The key is: *questions and answers must be woven into the fabric of the story so they seem natural and consistent.*

Natural and consistent.

The easiest approach is to understand what dialogue questions and answers must and must not do. They:

> must propel the plot forward; Robyn Carr says this is so that we "get to know the characters through the way they react to external stimuli";
> must avoid pointless, extraneous debate;
> must not be overused; Peggy Simson Curry says too many questions and answers "give the dialogue a lack of forward movement";
> must not do the job of exposition.

In an earlier chapter we saw Arturo Vivante portray certain questions and answers as "passport dialogue"—"what's your name?"…"where do you live?"…and so forth. His reasoning was that these items simply do not move the story along. They are extraneous to the action and could be summarized much more simply in narration, or in certain cases not even mentioned. We must ask ourselves…are these questions and their answers important to the story? Do they, in Anthony Trollope's words, contribute to the telling of the story?

To write a good story, it's necessary to limit these "passport" questions and answers, as Vivante makes clear, but, if we use them, we have to make sure they will propel the story forward. Yet in the hands of a highly accomplished writer even "passport" questions and answers can work well. See how Frank O'Connor, the Irish short-story writer, does it with his tale, *The Pretender*. Michael and Susie, aged about twelve, brother and sister, are informed by their mother that she's invited Denis, whom they have never met, for dinner. Afterwards, the children are upstairs talking, and Denis stares at the toys Michael and Susie have. Michael is the narrator:

> "Haven't you any toys of your own?" I asked.
> "No," he said.
> "Where do you live?" asked Susie.
> "The Buildings."
> "Is that a nice place?"
> "Tis all right" Everything was "all right" with him.
> Now, I knew The Buildings because I passed it every day on the way to school and I knew it was not all right. It was far from it. It was a low-class sort of place where the kids went barefoot and the women sat all day on the doorsteps talking.
> "Haven't you any brothers and sisters?" Susie went on.
> "No. Only me mudder...and me Aunt Nellie," he added after a moment
> "Who's your Aunt Nellie?"
> "My Auntie. She lives down the country. She comes up of an odd time."
> "And where's your daddy?" asked Suzie.
> "What's that?"...

Most of Suzie's questions and Denis's answers are of the "passport" variety, but somehow they work well. The first thing to note is that the characters are children, and as with so many other circumstances, we tend to forgive children for those things we might condemn in their parents. In other words, kids ask a multitude of questions. We expect it, and we're not put off by it. Kids don't have the inhibitions we adults do, so a conversation like this is customary, and entertaining.

Secondly, see how these questions actually do propel the plot. They tell us quite a bit about Denis—where he comes from, that he has no toys, that he lives with his mother and Aunt Nellie. As we get to know Denis, we see the vast difference between him and Michael and Susie, and it is the difference that moves the story along.

There is another thing to be aware of here, too: O'Connor breaks up his questions and answers with a passage of narration, and this serves to change the pace and to underscore some of the information the earlier questions and answers provided. It also prevents the action in the story from growing static, and it injects an ominous note ("a low-class sort of place …kids went barefoot"…) which then can be the springboard for succeeding questions and answers.

All of this in one short passage. But we should be careful because what works with kids often does not work with adults. Put these same questions and answers in the mouths of adults and see the difference.

Boring, we'd say. No movement, no story push.

The classic question-and-answer situation in literature is in the courtroom. The action revolves around questions and answers, and the drama is often supplied by the atmosphere itself. Yet unrelieved questions and answers will eventually lead to boredom, too. So we have to know how to break things up and give the reader a different perspective.

Not much, actually, is required because the courtroom drama is generally intense in and of itself. But for change of pace and to add to characterization, the most appropriate technique is to provide gesturing to the characters.

Why gesturing?

So we can get a better handle on their feelings as they speak.

Let's take a look at the famous court-martial scene from *The Caine Mutiny* by Herman Wouk. Commander Phillip Queeg is on the stand, and he's being questioned about the incident where he dropped a yellow dye marker off the beach at Kwajalein Island as he led a flotilla of invasion boats towards shore. He was supposed to stay with the boats until they made their final run for the beach, but the accusation is that he came about and left the scene early, thus leaving the boats without protection. Queeg is being questioned by Captain Blakely, in charge of the court-martial board:

"From the time you made rendezvous with the boats, Commander, until the time you dropped the marker, what was the widest gap between you and the boats?"

"Well, distances are deceptive over water, particularly with those lowlying boats."

"Did you stay within hailing distance of them?" Blakely said with a slight impatient tone.

"Hailing distance? No. We communicated by semaphore. I might have swamped them if I'd stayed within hailing distance."

Blakely pointed at the red head officer at the far left of the bench. "Lieutenant Murphy informs the court that he was a boat officer in similar situations in these invasions. He says the common practice was to stay within hailing distance, never more than a hundred or a hundred fifty yards apart."

Queeg slumped in his seat, looked out from under his eyebrows at the lieutenant. "Well, that may be. It was a windy day and the bow wave made a lot of wash. It was simpler to semaphore than to go screaming through megaphones."

"Did you have the conn?"

Queeg paused. "As I recall..."

Note the gestures: *Blakely said with a slight impatient tone... Blakely pointed...Queeg slumped...looked out from under his eyebrows...Queeg paused...*Each of these breaks up the rapid-fire question-and-answer process, but not to the extent that the impact of the dialogue is lost. Instead, we get a small change of pace, coupled with a sense of how the characters are feeling as they say the words. Once we know that Blakely is impatient or that Queeg is slumped in his chair, we can imagine one character's loss of sympathy coinciding with another character's growing defensiveness. The conflict, in other words, becomes heightened, and the drama grows more intense.

Those of us who have spent more than a few moments in a courtroom know the action is often tedious. There isn't much body movement, words themselves are the source of what is happening. So, as writers, we have to make those words become the story. How something is asked and the way it is responded to are the crucial items, and we try to color the questions and answers with characterization:

"What did you do next?" His eyes bore into hers implacably…

"And I suppose you didn't try to stop him?" he said, staring out at the spectators…"I didn't think he'd understand," she said, massaging her empty ring finger …

Questions and answers with gestures; there are no dead spots now.

One thing we must be careful with is to avoid letting our questions and answers do the job of narration, or exposition. Each question and each answer should be designed to move the story forward. Let's leave major explanations, such as chronicles of family history, lengthy, complicated anecdotes, detailed physical descriptions, arduous journeys, to narration, and concentrate on building tension and character with our dialogue.

Dialogue, in other words, should not be packed with extraneous matter. Questions and answers, useful as they are, are simply a tool for moving the story along. The shorter we keep them, and the more focused, the less likely we will be to slip off the path.

"You think he'll come back for us?"

"That's a dumb question."

If the characterization is clear, no further words are needed to tell us what's going to happen. We demand:

— no lengthy explanations;

— no pointless debates.

We understand.

That's what good questions and answers in dialogue are supposed to accomplish.

11. What About Terms of Art and Slang?

"I guess I better *stump the pew*..." (to pay a debt)
"Lookit 'im, old *gotch-gutted*..." (pot-bellied)
"A real *pea wacker* we're in..." (heavy fog)

Strange words and phrases to us in the twentieth century, relics of another day, arcane reflections of speech patterns that once were in everyday use.

Slang!

Did people really speak this way? Of course they did, but as with many other aspects of the language, the words and phrases people use change and change again as the years go by.

We see it in our lifetimes. Is anyone a *beatnik* these days? Do we still gild the lily? How about catching the *milk run*?

When we put words in the mouths of characters, we have to be careful with the colloquialisms we use—slang, in other words. Every period of history has had its peculiar idioms, and we have to know which ones apply to which set of years.

Raleigh held her close, shielding her from the scaffold construction in the courtyard. "Prithee, dear Lady," he consoled, "the media will cover this hanging well..."

Is *media* a proper word to use with this scene? The media are a product of the second half of the twentieth century, and they don't fit a medieval castle scene. This, obviously, is an extreme example, but it points to the importance of weighing our colloquialisms carefully so we don't have our characters sounding as if they've been asleep for twenty years or more.

And the problem is compounded by the fact that what is slang today may disappear quickly, only to be replaced by something else. What comes into the language also leaves it, and if we put old words in the mouth of a new character, we're liable to have the reader shake his head ...*doesn't this writer know anything?*

We lose the respect of the reader, and then we lose the reader. Simple as that.

One thing to watch out for is slang that seems to have blossomed with a heady burst, more on quickness than on longevity. Trendy words and phrases, for example. Here's William Zinsser on the subject:

The only trouble with accepting words that entered the language overnight is that they have a tendency to leave as abruptly as they came. The 'happenings' of the late 1960s no longer happen, 'out of sight' is out of sight, nobody does his 'thing' anymore, 'relevant' has been hooted out of the room, and where only yesterday we wanted our leaders to have 'charisma', today we want a man who has 'clout' . ..

Slang definitely has a place in dialogue; it's the means by which we reach the reader and encourage his or her sense of identity. We use comfortable, familiar words, we set an informal tone, and then we settle back—reader and writer—and pursue the story together. There is, however, good slang and bad slang, and when we choose our idioms, we must be conscious that what was a character's *cup of tea* thirty years ago might have been his bag ten years later.

Bad slang can take several forms: it can be offensive, in the sense that any crude word or phrase is offensive; it can be inappropriate, in the sense that it is no longer pertinent; it can be uncharacteristic, in the sense that certain characters would simply not use these idioms; it can be overbearing, in the sense that the word or phrase is used to the point of gagging us, and we want to scream "enough! enough!"

Good slang, though, can inject life and immediacy into a story. It can turn a commonplace tale into high drama. This is what Irwin Faust does with his *The Year of the Hot Jock*, told in the idiom of the thoroughbred jockey, without quotation marks. Pablo is to ride Wineglo in the Preakness, and he runs into his old friend Rafael in the lobby of the hotel:

Listen, he says fast and jerky, don't win.

Stare, open mouth, close, open. Did I hear what I heard?

Don't win, Paul.

Face gets hot, keep voice down. Soft, low: this horse can't miss, Rafe.

Eyes stop shifting gears, voice levels off. You got the hands Paulie, you can do it.

Don't answer, not yet, maybe he exits while he can. Sits there, not going anywhere. He once told me: In this world anything can happen. Think of that, finally, say it. Rafael, you asking me to pull my horse?

I'm asking you not to kill him to win.

You asking me to pull him?

Don't be so damn technical...

The situation is stereotypical—a jockey being asked to prevent his horse from winning—and there are only so many ways this can be presented. Ultimately, the proposal has to be made —*pull the horse, don't let him win*—and the reaction has to be portrayed—*I will (or won't) do as you ask...*

But note the style. It reads like a telegram, abbreviated phrases, words running together, everything intensified. The slang phrases are here—*horse can't miss...you got the hands...not to kill him to win...pull my horse?...*What's important is that the slang fits with the general dialogue, and is perfectly appropriate for the mood of the story.

The slang is as natural as the story itself.

Good slang because it blends well.

Doesn't the story benefit from the slang? The immediacy and the drama are right before our eyes. Anything less colloquial would take that away.

Let's substitute—*this horse is the best in the field...we want you to lose...you know how to do it...*

Is it the same?

There's a hollowness in there, a lack of authenticity. That's what good slang is designed to avoid.

Good slang allows us to use familiar colloquialisms, but what about those times when we have unfamiliar words and phrases, and there just isn't an effective substitute? Or when we want to use unfamiliar words and phrases to add to the mood of our story?

We call these "terms of art," and they represent a body of language which must be carefully weighed before being used. We see these terms appear when something of a scientific nature is discussed, or something medical or something artistic...anything, in fact, which has developed its own language so that a non-member of the group would be at a loss to understand. Suppose, for example, we're in a courtroom, and the opposing lawyers are discussing a point of law before the Bench:

"I think it's appropriate to bring in *res ipsa loquitur*" Your Honor..."

"Not unless the *Parole Evidence Rule* has been repealed. There's no way we're going to impeach our *extra-judicial* testimony..."

"Gentlemen," the Judge reminded them," this is not a *Court of Equity*..."

The italicized words, of course, are terms of art, the lawyer's art, but under different circumstances they could be the physicist's art, the trumpet player's art, the advertising man's art, and so forth. The point is that whenever we have a character with a specialty, and the action revolves around that specialty, we have to know when to use the specialty's terms of art, and whether to explain such words and phrases to a quizzical reader. It's the same judgment we make with bad slang: if we lose the reader's respect with bad slang, we cause the reader to become confused with esoteric terms of art. In either case, the result is the same:

We lose the reader.

Terms of art, then, must be carefully offered. The first and most important thing to remember is never to overdo it. When in doubt, cut back on the terms of art, keeping them around only to propel the story forward.

And, if possible, provide some form of explanation, or at least offer reasons why the terms of art are relevant.

See how Edward Stewart does it in his book, *Ballerina,* the story of young ballet dancers in an international ballet company in New York. Chris, one of the dancers, is to work on a new ballet with Wally Collins, a highly respected male dancer. Marius Vollmar, the ballet master, is to rehearse them:

Vollmar let the music continue to the end. He thanked the pianist, got to his feet and began pacing, waving his arms.

"Music is our staircase. This is simple music; it makes a simple staircase. No spirals, no zigzags, no drooping over the banister. We go up, we come down again. We have two tempos: die *andante,* the '*piu mosso.* They are repeated. Same stairs up, same stairs down. Wally—where is our emotional climax? Where are the stairs steepest?"

"The last *allegro*"

"Christine?"

She hesitated to disagree with her partner, but…

"The second *andante.*"

"What phrase in the second *andante?*"

"The two silences…"

*Andante…allegro…'piu mosso…*there is no attempt to define or explain these musical terms, yet they are essential to the ballet the characters will learn. Would someone without musical training understand them? Or, more importantly, does a failure to understand them affect an understanding of the plot?

Probably not. We know several things from this passage: the characters are learning a new ballet, and they must learn the music that goes with it; Chris and Wally disagree about the location of the emotional climax; the music has an "up tempo" and a "down tempo," and these are the only tempos and it is simple music.

We also get some implied explanation of the terms of art; note Vollmar's description of the music—a "simple staircase." Don't we "hear" how it sounds, can't we imagine the dancers moving to this music?

And isn't this all we need to know to keep up with the plot? The terms of art add a certain mood to the scene, but for us who have no musical background, it's enough to know the general trend of the music and to see that Chris picks up its subtleties more easily than Wally.

The point is this: unless it is necessary for an understanding of the story, detailed explanations of terms of art are not necessary. We can imply meanings, if we wish, but even this should be done only when we wish to nudge the plot along.

There are times, though, when we must add an explanation to the unfamiliar terms we use. We should ask ourselves: would I be confused if I didn't get an explanation? This is especially true where several terms of art appear within a short space; some, at least, should be explained, so that the reader can get the drift of what is happening.

In Gerald Green's *The Hostage Heart*, we see an example of explanation and non-explanation, but there's little doubt about what's happening. In this passage Dr. Eric Lake is about to operate on Walter Trench for a coronary by-pass:

Dr. Lake put his scalpel at a point on Trench's aorta about one inch above the heart. "Right here for the graft to the LAD," he said. He moved the scalpel up an inch. "And here for the graft to the diagonal. How does that look, Jack?"

"Looks fine, Eric."

Mihrab nodded. Lake would put the grafts where he wanted. But he always included the junior surgeons in his decisions.

"There's an artery that's really shot," Lake said. He touched the wider end with his gloved fingers. "Beading. A good part of the way down Just a matter of time before it closed off. Feel it, Jack." *Beading* described the bits of hardness in a vessel grown narrow, obstructing the flow of blood...

Green does not explain his reference to LAD, but he does give us a full explanation for "beading." What's the difference? It's probably a case of not letting too many terms of art go on without remembering the reader. Then, too, "beading" is a condition that affects the particular patient's health, a key symptom; LAD refers to a piece of tissue, something common in all of us. "Beading" is special, different, uncommon, LAD is none of these things.

So we get an explanation of the less familiar term of art. And it doesn't interrupt the flow of the story, does it? In fact, by understanding "beading," we feel a greater sense of immediacy:

The condition is serious!

The man might die!

Thank God, we operated in time!

Terms of art should be sprinkled delicately," says the writer...

"Terms of art help me to understand," says the reader...

And slang brings us together.

12. Suppose I Open With Dialogue? Suppose I Close?

The lead.

The end.

So much goes on in a story after the lead and before the end that we might forget how crucial the opening and the closing really are.

The way we open a story sets the story tone.

The way we close a story provides the final impression the reader takes away.

Crucial. Key. Decisive.

Journalists speak of the lead as the most important sentence in an entire work, and fiction writers talk about endings in terms of satisfying the reader. In both instances the inherent quality of a piece of writing is being held up to scrutiny, and a standard is being set. Does the lead set the tone…does the end fulfill most expectations?

As writers we strive to answer with a resounding yes!

But sometimes—the cliché goes—it ain't so easy.

Dialogue, however, is a tool that can help. Because of the sense of immediacy it carries and because it can pack a lot of drama in just a few lines, dialogue can do the job that many more lines of narrative might struggle with.

"It has to be an albino skunk!" Helen said to her pouting mother from the verandah step.

"Can't be," said her brother, Harley Hanscomb. "Circus claimed it was a West African tree squirrel."

"I don't see why you won't move back home for a little while," said their mother to Helen. "How can working in a circus be good for you?"

"You can see the stripe marks down his back," said Helen…

In a few short lines we have moved right into this story, we get the tension between Helen and her mother, we find out Helen works for a circus, we learn she has a brother. Would we like to read on?

That, of course, is the point. An opening that doesn't encourage us to read further doesn't make for much of a story. And an ending that doesn't leave us with satisfaction doesn't do its job. While there aren't exact rules on how all of this is done, there are two general principles we should remember:

Openings must be attention-catching.

Closings must provide a slight surprise.

In our lead, if we hook the reader, we have him or her for at least the next few paragraphs, where we must continue the process of imbedding the hook.

In our endings, we want the reader to walk away thinking how it all came out wasn't quite what was expected. Not a huge twist, mind, but something a bit different yet perfectly reasonable. Why a surprise at this point? Remember, the ending is the final impression the reader takes away, and wouldn't we want him or her to feel that the story has to be followed to the end, that stopping before that reduces the pleasure? We want that reading pleasure to be paramount, and therefore we continue to develop the story to the end, so the pleasure is maintained.

Let's go back to openings. In J.F. Powers's story, *The Valiant Woman*, we have three people seated around the dinner table: two priests and the rectory housekeeper. Remembering that we want to catch the reader's attention rapidly and hold it, watch how Powers begins:

They had come to the dessert in a dinner that was a shambles. "Well John," Father Nulty said, turning away from Mrs. Stone and to Father Firman, long gone silent at his own table. "You've got the bishop coming for confirmation next week."

'Yes," Mrs. Stone cut in, "and for dinner. And if he don't eat anymore than he did last year—"

Father Firman, in a rare moment, faced it. "Mrs. Stone, the bishop is not well. You know that."

"And after I fixed that fine dinner and all." Mrs. Stone pouted in Father Nulty's direction...

The tension is palpable. Mrs. Stone is complaining and the priests are defending. There's disagreement and dissatisfaction, and we'd like to know more. Why is the bishop coming, will Mrs. Stone continue to complain, will the priests finally exert authority over her and stop the complaining, will the complaining lead to other difficulties, how can the priests co-exist with Mrs. Stone? What we have here is quick tension, and the reader should be hooked by the second dialogue passage.

There are other ways to catch the reader's attention, though tension-filled dialogue is certainly the quickest and easiest. But note how Ray Bradbury accomplishes it with his story, *The Veldt*. George and Lydia Hadley are living in some indefinite time in the future, and in their home they have a large room they call the "nursery." The story opens:

"George, I wish you'd look at the nursery."

"What's wrong with it?"

"I don't know."

"Well, then."

"I just want you to look at it, is all, or call a psychologist in to look at it."

"What would a psychologist want with a nursery?"

"You know very well what he'd want." His wife paused in the middle of the kitchen and watched the stove busy humming to itself, making supper for four.

"It's just that the nursery is different now than it was."

"All right, let's have a look"...

Is all of this attention-catching? Could we stop reading after the first few lines? Would we *want* to?

Bradbury uses at least three techniques to hook us:

Questions and answers. There's inherent tension in this approach; it's almost always adversarial.

Bizarre circumstances. Who ever heard of an inanimate object like a nursery needing a psychologist?

Unexplained change. The nursery is "different" from what it was; why? what happened? and even more important, what's going to happen?

The dialogue here catches us a bit off balance because it's a quiet, seemingly innocuous conversation between husband and wife; it's only when we focus on what they are saying that we realize something weird is going on. That weirdness is what imbeds the hook and pulls the reader along with the story. Most writers know that hooking the reader is a delicate art, and it must be accomplished within a few paragraphs, at most. Bradbury does it here with consummate skill, maintaining, at the same time, the forward pace of the story and the first touches of characterization.

Would we want to read on?

Sure enough.

When we come to endings, the key element remains to provide a small surprise for the reader. It must be logical, of course, and it must be satisfying—no hanging threads of the story should be left untended. But surprise is what makes the story ending memorable.

This is what William Wharton did with his highly acclaimed novel, Birdy. Al and Birdy are boyhood friends, and they both find themselves under treatment in a U.S. Army psychiatric hospital during World War II. Birdy has had obsessive boyhood fantasies about becoming a canary, and he dreams of flying off into freedom. They are treated by the hospital psychiatrist, and as the last scene begins the fantasies return. Birdy sees himself with Al standing on the hospital roof throwing baseballs at the sky. The psychiatrist appears and slowly sheds his skin, becoming a golden duckling and urging the young men to follow him into the sky. Al speaks:

"Not me, Birdy. I'm not even going near the edge. I'm not going to jump off a building and get myself killed."

"I'm not either, Al."

"Well, we take the suit that Weiss molted and we put it in the box with what're left of the moldy baseballs. We go back downstairs and check the box at the entrance. Then we walk right on out of here, out the gates."

"Just like that?"

"Just like that."

"And so what happens, then?"

"Nothing, Al, just the rest of our lives."

"Is that all?"

"That's all."

"And that's the way it ends?"

"Not really, Al. It's never that easy. Nobody gets off that easy."

But it's worth trying.

The end. The surprise is this...although Birdy's obsession was to fly like a bird, in this, his final fantasy, he reaches for freedom by walking. The question we're left with is: does this mean Birdy is cured? The answer, of course, is more elusive, and Wharton, like any good writer, allows us to fashion a final scenario for ourselves. But whatever we come up with, it's clear that the final dialogue passage does not interfere with the logical progression of the story, nor leave us wondering and waiting for more. The ending is satisfying because it concludes the fantasy and with it the obsession... perhaps.

Notice that this is a surprise only in the sense that one would expect Birdy and Al to fly after the psychiatrist, given the obsession that Birdy holds. But the fact that they choose to walk out the gate is not so unexpected nor so vast a change. It is, after all, the goal of any psychiatric hospital to try to make the patients whole, and Birdy and Al have been undergoing treatment for an extended period. Now, all of a sudden, they seem cured—at least in the fantasy.

Surprise!

Sometimes we can couple tension with modest surprise and bring about an even more satisfying ending. A disagreement, say, or a confrontation, or a discovery can be portrayed with tension, and at the last moment a surprise can enter and provide a turntable effect so the characters must readjust immediately.

Remember, though, we must make it logical and satisfying.

See how James McKimmey does it with his mystery-suspense story, *A Proper Environment*. Ambleton killed his wife, and Harms, a household servant, discovered it and agreed to cover up the killing so long as Ambleton paid him money every year. Harms was a huge man, who enjoyed killing and tearing wild animals apart. Harms left Ambleton's employ, and every year the money was paid as promised. One day Ambleton's son, Kevin, overhears his father and Harms on the telephone talking about the murder. Kevin, an avid collector of magic tricks, puts disappearing ink into the inkwell of his father's desk, knowing the next delivery of money to Harms would be addressed with this ink. Later, Kevin confronts his father about murdering his mother:

"Killer," Kevin said.
"If you'd only been old enough to know what she really was."
"You didn't give me the chance," Kevin said cooly.
Behind Kevin, as he spoke, Edward Harms appeared in the doorway, looking much as he had the day seven years before when the boy had been asleep in his room.
"No!" Ambleton told him. "No no no no no!"…

This is the tension of confrontation-between father and son— and some way has to be found to resolve it. The story simply cannot end with father and son glaring at one another and throwing epithets about.

Enter Edward Harms. We know he's vicious and brutal, and we know what he intends to do. This will resolve the confrontation, certainly, and it will also provide a nice, logical, satisfying end to the story. There's surprise, too, in the sense that Harms's entry at this moment may not have been anticipated. But he has motivation to be in the house (because he didn't receive his money, since the ink on the package had disappeared), and the father, who had prevailed through the years by paying blackmail and covering up a murder, was now to be killed. Simple justice, after all.

The ending works, doesn't it? And it has the elements we've discussed: surprise, logic and satisfaction.

The most effective type of surprise for our endings comes in the form of a reversal of what we've come to expect. That is, things go along in one direction, and then, in the end, things get reversed. We mentioned the "turn-table" effect, and this is really only an extension. But it's effective and it's common.

See how D.H. Lawrence uses it in his story, *The Captain's Doll*, about a romantic triangle involving a refugee German baroness and an English Army captain and his wife. The baroness makes dolls. She created one of the Captain which both he and she cherished. Finally, the romance ends, and the Englishman and his wife return to England, while the baroness continues to live on the continent. Years pass, the wife dies, and the Englishman finally locates the baroness in Salzburg, Austria. They reunite and, during a quiet boat ride, discuss whether they should marry. The baroness says she will marry him, but she won't promise to honor and obey him. The Englishman says in that case the marriage will never take place. The boat comes to a stop at the dock of the baroness's villa.

"You'll come in?"

"No, I'll row straight back."

"But you won't have me even if I love you?" she asked him.

"You must promise the other," he said, "it comes in the Marriage Service."

"Don't be a solemn ass. Do come in."

"No," he said, "I don't want to come in."

"Do you want to go away tomorrow? Go, if you do. But anyway I won't say it before the marriage service. I needn't need I?"

She stepped from the boat.

"And come to me tomorrow, will you?" she said.

"Yes, in the morning."

He pulled quietly into the dark...

In the end, she agrees to the Marriage Service and to including the words "honor and obey." It is a reversal of her longstanding point of view, and since it comes at the end of the story, it is surprising. But there's motivation: she does love him, and she wants to be with him. If this is the only way it will happen, she will go along…reluctantly. But note something else. In the earlier years the baroness had her English Captain doll, and it was satisfying for her. She made the doll and she controlled it. Now, suddenly, she has become his doll. "Honor and obey" put her in this position, and the roles have been subtly but definitely reversed.

This is Lawrence at his best, and we can appreciate how deftly he maneuvers his characters. But what of the ending? Is it logical, is it satisfying?

An old love offers an aging beauty security and deep feeling. All she has to do is say a couple of words.

The baroness gets what she wants. The English Captain gets what he wants.

We, the readers, get what we want—a story we'll remember.

13. Should I Be Aware of the Rhythm of My Dialogue?

Here's a famous passage from a famous story:

> "The cannonading has got the wind up in young Raleigh, sir," said the sergeant Captain Mitty looked up at him through tousled hair. "Get him to bed," he said wearily. "With the others. I'll fly alone." "But you can't sir," said the sergeant anxiously. "It takes two men to handle that bomber and the Archies are pounding hell out of the air. Von Richtman's circus is between here and Saulier." "Somebody's got to get that ammunition dump," said Mitty. "I'm going over. Spot of brandy?"…

What makes this story memorable? Is the dialogue unusual, does it create unforgettable images in our mind? Are we overwhelmed with wordsmanship?

The simple truth is that this passage flows smooth as silk; there is nothing magic in the dialogue, other than its leanness and its rich tone. We can believe what the characters are saying because it seems so real, yet we also understand how unreal it all is. This, of course, is *The Secret Life of Walter Mitty,* by James Thurber, and what we see here is plain fantasy.

And it holds together so well! No awkward phrasing, no uncertain cadence, no abrupt changes of pace or tempo.

The rhythm works!

Every story has to be concerned with rhythm. It is to the writer what time is to the musician and angles are to the sculptor. It is the way a story moves, the way its audience is caught up.

Bad rhythm causes us to sense something out of place, something distasteful. The only reason we would ever use bad rhythm is when we *want* to create the desired effect in the reader. But to use bad rhythm we have to know why it's bad and when it's bad.

For example, we could have a character say:

"What in the world are you doing?"

The rhythm is clean, the tempo even. It's a simple phrase, simply said.

But suppose, instead, the character announces:

"The world knows you're doing something, I think, aren't you?"

Things don't flow here, the pace is uneven, there is no smoothness. The rhythm is bad. Take out "I think," and it still doesn't have the evenness of the earlier phrase.

Rhythm affects not only what the reader sees but what he or she hears. That's right...*hears!* William Zinsser, in his book, *On Writing Well*, puts it succinctly:

Also bear in mind, when you are choosing words and stringing them together, how they sound. This may seem absurd: readers read with their.eyes. But actually, they hear what they are reading—in their inner ear—far more than you realize.

See how the following passage affects us in this way. It's from Russell Bank's novel, *Continental Drift*. In the story, a young Haitian woman and her baby son and young nephew are in a frantic escape from Haiti, on a perilous journey towards Florida. The three Haitians are in the hold of an island freighter when the freighter picks up some other Haitians whom the captain orders into the hold. The Haitians want to stay above deck, but the Captain tries to convince them otherwise:

"Got sumpin down dere better'n up here, mon."
"Yes?"
"Got a gal. Haiti gal down dere, jus' waitin' for a big ol' black Haiti mon to come down an' chat wid her."
" Yes?"

"Haiti gal an' her pickney an' a pretty bwoy down dere wid her."

"Yes? A pretty boy, eh? *Massisi?*"

The fat man laughed. Yas, mon, him a pretty bwoy, all right, but de gal, dat de real beef. Make the journey sweet."

"Yes. So we dry and warm ourself in the morning sun, eh? Then we go chat up the Haiti gal and pretty boy, eh?"

"Eh-eh-eh," the Captain said, laughing, walking aft towards the wheelhouse ...

Don't we hear the growing interest in the Haitian, and don't we sense the growing terror in the woman as she hears this conversation? Can't we hear these words, as well as read them?

Why?

First, listen to the dialect. It's almost a singsong cadence. Say the words out loud, speak them. They have a natural tempo, a fluid pace. If the same phrases were stripped of dialect and read as dictionary English, they would lose their flavor—and their rhythm.

Second, note the repetitiveness of "yes?" It sets up a regular beat, a short response after a long phrase, a dum/dum/dum/DUM! This is rhythm because it is so regular and because it follows a pattern.

Third, see how the Captain's speech rhythm differs from the Haitian's. The Captain talks in longer sentences, he sounds more expansive. The Haitian speaks in short bursts, as if too many words would make him vulnerable. This contrast in rhythm provides us with another insight: it shows us character, and this, in turn, makes us *hear* not only *what* is said, but how it is said.

Writers, Sometimes, forget the importance of rhythm in developing the tone of their stories. Good rhythm means a story fits together well; bad rhythm means it is lopsided and uneven. To John Gardner, the late novelist, awareness of rhythm is crucial. Even famous writers, he says:

...write with no consciousness of the poetic effects available through prose rhythm. They put wine on the table, put the cigarette in the ashtray, paint the lovers, start the clock ticking, all with no thought of whether the sentences should be fast or slow, light hearted or solemn with wedge-in juxtaposed stresses...

How would we slow down a line of dialogue? Let's take a simple phrase:

"I'm not sure I want to go."

We can lengthen it and complicate it:

"The problem certainly is me, and deciding to go is difficult."

Or we can use multisyllable words (note the same number of words as the original, however):

"I'm undecided whether the effort's worth it."

In either case we have slowed things down, and this, then, says to the reader in the subtlest manner that the tempo and the pace of the story may be changing—at least in this short passage. The writer must know, of course, why he wants the pace to change and what he hopes it will accomplish. But if he's aware of what he's doing, his work will carry his intentions much further.

What if we want to speed things up? What if we want our sentences to move rapidly? Take a look at this passage from Ernest Hemingway's *The Short Happy Life of Francis Macomber*. This is the way the story opens:

It was now lunch time and they were all sitting under the double green fly of the dining tent pretending that nothing had happened.

"Will you have lime juice or lemon squash?" Macomber asked.

"I'll have a gimlet," Robert Wilson told him.

"I'll have a gimlet, too. I need something," Macomber's wife said.

"I suppose it's the thing to do," Macomber agreed.

"Tell him to make three gimlets"...

Note the tautness and the tension here. *Something* has happened, and the characters are obviously affected by it The thing that builds the atmosphere is the staccato-like dialogue, the clipped phrases, the short, quick responses. It is the rhythm of the dialogue that sets the mood and gives added body to what is said. The sentences are short and pointed, and the words are uncomplicated. The characters ask, tell, say and agree…no one *wonders…shudders. …shouts…cries…*it is a civilized scene, yet underneath that patina of civility lies a mass of raging emotions. It is this controlled tension that Hemingway's words so well portray, and it is the rhythm of his writing that gives us the mood without his having to spell it out in detail.

The key is something we should remember: Hemingway is showing us the drama, not telling us.

William Sloane believed that people have at least two vocabularies and that they switch in and out depending upon to whom they are talking and what they are talking about. What he really means is that our reactions are controlled by the environment within which we find ourselves. "A convict talks one way to his mother," he writes, "another way to his girl or to the warden or to a fellow inmate. A woman tells the same thing differently to a man and to another woman."

Does one talk about the sordid reality of prison life with the same degree of venom no matter who the listener? If it's Mother, don't we say things differently than if it's Cell Mate? It's a two-step process, really: first, we have to decide what we're going to say; then we have to decide how we're going to say it We might use almost the same words with both listeners—*I hate this foul place!*… though we might add an adjective with Cell Mate that we wouldn't with Mother.

With Mother, we are looking for sympathy, stroking, nurturing, so our tone of voice would be prodding and plaintive…*I hate this find place*, he sobbed…

With Cell Mate, we are looking for agreement and approbation…*I hate this miserable foul place*, he spat out . .

Different vocabularies, different rhythms…though the same words.

The tone we use would be different; with Cell Mate it would

be aggressive, disgusted, certainly mean-sounding; with Mother it would be angry, dispirited, probably seeking help. If we expanded the dialogue, the words with Cell Mate would be short, snappy, harsh, building an atmosphere of blinding fury, and the words with Mother would be lengthier phrases, softer on the ear, slower moving, to give effect to the sense of despondency.

Tempo and pace are what we mean by rhythm. We must be aware of and control these elements to achieve the best dialogue. John Sayles puts it well when he writes:

...Rhythm applies to the individual speaker's style and to the pace of the story. People speak in different tempos, breathe more or less in phrasing a sentence, put their sentences together simply or in a more complex way...If you control the rhythm of your dialogue, of your story, you can better hold the reader where you want him, make him want to listen to you.

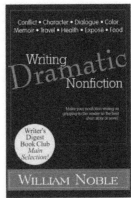

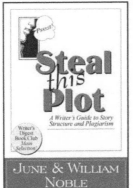

THANKS TO CLAUDINE SHARP

Art direction: Kamy Pakdel, Studio Autrement

Clarion Books
a Houghton Mifflin Company imprint
215 Park Avenue South, New York, NY 10003
Copyright © 2002 by Autrement Jeunesse
Translation copyright © 2004 by Clarion Books
Originally published in France under the title *Un Roi Tout Nu.*
First American edition, 2004

www.houghtonmifflinbooks.com

Printed in France

Library of Congress Cataloging-in-Publication Data

Gibert, Bruno
The king is naked! / story and pictures by Bruno Gibert.—1st American ed.
    p. cm.
Summary: After the lion, king of beasts, takes off his fur coat on a very hot day,
the other animals make fun of him and someone steals his fur.
ISBN 0-618-41067-8
[1. Lions—Fiction. 2. Jungle animals—Fiction.] I. Title.
PZ7.G339253Ki 2004   [E]—dc22   2003014424

10 9 8 7 6 5 4 3 2 1

The King Is Naked!

Story and pictures by
B RUNO G IBERT

Clarion Books
New York

It was such a hot day . . .

"Oh, it's hot," sighed the lion,
king of the jungle, under his mane.

He scratched himself
and discovered . . .
a zipper!

The lion hid his skin
behind a bush

. . . and went for a walk.

"I'm much more comfortable now!" he said.

Along the way he met a rhinoceros and an elephant.

"Hey, look at that cat in his underwear!"
said the rhino.

"Hee, hee! Very funny,"
said the elephant.

Other animals he met
made fun of him, too.

"Good grief," he grumbled. "These stupid creatures don't recognize me!

"I AM YOUR KING!" he cried.

But when he tried to roar,
only a little meow came out.

RRRmeeooow

And with
the gazelles and zebras
he had hunted so often
thundering after him,

he fled.
"HELP! HELP ME!"
he shouted.
What a nightmare!

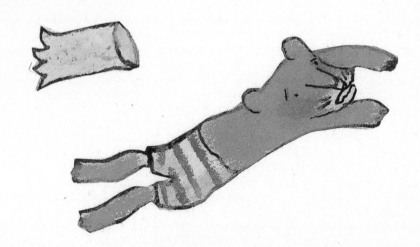

The lion wanted to put his fur back on, but—

OH, NO!

——it was gone!

All night long, he wept and wailed.

"Boo-hoo! I used to be king,

but now I'm miserable,
and it's my own fault!"

"Very well," said the big fat lion.
"Promise me that from now on
you'll eat only dog biscuits,
artichokes,
turkey,
and grated cheese."

"Er—I promise," said the king.

"All right, then. **Here's your skin!**"